BEFORE THE BADGE

BEFORE THE BADGE

HOW ACADEMY TRAINING SHAPES POLICE VIOLENCE

SAMANTHA J. SIMON

NEW YORK UNIVERSITY PRESS

New York

NEW YORK UNIVERSITY PRESS
New York
www.nyupress.org

Please contact the Library of Congress for Cataloging-in-Publication data.

ISBN: 9781479813278 (hardback)
ISBN: 9781479813315 (library ebook)
ISBN: 9781479813285 (consumer ebook)

This book is printed on acid-free paper, and its binding materials are chosen for strength and durability. We strive to use environmentally responsible suppliers and materials to the greatest extent possible in publishing our books.

Manufactured in the United States of America

10 9 8 7 6 5 4 3 2 1

Contents

Preface   vii

1 The Academy   1

2 A Few Good Officers   21

3 Us vs. Them   61

4 Police Work as Warfare, Officers as Warriors   101

5 Training for War   139

6 Pushed Out of Policing   180

7 The Future of Policing   206

Acknowledgments   221

Methodological Appendix   223

Notes   249

Index   271

About the Author   289

Preface

On a hot Texas morning in September 2016, I found myself on a six-hundred-acre ranch to attend an all-day License to Carry class. At the time, civilians in Texas needed a license to carry a firearm, which they could get by filling out an application, taking the state-mandated one-to two-day course, completing a short exam, and paying the required fees. Gary, the instructor for this class, had emailed me detailed, but confusing, driving directions to find his ranch in a rural area about fifty miles from my apartment. Per his directions, I drove through the front gate, past a small cemetery, through a second gate, and down a long, dirt road until I saw an old white farmhouse in the center of the property. Gary stood out front, wearing dark-blue Wrangler jeans, a long-sleeve light-blue Wrangler shirt, and brown work boots. Gary was white, in his early seventies, and had spent twenty-eight years in the Army. Around the time that Gary retired from the military in the late 1990s, many US states, including Texas, passed new laws that allowed civilians to obtain a concealed handgun license (CHL). Since then, several regulatory changes have made gun ownership and carry even more easily accessible and popular among the public. I spent the summer and fall of 2016 as a research assistant attending classes taught by Gary, and many others like him, to understand how this seemingly never-ending expansion of civilian gun ownership was related to changing conceptions of self-defense, safety, citizenship, and democracy.

Gary's living room and kitchen were arranged for today's class, with several wooden tables and folding chairs facing a makeshift screen set up for the PowerPoint presentation. Two pots of coffee and a large box of donuts sat untouched on the kitchen table while the classroom steadily filled up. By 8:00 a.m., all twenty seats were taken, mostly by older, white men, with a few white women scattered throughout the room. Gary began his instruction for the day by pulling up a one-thousand-slide PowerPoint presentation that covered topics like the use of force, the legal definitions of self-defense, what "castle doctrine" meant, and what steps to take immediately after shooting someone.

A few hours into Gary's instruction, he introduced the class to Dale, a retired police officer from a department nearby. Dale was there, Gary explained, to provide a police officer's perspective on the topics covered in the class curriculum and to serve as a safety range officer during the shooting portion of the test later that afternoon. Dale was about six foot five, in his sixties, and white and had a large, round belly and light-brown hair. For the next hour, Dale discussed how we should interact with police officers if we end up using our firearm. When you talk to the 911 dispatcher, he explained, you should tell them that the "situation has been neutralized" so that the responding officers know there is no longer an active shooting in progress. He went on to tell us that "attitude is everything" when interacting with the police, so even if we ask for an attorney immediately, we should do so calmly and politely. He also provided some tactical advice, encouraging us to always look for "cover" in a gunfight and to "always shoot multiple rounds" at our opponent.

After listening to Dale's instruction, I wanted to learn more about how he, as a police officer, thought about civilian gun ownership. A few weeks after the class, I emailed Dale to ask if he would be willing to participate in an interview as part of the study. He replied that he would be "honored," so we set up a time to meet at the small, rural police station where he had retired as the chief of police—the current chief, he explained, still let him use the office from time to time. For about two hours, I asked Dale about his first exposure to guns, how he got into law enforcement, and the process of becoming certified to teach civilians about firearms. During the interview, Dale brought up his experiences training police officers and how that expertise dove-tailed nicely into training civilians. "Do you have different strategies in teaching civilians versus police officers?" I asked. "Training police officers is a lot more advanced," Dale explained. "We go into cover concealment, left hand / right hand, barricade shooting, different po-sitions, kneeling, prone, sitting, standing, running. You just try to give a police officer every element of training that you can conceivably give him that might happen in the real world. That's ten times more ad-vanced than a civilian will get."

Gary was one of many police officers I met in the summer and fall of 2016 who trained civilians as a side job or as a part-time gig after retirement. As I watched these police officers teach civilians how to think about and use guns, I began to wonder what this kind of train-ing looked like for police officers. These classes taught civilians to be afraid of the world around them, to maintain a sense of constant vigi-lance, and to be comfortable using weapons.[1] Gender and race were deeply embedded in this worldview, in which white men gun owners expressed feelings of insecurity and a sense of responsibility to protect (white) women and children from racialized others. If this is what ci-vilians were learning, I thought, what were new police officers being taught at the academy by these same, or similar, instructors?

My interview with Dale took place about four years after George Zimmerman, a twenty-eight-year-old white and Latino neighborhood watch volunteer, shot and killed Trayvon Martin, a seventeen-year-old Black teenage boy. More than a month later, Zimmerman was charged with second-degree murder and manslaughter. Zimmerman firmly maintained that he acted in self-defense, pointing to Florida's 2005 "Stand Your Ground" law, which eliminated a person's duty to retreat from a dangerous situation and authorized the use of deadly force if a person believes it necessary to prevent harm.[2] The case went to trial, and on July 13, 2013, after sixteen hours of deliberation, the six-person jury acquitted Zimmerman of all charges.[3] That same day, Alicia Garza, a Black, queer activist, took to Facebook to express her frustration, anger, and grief about the verdict, writing, "I continue to be surprised at how little Black lives matter. . . . Black people. I love you. I love us. Our lives matter."[4] Garza's Facebook post was the first time the phrase "Black lives matter" appeared on the internet, marking the birth of a movement that would, in many ways, define the decade.

Just one year later, in August 2014, Ferguson, Missouri, police officer Darren Wilson shot and killed Michael Brown, an eighteen-year-old Black teenage boy. The killing of Brown, and the much-longer history of racial injustice that it represented, elicited a resounding, powerful reaction from the public. Uprisings in and around Ferguson began the day after Brown's killing and continued for several weeks. According to the Pew Research Center, in the three weeks following Brown's killing, the #BlackLivesMatter hashtag appeared close to sixty thousand times per day.[5] A disturbing sense of déjà vu overcame the public when Wilson, just like Zimmerman, was not indicted for killing Brown. Protests and demonstrations immediately ensued in Ferguson and around the country, with the use of the #BlackLivesMatter hashtag reaching a feverish pace, with 1.7 million appearances online in the following three weeks.[6] A few months later, in December 2014, President Obama assembled the Task Force on 21st Century Policing to, in his own words, address the "distrust" between the police and communities of color, "build confidence" in law enforcement, and "determine what the problems are and . . . try to come up with concrete solutions."[7]

Despite this public pressure, news stories covering police killings of Black boys and men around the country continued to break over the next several years: Freddie Gray in 2015 in Maryland; Walter Scott in 2015 in South Carolina; Philando Castile in 2016 in Minnesota; Alton Sterling in 2016 in Louisiana; Stephon Clark in 2018 in California; and Botham Jean in 2018 in Texas; among many others. It was against this backdrop that I continued to think about the police officers I had met at civilian firearms-training schools and the emphasis on fear, distrust, and violence in their instruction. I thought about how masculinity and whiteness were wrapped up in these wider patterns of violence. I wondered if there was a connection between these kinds of sentiments and the repeated instances of racist police violence that continued to make national headlines. I, like so many others, urgently wanted to know why racist patterns in police violence persisted, and I knew that to answer this question, I would need to look to the organization itself to find out what ideologies, practices, and processes dictated who was allowed to be a police officer and how they were taught to do their jobs. I knew that, if nothing else, the training of new members could tell us something about the values, worldviews, and aims of contemporary US policing.

It was with this goal that, in 2018, I began studying police training academies. Two years after I completed the fieldwork for this book, racist police violence was once again on full display with the 2020 police killings of Breonna Taylor and George Floyd. This time, however, the entire country was in lockdown to slow the spread of the COVID-19 virus and an intensely polarizing presidential campaign between Donald Trump and Joe Biden was in full swing. The simmering frustration, disappointment, and anger building over the preceding several years boiled over, and demonstrations protesting racial injustice in the criminal legal system popped up all over the country. According to one estimate by the *New York Times*, in the summer of 2020, nearly half a million people participated in demonstrations for racial justice in roughly 550 cities and towns across the United States, making it the largest social movement in US history.[8] The topic of police reform dominated the news cycle, and the idea of "defunding the police" gained some traction, although virtually no cities followed through with cutting police budgets.[9]

This is the context in which I have written this book. The United States is, as it has often been throughout its history, in a period of social unrest. Although the police are just one part of this larger story, they are an essential element. In this book, I provide a window into how police officers—the people whom we, as a society, have granted the authority to use state-sanctioned force—are selected and trained. Spending a year watching police academy training revealed to me the belief systems, ideological commitments, and organizational practices that structure and sustain US policing. Examining these processes is a key part of understanding the current state of policing in the United States and how we might, as a nation, think about the future of policing.

When I finished my interview with Dale, I left the small police station, got into my car, and pulled out my phone to navigate back to my apartment. As I did this, Dale also began walking toward his car but changed course to knock on my driver's-side window. I rolled down the window, wondering if I had perhaps left something of mine inside that he was returning. "I want to thank you for not asking that question," Dale said to me, solemnly. Confused as to what he meant, I asked, "What question?" "Have I ever taken a life," he clarified. I was completely taken off guard by this interaction and feeling flustered, simply replied, "Oh, of course." Dale reached through the open window to shake my hand, told me he really appreciated it, and turned around to walk to his car.

About a week later, I emailed Dale to thank him again for taking the time to participate in an interview and to follow up on our last exchange. In my email, I told him I was really struck by his comment and wondered if he might be willing to talk with me about how he feels when he is asked about instances when he has used his firearm while on duty. Dale promptly replied that it had been a pleasure to meet but that he would respectfully pass on any further discussion about that particular topic. He closed the email by telling me to "stay safe" and including a phrase that he said resonated deeply with him: "I pray to God you will never fire but hope to hell you will never miss."

1 THE ACADEMY

On my first day at Terryville Police Department's academy, I arrived at the training campus at 7:25 a.m., right as the sun began to peek over the horizon. The cadets were parking their cars and nervously gathering their belongings in preparation for their first day. I made my way to the main building, where an officer swung the front door open for me. Inside, I saw all of the academy instructors congregated in the front hallway dressed in their formal uniforms, which included a navy-blue long-sleeved shirt, a matching navy-blue tie, a tie clip, and a peaked cap. I watched as the instructors spent a few minutes straightening each other's uniforms as they got ready to greet the new class for the first time.

At 7:40 a.m., the instructors exited the front door and immediately began to bark commands at the group of new cadets. "Drop your stuff," Davis shouted. "Form up!" another yelled. The cadets scurried into a chaotic formation, and unsatisfied, Kevin instructed them to get into five squads of six people. The cadets' eyes widened, and they shifted their heads around nervously trying to follow the command but clearly unsure of what a "squad" meant. Kevin continued to yell, eventually conveying that "squad" referenced the horizontal lines of the formation. Once they got it right, Kevin paced around the group to make sure each line of cadets was perfectly straight.

Four of the instructors then spent about twenty minutes carefully inspecting each cadet, scanning the front and back of their bodies to make sure their buttons were fastened, their belts were tight, their name tags were straight, their boots were shined, their hair was within regulation, and they were not wearing any nail polish. The officers scribbled down each infraction they saw into a small notepad, and once the inspections were complete, Kevin reprimanded the class for their missteps. "Did you get the cadet manual last Monday?" he asked. "Yes, sir!" the cadets responded. "Did you read it?" he yelled. "Yes, sir!" the class confirmed. "So then why are you not all within the dress regulations?" he posed. No one in the class responded. "Front-leaning position!" Kevin shouted. The class did not yet know what this meant, so Kevin yelled for them to get into a push-up position. "Down!" Kevin barked. The cadets lowered their bodies to the ground and in unison counted, "One!" "Up!" Kevin commanded, and the cadets pressed their palms into the ground to push their bodies back up. The other instructors shouted for the cadets to get their knees off the ground and their butts out of the air as they began to struggle. Standing directly above a cadet, one officer asked, "Are you not strong enough, or do you weigh too much to push yourself up? It's one or the other!" When the group reached twenty-five push-ups, Kevin finally relented.

Eventually, the instructors told the cadets to drop their stuff in their lockers and meet in the classroom, where there were four rows of tables set up on either side of an aisle. I sat in the back row so that I had a good view of both the instruction and the cadets. Hannah was assigned to the seat next to me, so we sat together on that first day and every day after. Hannah was very petite, standing at around five foot two and weighing maybe one hundred pounds. She had very fair skin and light-blond hair, with freckles sprinkled across the bridge of her nose and upper cheeks. Despite her small stature, she held herself with a relaxed confidence. Later that day, when the cadets were asked to introduce themselves, Hannah shared that while she was growing up, her mother had been in and out of jail, so she decided to pursue a career in law enforcement to help other kids in similar situations.

About six weeks later, Hannah and I were paired up for an afternoon of defensive tactics (DT) training. The cadets had been working on a series of skills that fell under the category of "mechanics of arrest," and this afternoon was devoted solely to working on handcuffing techniques. When we got to the DT gym, Davis yelled, "Up top!" and we all ran to the middle of the room to watch him demonstrate the skills we would be learning that day. Last time, Davis reminded us, we learned how to apply handcuffs starting with the bottom cuff. Today, he went on, we would learn how to cuff starting with the top one. Using a cadet to demonstrate, Davis talked us through the process: make sure your cuffs are arranged in your duty belt correctly, start giving commands, position the other person's body so that they are at physical disadvantage, and then cuff them. Davis demonstrated this process about a dozen times before instructing us to break out into our pairs to practice on one another.

Hannah and I took turns pulling the handcuffs out of the pouch on our duty belt, holding the middle chain with our right fist, and hitting the single bar of each cuff against the hard piece of bone on the pinkie side of each other's wrists. After about twenty minutes of this, my wrists became red and raw from the many times Hannah slammed the cuffs incorrectly, preventing the cuff from swinging around and clasping in place. We repeated the exercise five times with commands, ten times without, and then switched. Hannah fumbled over her commands, hesitating and mixing up her words. "Turn around," she said. "Put them behind your back." I helped her along: "My hands?" Hannah was supposed to say the following lines firmly and authoritatively: "Turn around for me, ma'am. Put your hands behind your back, palms up. Spread your feet. Bend over at the waist. Do not move." When everyone else started giving commands, I could barely hear her. "Ugh, sorry," she apologized. "I'm still uncomfortable giving commands. I need to practice it more."

Three months later, I watched Hannah, and the other two dozen cadets in her class, complete scenario-based training at the academy. They had spent the previous two days in a classroom learning about case law, the code of criminal procedure, and departmental policies that dictate when and how they could use force. Before this particular scenario started, an instructor told each pair of cadets that they were responding to a domestic disturbance between two brothers. The cadets entered the gym to see two large men—who were actually police officers, volunteering as "actors"—shouting and pushing each other. When the cadets tried to separate the two, a fight broke out. I watched Hannah, who had expressed discomfort giving commands just a few months ago, wrestle a man who weighed at least a hundred pounds more than her, shouting repeatedly at him, "Stop fighting!" and "Put your hands behind your back!" Panting, completely out of breath, struggling to get out of pins, and doing her best to control his movement, she continually shouted commands while using the tactics she had learned in her training. Eventually, she and her partner got him on the ground and into handcuffs.

At the beginning of the academy, Hannah did not know how to use her voice to communicate authority, position her body and operate handcuffs to confine someone's movement, or use violence to incapacitate another person's body. By the end of the academy, she did. How did this transformation happen? How did Hannah, who was uncomfortable even raising her voice loud enough for me to hear her commands, come to be confident in authoritatively shouting orders while physically taking someone to the ground? And, perhaps most importantly, what are the larger implications of the transformation that Hannah, and her classmates, experienced at the academy?

A few months after that scenario-based training, Hannah graduated from the academy and began patrolling the streets of Terryville. She made it past the highly selective and extensive hiring process, the grueling physical-fitness and defensive tactics training, and the biweekly exams testing her knowledge of the code of criminal procedure, case law, and departmental policies. Over the course of eight months, Hannah learned how to complete the basic tasks of her new job, including writing reports, using the computer system, and driving a patrol car. Just as importantly, however, Hannah also learned how to look, think, and act like a police officer.

As a researcher studying police hiring and training, I had a front-row seat to Hannah's transformation from civilian to police officer. I spent close to six hundred hours over the course of a year watching Hannah, and other cadets like her, move through these organizational processes to get hired, and then trained, to be a police officer. Over the course of that year, I learned what kinds of qualities and life experiences, according to police departments, made someone a good fit for police work, what skills and ideologies cadets needed to master to make it to graduation, and what kinds of nonconformity put cadets at risk of being pushed out of the institution. I found that each stage of these organizational processes—from recruiting to hiring to training—emphasized a willingness and ability to use violence. This process, which I call the *socialization of state violence*, ensured that those who made it to patrol were proficient in, and eager to use, violence.

* * *

I conducted this research at four large, municipal police departments all located in the same southern state. Maintaining the confidentiality of these departments and the cadets and officers within them was a key part of my getting permission to do this project, so I have assigned pseudonyms to all of the departments and participants. These departments, which I call Terryville, Rollingwood, Clarkston, and Hudson, granted me different levels of access to their hiring and training processes. Terryville, for example, allowed me to participate in any and all activities, whereas Rollingwood permitted me to observe but not participate in the training. Taken together, I watched applicant testing and interviews, recruiting events, classroom instruction, and scenario-based training and participated in physical conditioning, defensive tactics, and shooting drills.

These four agencies were different sizes and served cities that differed in their demographic compositions and political leanings; the length of their training academies and the demographic makeup of their police forces also varied. However, the departments had a lot in common: they were all located in the same southern state; they were all located in mid- to large-size cities; the hiring processes at each department were similar; they recruited at many of the same events; they all taught the same six hundred hours of state-mandated instruction to cadets; they each had instructors who specialized in classroom curriculum, defensive tactics, or firearms; and they each added a substantial amount of training to their academies that was not mandated by the state, primarily focusing on department-specific policies, physical training, tactics, and scenario-based training. For a detailed overview of this information, refer to table A.1 in the methodological appendix.

I also interviewed thirty-eight police officers and two cadets who did not complete the academy. The officers I interviewed worked in hiring, training, and patrol units at one of nine different police departments, which included Terryville, Rollingwood, Clarkston, and Hudson as well as Fairview Sheriff's Office, Bristol, Marion, Riverdale, and Greenview. With the exception of Bristol, which was located in a southwestern state, the remaining eight police departments were all located in the same southern state in which I completed fieldwork.

Conducting ethnographic fieldwork and interviews allowed me to see, and often feel, the entire hiring and training process, from when a candidate expressed initial interest at a career fair to their graduation from the academy. This deeply embedded, embodied approach to research has its roots in Black feminist traditions that regard the body as an important site of knowledge production.[1] Sociologists often call this embodied method "carnal ethnography," and scholars who engage with it use their bodies to understand the social phenomena they study.[2] Through this approach to research, I was able to experience parts of the transformative processes that occur within the academy context. I watched as the cadets' demeanor, posture, tone of voice, self-presentation, and ideologies developed and changed. This immediate proximity to cadets and instructors gave me the opportunity to see and experience the socialization processes at work in these academies.

* * *

Hannah began the Terryville police academy in the spring of 2018, four years after a Ferguson, Missouri, police officer shot and killed Michael Brown and two years before a Minneapolis police officer killed George Floyd by kneeling on his neck for almost nine minutes. The killings of Michael Brown and George Floyd were two of the most recent instances in a long history of racist patterns in policing. Their killings, and the history of racist abuse that they exemplified, sparked massive public responses. Following Brown's 2014 death, thousands of protestors filled the streets of Ferguson; the Black Lives Matter movement gained momentum; the US Department of Justice opened an investigation into the Ferguson Police Department; and then-president Barack Obama created the Task Force on 21st Century Policing.

Despite these efforts, six years later, racism and violence in policing were once again on full display with the police killings of George Floyd and Breonna Taylor. With a global pandemic leaving millions of people dead and a highly polarizing presidential election around the corner, Floyd's and Taylor's violent deaths struck a chord with the American public on an unprecedented scale. Polls estimated that during the summer of 2020, between fifteen and twenty-six million Americans in over two thousand US cities and towns in all fifty states participated in protests advocating for racial equality, making the Black Lives Matter movement one of the largest—if not the largest—social movements in US history.[3]

Although 2020 was in many ways unique, the police killings of Breonna Taylor and George Floyd reflected a very long history of targeted violence by US police forces. The police have historically protected the interests of the controlling classes, a function that has taken many forms over time, like suppressing opposition voting for political parties, breaking up workers'-rights organizations and strikes, raiding queer bars and other community spaces, and enforcing laws that encode a racial hierarchy by capturing, hurting, humiliating, and killing those who are considered to be nonwhite.[4] These racialized forms of police violence have manifested themselves in many different ways over the course of US history. The Texas Rangers, for example, played a key role in violently pushing Native American and Mexican populations off their land in the interests of white colonial expansion.[5] Contemporary US police forces have continued in this tradition by disproportionately profiling, harassing, and killing Latino people.[6] The US Border Patrol, an arm of US law enforcement, was specifically created to enforce the National Origins Act of 1924, which established a system of immigration quotas based on national origin, in effect legislating anti-Asian sentiments.[7] And, in the early 2000s, the New York Police Department (NYPD) formed their "Demographic Unit," which sent plainclothes detectives into traditionally Muslim neighborhoods to spy on community members' habits and private conversations.[8]

Although the police have historically targeted, and continue to target, many different marginalized groups, this has been uniquely true for Black communities because of the United States' history of colonization and slavery. Some of the first law enforcement agencies in the United States were designed to regulate the movement of people who were enslaved and squelch any uprisings or rebellions.[9] Historian Sally Hadden traces the origins of slave patrols back to sixteenth- and seventeenth-century Spanish and English colonies in the Caribbean and Latin America. As the population of people who were enslaved in Caribbean colonies grew, white fears of rebellions swelled, and white colonial officials enacted laws to regulate and control the populations of people who were enslaved. Hadden explains that these early patrol systems in the Caribbean were an important precursor to more formalized slave patrols in the American South, writing that "once a Caribbean patrol system existed that could be elaborated on, colonists in the Carolinas and Virginia developed their own distinctive slave patrols in the eighteenth century."[10]

The formation of southern slave patrols mirrored a larger historical shift in systems of social control from informal collectives to formalized institutions. In the Northeast, for example, sixteenth-century
day and night watches, primarily composed of community volunteers,
evolved into some of the first formal US police departments by the
early 1800s.[11] In the South, increasingly formal systems of patrols began
enforcing slave laws, a legal responsibility that had previously fallen
on private citizens.[12] The first of these formal slave patrols emerged in
South Carolina in 1704, and by the nineteenth century in the American South, municipal police and new town charters managed the slave
patrols. Sociologist Philip Reichel explains that these "patrollers had a
defined area which they were to ride in attempts to discover runaway
slaves, stolen property, weapons, or to forestall insurrections."[13]

Even after slavery was abolished, this system persisted. Informal
slave patrols were created, including vigilante groups, and police
squads revived patrolling practices. Many southern police squads continued to use horrific violence when stopping Black people and often
searched their homes to confiscate weapons. Southern states quickly
implemented "Black Codes" to maintain control of Black residents,
and the Ku Klux Klan gained prominence as it continued to enact violence and terror on Black communities. This violence largely went
unchecked by southern police departments, which refused to protect
Black people or prosecute Klan members. White authorities often beat
Black people who were newly freed, believing that they were by definition law breakers.[14]

After emancipation, criminal law became a means of continuing
to enforce the caste system created by slavery in the United States.[15]
Historian Khalil Gibran Muhammad explains that in the decades following emancipation, criminal sanctions—for example, Black Codes—
were designed and enforced in ways that correlated Blackness with a
propensity for crime. This was true in northern states as well, where
the police enforced racial and economic hierarchy, even within white
populations. As Black populations grew in northern cities in the early
twentieth century, the police began disproportionately arresting Black

people, often for manufactured charges, like suspicious character. This unequal and targeted enforcement of laws was then reflected in newly created systems of statistical data collection, like the census and the Uniform Crime Report, further entrenching, and providing an allegedly objective basis for, anti-Black conceptions of deviance and criminality.[16]

This racist legacy—of the police but also of the country itself—has not vanished over time, despite dominant narratives that purport otherwise. It is true that slavery is no longer legal; that the Civil Rights Act of 1964 prohibited discrimination on the basis of race, religion, and sex; and that multiracial, Black Americans have been elected as president and vice president of the United States. Although each of these historical moments is undoubtedly meaningful and important, they are not evidence that the United States is operating in a post-racial landscape. Racist systems still structure every part of US life, including housing, credit, education, employment, health, and civic engagement. Black and white people live in highly segregated neighborhoods.[17] Black and Latino/a people experience discrimination in housing and lending markets.[18] Black people are subject to discrimination in hiring and earn less than white people at every educational level.[19] Majority-white school districts have more funding than comparable schools with larger populations of students of color.[20] Voter suppression and disenfranchisement efforts specifically target and affect Black populations.[21] Black women experience higher rates of maternal morbidity and pregnancy-related deaths.[22] And the life expectancy of Black people has been, and continues to be, significantly shorter than that of their white peers.[23]

The police, as an institution, are not alone in their mistreatment and abuse of Black communities in the United States. Recognizing this larger reality, however, does not absolve the police of their role in maintaining a system of racial inequality. The images of Black criminality manufactured by postemancipation criminal sanctions continue to pervade contemporary media and policing, with real consequences. Criminologist and lawyer Katheryn Russell-Brown explains that these narratives in the media sustain criminalizing images and stereotypes of Black men and work to stoke white fear.[24] Importantly, these cultural images shape police practices. Law professor Jeannine Bell explains that police officers see Blackness itself as a threat, conceptualizing Black men as "always suspicious and always potentially up to no good."[25]

Whether it is possible to draw a direct causal arrow from this racist imagery to policing outcomes, it is true that the police disproportionately harass, stop, abuse, arrest, assault, and kill Black people.[26] Black adolescents describe being routinely harassed, treated as suspects regardless of their involvement in delinquency, and physically abused by the police.[27] Young Black women report being regularly stopped for curfew violations, harassed by police when they are with young Black men, and subjected to police sexual misconduct.[28] There is a mountain of empirical evidence demonstrating that the police treat Black people differently and, more specifically, unfairly. Although public debates about racism and policing often question the legitimacy of this claim, I, and a large group of sociologists and policing scholars, do not. It is essential that this very real social reality is established at the outset of this book.

Boys in Blue: Gender and Race in Policing

Hannah entered the academy at a time when police departments around the country were expressing a renewed commitment to diversifying their forces. Coming out of the Ferguson uprisings in 2014, proponents for these demographic diversity initiatives argued that hiring more racial-minority officers would help foster trust between the police and communities of color and that hiring more women would make the police more compassionate and less violent. These diversity initiatives tend to treat gender and race as two separate, disparate categories. However, according to this perspective, having a more diverse police force—with regard to both gender and race—could potentially "fix" the problems in policing that were on full display in the killing of Michael Brown.

These efforts to demographically diversify the police reveal the assumptions of whiteness and maleness that have undergirded policing for most of its history. For many decades, the police only considered white men to be appropriate candidates for the job, maintaining this demographic composition by implementing exclusionary hiring practices and creating a hostile environment for anyone who was not white, a man, heterosexual, and masculine.[29] The ideal image of a police officer—someone who runs toward danger, fights crime, and saves innocent people—is steeped in highly gendered and racialized conceptions of bravery and morality, reflecting a deep organizational investment in normative conceptions of whiteness and masculinity.

Women who entered policing early on experienced intense resistance from their coworkers who were men and encountered many barriers to employment, like higher entrance requirements, admission quotas, and separate promotion lists.[30] Some of the first women officers carved out a space for themselves at police departments by relying on white, middle-class ideologies of domesticity and respectability.[31] These police reform movements of the early twentieth century pushed for the incorporation of white women in policing by arguing that they were naturally better than men at filling social service roles. These arguments were convincing enough that in 1910, the Los Angeles Police Department (LAPD) commissioned Alice S. Wells, making her the first white woman to ever be sworn as a police officer with the powers of arrest.[32] On the other side of the country, Mary E. Hamilton, one of NYPD's early white women officers, explained that her department's decision to hire white women officers to deal with runaways, missing persons, and women offenders served as an example of correctly utilizing women's skills in police work.[33] Hamilton relied heavily on conceptions of white women as being maternal and caring, and their expected role as mothers and homemakers, to argue that incorporating white women into police departments would simply be an extension of their existing duties at home.

At the same time, Black women were pushing local government officials and police departments to hire Black women officers. These activist groups also relied on normative conceptions of gender in their framing of the issue but argued that Black women were needed on the police force to address the unique needs of Black women, most notably their being subjected to racialized sexual exploitation.[34] In 1915, a delegation of Black women in Los Angeles petitioned then-mayor Charles Sebastian and then-chief of the LAPD Clarence Snively to hire Black women officers and to create a Black City Mother's Bureau to mirror the LAPD City Mother's Bureau formed by white women a few years earlier.[35] Their efforts paid off, and in 1916, Georgia Ann Robinson became the first Black woman police officer in the United States. Although women were formally allowed into the institution, women officers—both Black and white—were still assigned only to nonpatrol positions involving "women's issues," like sexual assault or child victims.

Even with these milestones, the police remained an overwhelmingly white and male occupation for the next fifty years. A shift in the demographic composition of the police force finally came in the 1970s, when an increasing number of men of color and women began entering the field of law enforcement.[36] This shift was the result of both cultural and legislative developments in the United States, perhaps most importantly, the 1972 amendments to Title VII of the Civil Rights Act of 1964 and the Crime Control Act of 1973. These changes to Title VII made discrimination on the basis of sex and race illegal for government employers, including police departments. The Crime Control Act of 1973 prohibited discrimination against women in the employment practices of agencies that receive funding from the Law Enforcement Assistance Administration, which led to the abolishment of minimum height requirements instituted by police departments that effectively excluded women applicants. Between 1978 and 1986, the percentage of officers who were women grew from 4 percent to almost 9 percent, about two-thirds of whom were white.[37] By 2019, that percentage had grown marginally and now persistently hovers around 12 percent.[38]

The 1970s also brought with it an overall increase in the number of Black police officers working in law enforcement. Prior to the 1960s, southern states systematically excluded Black people from applying to police departments. Departments in the North that did employ Black officers primarily assigned them to foot-patrol positions in Black neighborhoods and, in some cases, barred them from arresting white people.[39] In 1967, two major uprisings in response to racial inequality in Newark and Detroit led President Lyndon B. Johnson to assemble the National Advisory Commission on Civil Disorders, more commonly known as the Kerner Commission. In the commission's final report, it highlighted the persistent racial inequalities that characterized US policing, including racial discrimination in hiring and promotion. The commission also highlighted that police forces were disproportionately white, even in cities with large Black populations, like Cleveland and Oakland.[40] This racial composition started to shift over the next few decades: between the early 1960s and the late 1980s, the percentage of Black officers grew from 3.6 percent to 7.6 percent, with higher percentages in cities with populations over 500,000.[41] By 2006, Black officers made up 20 percent of police forces in cities with populations over 250,000.[42]

Despite these changes, men of color and women who entered policing early on were certainly not welcomed with open arms. Gender and policing scholar Susan Martin explains that because police work offered men a way to assert their masculinity, women's integration into policing threatened "the work, the way of life, the social status, and the self-image" that men officers enjoyed.[43] Once women officers gained entry to patrol positions, the policing organization placed them in a bind: women described feeling a sense of conflict between their gender and occupational expectations. These women explained that they had to pick one: they could either be a feminine woman or a respected officer but not both. Women officers also described feeling frustrated by male colleagues who insisted on enacting a protective, paternal role, making it impossible for women to prove themselves as independent, capable officers.[44] This dynamic left women officers stuck between being perceived as overly masculine and being seen as a liability, both of which were further shaped by race. Martin explains that although white men officers expected that both Black and white women would be liabilities on patrol, they drew on racialized stereotypes to conceptualize white women as "pets" or "mothers," while considering Black women to be "lazy."[45]

Black officers' treatment by their white coworkers, and by the institution more broadly, highlights the racialized logics of policing. Black officers report being routinely subjected to racism by their white coworkers, including being treated as though they are unintelligent and incapable of doing the job, hearing white coworkers use racial epithets and make racist jokes, and experiencing discrimination in job assignments, evaluations, and promotions.[46] Black women officers have had to contend with resistance to their presence from white people on the basis of their race and from Black men on the basis of their gender. Black women officers deal with racism from white women officers, for example, and sexual objectification and harassment from Black men officers.[47]

Police departments are predominantly filled by white men, but the organizations themselves are also gendered and racialized. To be a gendered or racialized organization means that the inner workings, including the guiding logics, practices, processes, policies, and rules of the organization, maintain forms of inequality.[48] In this context, sociologists consider gender and race to be organizational traits. Gender, for example, becomes a way of organizing practices, structures, and ideologies along gendered lines, rather than a way to describe an individual person. As sociologist Joan Acker explains, workers do not simply bring their gender and race with them to work. Rather, the organization itself is structured in ways that reproduce these social categories and their resulting inequalities.[49] These theories provide a way to conceptualize gender and race within organizations, like police departments, without relying solely on the demographic categories of the organization's occupants.

As an organization, policing relies on and reproduces normative conceptions of masculinity. Gender scholars tend to think about masculinity not as an individual-level characteristic or list of traits but rather as a system of discourses and practices that are often centered around dominance.[50] Men and boys in all kinds of contexts, including policing, the military, prison, fraternities, high schools, and civilian firearms-training schools, accomplish masculinity through dominance and the repudiation of anything deemed feminine.[51] Importantly, this repudiation of the feminine does not exclusively take its aim at girls and women but also at feminized boys and men. In a study of gender and masculinity at a high school, sociologist C. J. Pascoe found that teenage boys monitored each other for any kind of deviation from enacting an acceptable form of masculinity.[52] These infractions could include a range of behaviors, like expressing emotion or warmth, demonstrating a lack of physical strength, or something as small as dropping a pencil in a way that seemed to indicate poor physical coordination. In this way, masculinity is a site of constructed meaning and is primarily maintained through the collective assertion and degradation of what it is not.

Police work offers a pathway to accessing masculinity. When efforts to reform policing threaten this masculine ethos, those within the institution tend to push back. When police reform movements in the 1970s and 1980s, for example, advocated for a community policing model, many men officers refused to adapt. Community policing, which included increased foot patrols, community substations, and neighborhood watches, promised better, more meaningful interactions between officers and civilians.[53] Law professor Steve Herbert explained that community policing "implies a definition of the police role that runs counter to the masculinist crime fighter image" and is "so inconsistent with their masculinist self-image that many officers refuse to redefine their role."[54]

This gendered and racialized tug-of-war, in which policing's underlying white, male logics clash with their stated goals of diversifying their forces, permeated my fieldwork at police academies. Although formally allowed in, and indeed encouraged to apply, men of color and women are still required to adapt themselves to the existing institution. As I explain in the chapters that follow, the academy required that new officers align themselves with ideologies and physical embodiments that relied on violence and domination, regardless of whose body was filling the role. In this way, police work continues to shape-shift—at least discursively—in ways that sustain gendered and racialized domination, sometimes even without white men.

The Police Academy

Today's model of US policing can be traced back to London in the 1820s, when Sir Robert Peel presented the concept to Parliament.[55] In 1829, after many failed attempts by Peel, Parliament passed the Metropolitan Police Bill, establishing the first modern police department.[56] London's police model made its way to the United States by the mid-1800s, with cities like Boston and New York leading the way in founding their own formal police departments. That departments had become formalized did not, however, mean they were operating smoothly or ethically. During this period, aptly called the "political era of policing," officers were appointed by local politicians, police corruption ran rampant, and police brutality and violations of civil liberties often went unchecked.[57] As a reaction to this dysfunction, several police leaders began organizing a police professionalization movement as a way to legitimize the field of law enforcement. August Vollmer, then chief of police in Berkeley, California, spearheaded several of these professionalizing efforts, particularly those focused on improving training for officers.

As part of this larger professionalizing vision, Vollmer established the first formal training school for police officers in Berkeley in 1908. By the next year, New York City Police Department followed suit, and by the 1930s, formal training schools were popping up all across the country.[58] Some of the earliest police training schools, like those in Berkeley, New York City, and Louisville required roughly three hundred hours of training, which included courses focused on law and procedure, rules and regulations, geography, traffic, first aid, and hygiene.[59] Several major historical developments, including the establishment of state police agencies in the early 1900s and the formation of the National Academy of the Federal Bureau of Investigation (FBI) in 1935, helped create the infrastructure needed to make formal police training a standard practice.[60]

Over the next century, police academies continued to expand across the country. At least some of the impetus for this expansion can be traced to police reform efforts emerging from the civil rights movement in the 1950s and 1960s. It was within this context that President Johnson assembled the 1967 Commission on Law Enforcement and Administration of Justice to investigate and report on the state of the criminal justice system. In the commission's report, it made several recommendations, including developing better training for officers, adding a field training component after graduation, and implementing more standardized oversight of police practices.[61]

These recommendations came to fruition over the next two decades. In 1972, the San Jose Police Department developed the first formalized field training program for new officers, which paired newly commissioned officers with experienced officers for supervised, hands-on training.[62] The San Jose model gained popularity across the country, and today, the vast majority of departments have a similar program. In 1979, the Commission on Accreditation for Law Enforcement Agencies (CALEA)—the first policing accreditation body in the country—was established to create national standards for police practices, including those focused on training.[63] By the 1980s, most US states had also instituted their own Peace Officer and Training Standards (POST) organizations, whose function was to oversee the selection and training processes at police departments.[64]

Today, attending a police academy is a required step in becoming a licensed police officer. There are now close to seven hundred state and local law enforcement training academies operating in the United States that, over the past decade, have provided instruction to forty-five to sixty thousand cadets annually.[65] These academies take on a variety of forms: some are operated by municipalities or counties; others offer training for their entire region, which typically includes smaller cities and towns; and many others are organized by two-year colleges. These academies require, on average, a little over eight hundred hours of training as part of their basic curriculum, though most municipal departments add hundreds of additional training hours to their academy schedules. This training includes instruction focused on police operations, the law, defensive tactics, firearms skills, and miscellaneous special topics, like human trafficking or mental health. On average, cadets attending US police academies spend the most time learning about the law (eighty-eight hours), firearms skills (seventy-three hours), and defensive tactics (sixty-one hours). Not everyone makes it through this training. In 2018, roughly 14 percent of cadets who began an academy in the United States did not complete it, the majority of whom were nonwhite and/or women.[66]

As the police academy has developed into an established US institution, social scientists have become increasingly interested in understanding the role of the academy in contemporary policing. In their work, these scholars describe academy training as a process that teaches new officers the nuts and bolts of their jobs but also, perhaps just as importantly, as an introduction to the collective understanding, meaning, and emotional reality of policing. Cadets listen to veteran officers' "war stories," hear warnings of unpredictable danger, and watch graphic videos of officers being beaten and killed on duty.[67] Sociologist John Van Maanen described the police academy as a shedding and rebuilding of identity, where cadets detach themselves from old attitudes and acquaintances to adopt their new identity and enmesh themselves with their peer group. Van Maanen explained that it is at the academy where cadets begin to "absorb the subcultural ethos and to think like a police [officer]."[68]

I watched this socialization process unfold for cadets during the six to eight months that they spent training to be police officers. Importantly, this socialization emphasized, and indeed required, that cadets thought about and engaged in violence in ways that sustained this institution. One goal of this book is to show how this socialization of state violence operated at the academies I observed. This socialization process is a key component of understanding why, despite decades of reform efforts, patterns of violence in US policing continue to plague this country.

2   A FEW GOOD OFFICERS

Michael and Nathan both worked as full-time recruiting officers for Rollingwood Police Department, and as such, one of their primary duties was to attend career fairs across the country to attract applicants to their department. In the spring and summer of 2018, I joined Michael and Nathan at the seven career fairs they attended, four of which were specifically targeted toward military veterans. By the time I joined Michael and Nathan at a career fair at Fort Sill, an Army base located in Lawton, Oklahoma, I could anticipate the kinds of questions potential applicants would ask: What's the salary? What are the qualifications? How do I become a detective? What are the physical requirements? How long is the academy?

Tables advertising jobs in a range of careers were set up in a large basketball gym on Fort Sill's base. Engineering firms, construction companies, and several different police departments, among others, promised attendees fulfilling career paths after separating from the Army. The timing of this particular career fair was not ideal; Rollingwood had already closed its application portal, so anyone who expressed interest would not be able to start the academy for over a year. As we sat at our assigned table, which was lined with Rollingwood-branded pens, koozies, and calendars, Michael and Nathan expressed frustration about this timing—they lost motivation to aggressively recruit, they explained, once the hiring cycle was closed.

The combination of low motivation and poor attendance made for a fairly uneventful career fair. To treat our boredom, we passed the time by chatting about our own career ambitions. I had spent a significant amount of time with Michael and Nathan at this point in my fieldwork. I had interviewed each of them individually, watched as they tested and interviewed potential applicants, and—including the fair at Fort Sill—attended four career fairs with them. We had developed a relaxed and playful rapport over that time, and I felt at ease engaging in conversations with them about a range of topics, some of which were related to policing and others to everyday life, like movies, food, or local politics.

Michael and Nathan were both middle-aged, Black Army veterans. Michael retired from the Army after twenty-one years and, just one month later, joined Rollingwood. For the next ten years, he worked as a patrol officer, a field training officer, a mental health officer, and now, in recruiting. Nathan was in the Army for twelve years before switching to a career in law enforcement. Like Michael, he spent the next fifteen years at Rollingwood working as a patrol officer, a field training officer, a mental health officer, and now as a full-time recruiter. Both of them were approachable and charismatic, making them well suited to recruiting new applicants.

About an hour into the Fort Sill career fair, I asked Michael how long he planned to stay in the Rollingwood recruiting unit. As long as they kept him working as a recruiter, he replied. He much preferred this job to doing background checks on applicants, he explained. He did not want to be calling people to ask them if their friend or family member would be a good officer, which was a major part of doing background investigations on applicants. Curious as to why he disliked making those calls, I pressed him on this: Did he think it was boring, invasive, annoying, or something else? It was boring, he confirmed, but it was also frustrating. Sometimes you just knew someone would not be a good officer, he elaborated, but you could not justify it with anything in their application. You just could just tell they would not be a good officer, he repeated.

We then moved on to talk about my career plans. Repeating a question I received often during my fieldwork, Michael asked if I wanted to be a police officer after I finished graduate school. No, I replied, I wanted to be a professor. "Why not?" Michael asked. I told him that, honestly, I did not think I would be very good at the job since I do not do well under pressure. I turned the question around on him, asking if he thought I would make a good police officer. Michael leaned his head to the side, considering the question for a moment. He told me he thought I definitely had the communication down, that I could clearly talk to people. But, he added, he was not sure how I would react if someone punched me. "Have you ever been in a fight?" he asked. "Nope, never," I said. His lips tightened, his smile pulled to the right side of his face, and he let out an uncertain "Hmmm." Given my reply, he was not so sure, his face told me.

This interaction, and many others like it, made me wonder how officers could tell who would, and would not, be a good police officer. What kinds of characteristics, life experiences, ideological commitments, and physical embodiments make someone a good fit for policing? Who is allowed into this institution, who is denied, and for what reasons? In this chapter, I draw on my interviews with hiring and training officers and my ethnographic observations of recruiting events, applicant testing, and applicant interviews to explain how these police departments decided who to hire. These hiring decisions were based on organizational conceptions of what constitutes an ideal candidate for policing, which, as I will explain, required a specific set of characteristics, motivations, politics, and orientations toward violence.

Applying

Terryville Police Department's headquarters were located downtown in a large, beige, mostly windowless building. The first few floors housed the city's municipal courts, creating a lot of foot traffic in and out of the building. On my first visit there, I entered the main door, walked through a metal detector, put my backpack through an X-ray machine, and headed to the fourth floor, where the Terryville command staff worked. During my meeting with Commander Louis, who oversaw the hiring and training of new cadets, he walked me down to the third floor to introduce me to the hiring officers.

Terryville's hiring unit was composed of one full-time recruiter, one full-time background investigator, and a handful of retired officers who helped with background investigations part-time. Adrian, a forty-two-year-old Hispanic officer with twenty years of law enforcement experience, worked as the full-time background investigator.[1] Adrian usually dressed in khaki pants, a Terryville-branded polo, and today, since it was still winter, a zipped-up Columbia fleece. Adrian was very accommodating of my project, always friendly, and loved to poke fun at his coworkers. At lunch later that day, for example, when he and the administrative assistant playfully took jabs at each other, he suggested that she and her fiancé "might be related" since she was from West Virginia and he was from Arkansas. Rick, a fifty-three-year-old Hispanic officer with thirty-three years of law enforcement experience, worked as the full-time recruiter at Terryville. Rick was charismatic, animated, and generous with his time. He was almost always smiling, often reached his right hand out dramatically when emphasizing a point, and would gently hit my arm when delivering a joke.

I spent the rest of the day with Rick and Adrian, asking them about hiring at Terryville and, later that afternoon, watching applicants go through physical and written tests. When I asked Rick and Adrian how the hiring process worked, Rick replied, "I'll just go step by step." First, he explained, applicants needed to fill out a screening form:

They start off with the questionnaire, and that's . . . just basic information. It asks, "Have you ever been convicted of a class B or higher offense in the last ten years?" Because the criminal justice information system that we use to access criminal justice, if you have a class B, it has to be ten years from conviction to have access. If it's a class A or higher, you can't have access, so that's on the questions.

"Have you used any illegal drugs in the last twelve months, in the last twenty-four months, in the last thirty-six months?"

It talks about, "Have you had two or more moving violations in the last two years?" Now, you can have had three in a thirty-six-month period or two in a twenty-four-month period, and if you did a defensive driving, that gets knocked off. Obviously, that's probably, more than anything, that's a liability, and if you've had your license suspended in the last two years, which is probably pretty general as far as [other] agencies.

Each of the departments I studied had a similar initial questionnaire or interest form. To make it past this first step, applicants had to meet the basic eligibility requirements, which usually included being a US citizen between the ages of twenty years and six months and forty-five years and, depending on the department, having a high school diploma or GED or a certain number of college credits. As Rick indicated, immediate disqualifiers included illegal drug use, poor credit history, a criminal record, a certain number of driving violations, or a dishonorable discharge from the military. A large percentage of applicants—at Terryville, nearly one-quarter of the applicant pool for its incoming academy class—were disqualified at this stage.[2]

Applicants who made it past this initial screening then underwent a series of tests, starting with a physical fitness (PT) test. Rick explained that Terryville's PT test included the following:

A bench press, which males have to do 91.8 percent of their body weight one time, free weight, bar. Female applicants have to do 49.2 percent of their body weight one time. We have what's called the Illinois Agility Run. It's just a timed event [in which] you have to serpentine through some cones. Males have to do it in 17.79 [seconds] or faster, and females have to do it in 20.79 [seconds]. Then, we have a mile-and-a-half run. . . . Males have to do it in 13.33 [minutes] or faster, and females have to do it in 17.15 [minutes] or faster.

The specifics of the physical fitness test, and in what ways the requirements differed by gender, varied between departments. The test at each department included some combination of a one-thousand- or two-thousand-meter row, push-ups, sit-ups, a bench press, a vertical jump, a three-hundred-meter sprint, a one-and-a-half-mile run, clearing a five-foot wall, and/or completing an agility course. In general, these tests evaluated applicants' physical endurance, agility, strength, and speed.

The initial testing process also included a written exam. Rick described the written exam at Terryville as a "cognitive" and "personality test" and explained that candidates needed to earn a score of seventy or above to move past this phase. At each of these departments, the written tests were created by third-party companies that made bids to city governments for the contract. These exams typically included sections on reading comprehension, verbal reasoning, and quantitative skills. Although prior law enforcement experience was not a requirement to get hired at any of these departments, at Rollingwood, this test included a short section with questions specifically about policing procedures. If applicants failed any one of these tests, they were disqualified.

Next, Rick explained, "If everything's all right on their initial screen, there's nothing that would be a disqualifier, drug use or whatever, then we send them the application. Technically, we tell them, 'You have seven days to complete this,' but they need their high school transcript, college transcript. There's a lot of things that take time . . . [so] we'll give them two or three weeks." At Rollingwood, this was the stage when applicants first met with their assigned background investigator, who would go over the completed application with each candidate and ask probing questions to evaluate the accuracy of the information that they had provided.

Applicants who got through their testing days were then scheduled for a board interview. During the board interview, each applicant met with three police officers (at Terryville, a staff member from the city's Human Resources Department also sometimes attended), who asked them a series of interview questions for an hour or so. Rick described the board interview as including "ten to thirteen questions that are the same for every candidate." "They're gonna ask general questions," he elaborated, "like, 'What do you have to offer us? What have you done to prepare yourself for this position?'" Adrian chimed in, adding, "What are your strengths? What are your weaknesses?" Rick explained that the board interviewers tried to determine if applicants had "critical thinking" skills and if they could "think on their feet." At Terryville, roughly 8 percent of the applicants for its incoming academy class who had made it to the board interview phase failed their interview, leading to their disqualification.

The next stage of hiring was the most invasive and time-intensive, taking anywhere from four weeks to six months to complete. At Terryville, this sometimes happened concurrently with the board interviews to make the process move faster. Depending on the size of, and resources available to, the department, background investigations were done either by officers working as background investigators full-time or by retired police officers working part-time for the department. Each applicant was assigned a background investigator, who then spent weeks or months delving deeply into their lives to determine if they had been honest in their responses on the form and if there were any disqualifiers the department should know about.

As part of the investigation, each applicant completed a background history statement, which was a twenty-five- to forty-page questionnaire spanning the applicant's past ten years of employment, housing, education, and romantic relationship history, including the names and contact information for all previous employers, landlords, roommates, neighbors, and romantic partners. Applicants were also required to disclose information about financial debt, disciplinary action in school or work, family members' arrest histories, traffic violations and/or collisions, any illegal activity engaged in (regardless of whether it resulted in law enforcement contact), property or accounts that had been repossessed, and their typical use of alcohol and history of illegal drug use. The packet also asked applicants to list all law enforcement agencies to which they had applied and provide five additional personal references who had not been listed anywhere else in the packet.

The background investigators sent questionnaires to every person (family members, previous employers, coworkers, ex-partners, etc.) listed in the packet, scheduled phone calls with anyone they wanted to talk to more extensively, and, in some cases, conducted in-person interviews with neighbors and completed unannounced home visits at the applicant's residence. One cadet at Rollingwood, for example, told me that a background investigator visited his father's neighbor's house in a bordering state to ask them questions. Applicants were required to answer every question on the form, and if they skipped or missed one, their background investigator would highlight it, call them, and insist on getting an answer. If any of the applicant's previous employers, friends, family members, or neighbors did not fill out their questionnaire, the application was stuck in limbo until they did.

Rick explained that this process typically took Terryville recruiting officers forty hours per applicant. Rick recalled completing a background investigation on an applicant once who "had twelve different jobs listed." "They were all from different places," he continued. "He had moved all over the place, so you're contacting people in different states, contacting people all over the place." As is probably obvious, a significant percentage of applicants did not make it through this phase of the hiring process, either because of incomplete applications or because of information that emerged during the investigation.

The background investigators keep in touch with their counterparts at departments around the state. Applicants had to list the departments that they had applied to as part of their personal history statement, so the background investigators would sometimes call those departments to find out if that applicant had been disqualified and, if so, why. Adrian explained that the departments in his region "communicate with each other," elaborating,

> All these agencies, we call each other: "Hey, this person applied over there. What did they tell you on their personal history statement?

This is what they told me." We'll compare notes, and sometimes it helps them out, sometimes it helps us out, like, "Hey, they didn't tell us about this. Why not?" Some of the applicants, what they do, they get turned down from the agencies that they want to really go to, [and] they kinda start learning, "Oh, man, I think this is what I need to say" or "I'm not gonna say this, this, and that." They'll come to some agencies, and they won't say that they've applied to this other one they were turned down at.

Usually, we just send out an email or call. There's an email loop for most agencies: "Hey, has anybody worked this applicant before?" "Oh yeah, we got rid of him for this." We have to send waivers and disclaimers, all kinds of stuff. It's a pretty good network of law enforcement agencies, even though we're trying to steal applicants from each other. We still all talk with each other and say, "Yeah, this is what they told us" or "This is how they did at this part of the process."

This communication between agencies added an additional layer of scrutiny. Applicants were expected to be honest and consistent in the information they provided not only to one agency but also across agencies. If a background investigator determined that an applicant had been disqualified from another agency or had provided different information, the applicant's chances of getting hired at the current agency diminished considerably.

The applicants who made it through the background investigation had two final steps to complete before they could receive an offer of employment. First, applicants had to pass a polygraph exam. According to the recruiting officers, the polygraph exam provided one final opportunity for the department to test an applicant's truthfulness. Honesty, in this case, mostly meant consistency. Highlighting the role of the polygraph exam, Rick gave the example of a fictional applicant who lied about their drug use: "Obviously, with the polygraph, we've had people say, 'Oh, no, I haven't smoked in five years,' and they get down to a polygraph: 'Oh, okay, well, three months ago my cousin had a party, and I smoked a joint' or something." If the polygraph examiner determined that someone was lying, even if they had been consistent in their story previously, they could be disqualified. In cases in which the polygraph administrator was not sure whether someone was lying, the applicant's response was categorized as inconclusive. In those cases, the hiring officers used their discretion to determine if the applicant should be disqualified.

There is very mixed evidence as to whether polygraph exams can detect dishonesty, and the cadets I interviewed often mocked the exam once they were hired.[3] One cadet at Rollingwood, for example, told me that he was disqualified from another department because the polygraph results indicated that he had committed arson. He laughed as he told the story, indicating the absurdity of him being accused of arson. He then passed the polygraph exam at other departments, including at Rollingwood.

Following the polygraph exam, applicants then completed a physical exam and a psychiatric evaluation, both of which were organized by the department. At Terryville, just 5 percent of the total applicant pool for its incoming academy class made it past this entire hiring process, making them eligible to receive an offer of employment. From there, applicants eagerly waited until the next academy started, which could happen anywhere from once every two years to four times a year, depending on the size of the department.

Making the Cut

When I asked hiring officers what they were looking for in applicants, they would often tell me they wanted to hire the "best" candidates. Nathan had been working as a full-time recruiter at Rollingwood for two years when I interviewed him in his sergeant's office. I asked Nathan what he liked about his job, and he replied that he enjoyed going out with Michael to "try and get people to come join our department." He added that he and Michael were "trying to get the best of the best." What, in the context of policing, does it mean to be the best of the best?

The Right Personality

Police officers consistently listed the following personality traits in their explanations of what it meant to be a good officer: integrity, honesty, discipline, responsibility, and reliability. Officers tied these traits to the tasks, responsibilities, and authorities involved in police work, explaining that to be a good police officer, one must demonstrate a competence and commitment to each of these qualities. Throughout the hiring process, applicants were expected to show the hiring officers that they had the right personality, and those who did not—or, at minimum, did not successfully perform the personality—were at a significant disadvantage.

Adrian, the hiring officer at Terryville, explained that although there was "no perfect person," his department wanted to hire candidates who were "honest, [have] a sense of loyalty, and who will own up to what they've done." "A lot of it really is the honesty," he added. Being honest was integral to the job, Adrian explained, because the department was "trusting this person to potentially go into somebody's house, somebody's vehicle, have contact with all these people, and to do everything correctly, be honest about it, not lie." One lie during the application process, Adrian concluded, could mean more lies later: "If somebody is coming through the application process and they're lying to the background investigator from the beginning, how can [we] trust that person to go out there and be honest to the citizens that they're serving?" Adrian, and the other hiring officers I met, stressed that having integrity and being honest were essential because an officer's word is used in court as official testimony. If the public thinks that officers are dishonest, they explained, the department loses all legitimacy and authority.

If a hiring officer found out that an applicant had omitted information, been misleading, explicitly lied, or been inconsistent in the information they provided, the applicant was considered dishonest and promptly disqualified. During my fieldwork, a number of applicants were disqualified for dishonesty. I spent several days at Rollingwood's hiring unit with Nancy as she interviewed candidates and conducted background investigations. Nancy was about five feet tall and had blond hair and round, large blue eyes. She had a vibrating energy and was constantly moving and talking. She told me that her nickname in the unit was "Sherlock," because she was such a thorough background investigator.

Jason, a white applicant in his twenties, was assigned to Nancy, and by the end of her investigation, he was permanently disqualified from Rollingwood. Before Jason's board interview, Nancy and I sat in her office as she flipped through his initial background packet, highlighting anything she thought might be a red flag. Jason had been disqualified from three other departments, she told me, but she did not yet know why.

The day prior, after Jason completed his physical and written test, Nancy met with him and asked why he was disqualified from these other agencies. Jason said he did not know because the agencies refused to give him that information. The next day, Diane, a white sergeant in her thirties, led his board interview. She asked Jason why he was disqualified by three other agencies. In his response to Diane, Jason divulged information that he did not mention during the one-on-one meeting with Nancy the day prior: at one of the agencies, he could not get through the polygraph. It was three hours long, he said, and he just could not sit still the whole time. Diane, looking dismayed, asked him which part of the polygraph he failed. The two most important sections, he said: the questions asking if he was a gang member and if he had ever killed anyone. Everyone's eyes widened and heads shifted back slightly, including mine, in reaction to this new information.

Nancy immediately tilted her gaze in confusion, and chided Jason, "You never said any of that yesterday when I asked you, and I specifically asked you why you were DQ'd [disqualified]. See, that's the kind of stuff that just isn't going to work, Jason! It's going to get you DQ'd fast." Jason started to sweat as he tried to defend himself and apologize to Nancy, stuttering while he explained that he did not know she wanted that level of detail yesterday. "Of course, I did! I specifically asked!" Nancy shouted. Diane interrupted Nancy's reprimand to ask Jason about the second agency. Jason clarified that he was initially disqualified for a few months due to marijuana use. He continued the application process when he was eligible again but was then disqualified during the background investigation. He tried to find out why, he explained, but they did not give applicants that information. Nancy threw her arms up in the air and, looking flabbergasted, shouted, "Again, Jason! This is the first I've ever heard of this marijuana-use DQ. This is going to get you DQ'd if you keep it up!" Jason used a lot of "I apologize" and "ma'ams" in his attempt to explain himself, but Nancy did not cool off. After the interview, back in her office, she lamented that "nothing pisses [her] off more" than when someone lies and then tries to backtrack on it. Now, she explained, she thought he was deceptive, and she no longer trusted him. "What else could he be lying about?" she wondered.

Several weeks later, I spent a day at Rollingwood's hiring unit and caught up with Nancy about her ongoing background investigations. When I got to her office, she slammed her hands on the desk excitedly and told me she "had to" update me on Jason. It turned out that Jason had been disqualified from the other departments because he admitted to selling his prescription Adderall. Selling a controlled substance was an automatic disqualifier, so on top of the fact that he sold drugs, she explained, he also lied about it. "Nothing pisses me off more than someone lying to me," she griped. Even now, weeks later, Nancy's tone elevated, her cadence quickened, and her head swiveled back and forth as she recounted her irritation and resentment about Jason lying to her. She glanced at her office door, which was open, and in a hushed voice told me that Diane reprimanded her after Jason's board interview for "not keeping cool."

When Nancy "likes people," she told me, she usually calls them on the phone to break the news that they had been disqualified. Otherwise, she just emails them. Because Jason lied to her, she explained, she "had no respect for him" and so did not bother taking the time to call. After receiving the email from Nancy, Jason called her to find out why he had been disqualified. Smirking, Nancy played me the audio recording of their three- or four-minute phone conversation.[4] In the recording, when Jason asked why he had been disqualified, she said that she had called the other departments and found out that he sold Adderall. "What? Really?" he asked incredulously. There were several inconsistencies during the process, she told him, again complaining that he was not "forthcoming." Sounding defeated and confused, Jason replied, "Okay," thanked her, and hung up.

The moral element that officers attached to honesty was highlighted by Nancy's intense emotional reaction to Jason's inconsistencies. From Nancy's perspective, Jason withheld information from her, which meant that he was deceitful and untrustworthy and lacked character. She did not respect him anymore, she told me. Although Jason fit the mold for a police officer in many other ways—he was a young, relatively athletic, white man who felt a calling to help others, had broken up a physical fight, and presented markers of a conservative political identity—he was, according to Nancy, a liar, and liars could not be police officers. Jason did not fulfill the conceptualization of a good police officer and, as a result, was disqualified from the department.

* * *

Recruiters from police departments around the state attended many of the same career fairs, so after attending a few, I started to recognize faces at other departments' tables. Jim, a forty-eight-year-old Black recruiting officer at Marion Police Department, would usually come by the Rollingwood table to chat with Michael and Nathan at some point during the career fairs. Jim was animated, boisterous, and warm—once you got him talking, it seemed like he could go on forever. Jim had twenty-six years of law enforcement experience, fourteen of which had been spent recruiting new officers at Marion. I interviewed Jim over the phone a few weeks after meeting him to learn more about the recruiting process at his department, which was much smaller than the four that I had primarily focused on.

I asked Jim what kinds of questions he usually got from potential applicants, and in his response, he began describing what he looked for when he was recruiting. Jim emphasized that first and foremost, an officer must be "responsible." Jim elaborated that as a police officer, "you have to be responsible, because you have people's livelihoods [in your hands]. . . . If you have bad child support, that's a problem, because that's you not taking care of your responsibility. If you don't take care of that responsibility, what makes us think you're gonna take care of this responsibility?" In a similar way that dishonesty during the hiring process was read to mean that an applicant would also lie on the job, Jim explained that a perceived lack of personal responsibility in an applicant's personal life indicated the potential for irresponsibility while on duty.

While honesty and integrity were qualities that applicants had to actively perform during the hiring process, primarily by being consistent and displaying good intentions in the information they provided, being responsible was evaluated through proxies or during interviews. Having a clean criminal history, drinking alcohol only sparingly, and either never having used drugs or only using them within the department's allowed parameters were all markers that an applicant was responsible.[5]

Having one's finances in order, though, was the primary marker indicating that an applicant was responsible. This meant that applicants needed to have a good credit score, pay their child support, pay any debt consistently and on time, and not have let anything go to collections. Bruce, a forty-nine-year-old white lieutenant in Bristol Police Department's hiring unit explained that "poor finances" was a common reason for an applicant to be disqualified during the background investigation phase. Things like "multiple collections, multiple credit stuff, bankruptcies," he explained, were problems because they indicated that the candidate was "not responsible." Bruce, and other officers, equated poor finances with a lack of responsibility that could, down the road, make officers easily corruptible or susceptible to bribes. The credit check that departments required from applicants, then, served the function of helping hiring officers evaluate if, according to their way of understanding it, the applicant was responsible.

Although parenthood is culturally considered to be a major responsibility, aside from paying child support, being a parent did not enter the calculus of evaluating an applicant's personal responsibility. Having children only came up in the interviews I witnessed with women applicants and was discussed as a liability, rather than an asset. During Jessica's board interview at Rollingwood, for example, the interviewing officers warned her about the incompatibility of a police officer's work schedule and family life. Jessica was a white, forty-four-year-old applicant with two children. She was interviewed by Diane, Nancy, and Michael. Diane explained to Jessica that for the first several years, she would have to work evenings or nights and that this would be difficult with children. Nancy chimed in, warning that Jessica would need to adjust to the academy schedule and get used to telling her kids that "Mommy can't play right now." Nancy talked about another woman she recently hired who was really struggling to make it work with her family. Diane openly acknowledged the gendered assumptions in these warnings, explaining, "Would we be asking a male candidate these questions? No." Diane went on, justifying her line of questioning: "Women are different when it comes to children. It's just not the same for men and women. It's women's instinct to take care of everything." Michael added that they wanted to make sure Jessica was "mentally prepared" for this.

I asked several officers if their departments offered any kind of subsidized child-care options to help resolve this problem for parents, particularly for mothers, who still shoulder the lion's share of child care and household labor in the United States.[6] All the officers I asked about this reported that their departments did not assist with child care, though one officer noted that sometimes cadets' wives would take turns babysitting while their husbands were in the academy. It was on parents—and mothers in particular—to figure out a way to make it work, leading to more logistical difficulties for them to complete the academy.

* * *

Each academy class of cadets elected their own peer leadership toward the beginning of their training. The exact roles varied a bit, but at minimum, they included a president position. As soon as Jacob, a twenty-nine-year-old South Asian man, started the academy, he immediately began campaigning to be elected class president. His class elected him, and for the next eight months, in addition to leading his fellow cadets, he performed at the top of his class academically, physically, and tactically. Jacob had experience working in highly regulated, intense environments—he had attended the Naval Academy and served in the Navy for several years before applying to Rollingwood.

I watched Jacob go through the academy and interviewed him three months after he graduated. During our conversation, he drew from his experience in the military and law enforcement to highlight the importance of discipline in police work: "It [discipline] is important because you need to be able to trust someone to do what they're supposed to do when they're not being spoon-fed. . . . I was in the Navy. We had years of that, so now going into law enforcement, it's not very difficult. . . . That stuff is second nature, but for a lot of people, this is new to them. . . . If you're not making sure things like your TASER is charged, then you might need to use it to save my life, and you can't." Jacob explained that when someone has discipline, they will do "what they're supposed to do when they're not being spoon-fed." This came up in other contexts, where respondents told me that officers needed to have discipline so that they could make good decisions and follow the rules when they were on the street, unsupervised. This was easier for Jacob, he said, and for other applicants with previous military experience, because they already understood how to perform discipline and follow institutional rules, with an understanding that doing so may have life-or-death consequences.

As part of the hiring process, applicants demonstrated that they were disciplined primarily by expressing a commitment to physical fitness and showing a willingness to endure pain to prove that commitment. Applicants had to pass a physical fitness test and, during their board interview, were asked to describe their physical fitness regimen. The officers on the board were usually unsatisfied with whatever the applicants described and insisted that they take physical fitness more seriously before the academy started.

During the physical fitness (PT) test, applicants were encouraged to push themselves as hard as they could and to finish the exam even if they failed a portion of it. At Rollingwood, the PT test included a two-thousand-meter row with a time limit that was dictated by applicants' height, weight, and sex. On the day of the PT test, the Rollingwood hiring officers set up twenty or so rower machines in an otherwise-vacant room that resembled a cafeteria. The applicants all changed into workout clothes and sat at their assigned rower machine, waiting to begin. I stood on one end of the room with a few of the hiring officers, who periodically paced down the aisle, checking the monitors on the rower machines that measured distance traveled and urging applicants to keep going. Before they began, Tina, a white officer in her forties, advised the applicants, "If you feel like you need medical attention or you are going to throw up, raise your hand, and we will come to you." I asked Chris, the lieutenant who oversaw the hiring unit, if it was common for applicants to vomit during the fitness test. Someone vomits almost every time, he replied, and every now and then, someone faints or needs oxygen.

Tina warned the applicants that once the exam began, if they stopped early for any reason, they would be disqualified. Tina was about five foot seven and thin with small, condensed facial features and a blond pixie cut. She spoke with a slight southern accent and a firm, embodied confidence. When the test began, she shouted at the group to keep going and to push themselves even harder. As she walked by applicants who were struggling—their breathing strained, shoulders slumped forward, and faces flushed—she contorted her voice deeper and sharper, yelling, "Come on! Let's hustle! Do not quit! You didn't come here to quit! You don't want to go home a quitter! Keep it up—three hundred meters left!" One of the applicants raised his hand, an officer rushed over with a trash can, and the applicant vomited. At the end of the exam, another applicant said he thought he might need medical attention, but after sitting and resting for a few minutes, he recovered. This exercise tested the applicants' basic level of physical fitness, but it also evaluated if they were willing to endure pain and physical distress and complete the task anyway. The hiring officers wanted to know if the applicants had trained in preparation for this test—which demonstrated motivation and discipline—but they also wanted to know if the applicant was a "quitter." A good police officer does not quit and will endure physical pain to be a part of the institution.

* * *

Police work, according to the officers I met, also requires reliable team members. Police officers often work with partners or on teams, so it is vital that they can rely on one another, especially in stressful situations. In my interview with Paul, a forty-seven-year-old white sergeant at Rollingwood's academy, he told me that teamwork "comes into play when out on the street" because he has to "have confidence in the person who goes with [him] to the scene." Paul offered the following example to illustrate his point:

> I show up at a burglar alarm, and their front door's been kicked in, and I'm waiting for somebody else to show up. Then you show up, and I say, "Hey, Bert. You and I are going into this house to clear it, to make sure there's nobody in there." That could potentially be a life-or-death situation. So, I have to have confidence in you to work together with me, . . . as simple as being able to work together, to handle people's problems and stressful situations to the actual life-and-death situations of "we're in a scrap, I can count on you to give 100 percent just because I am and that if something were to happen and I get hurt, you're not gonna leave me." The teamwork creates bonds, and that bond is trust.

Being able to rely on other officers, Paul concluded, was key to completing daily tasks in police work, but it could also be the determining factor in whether he made it out of a situation alive. In his response, he highlighted that each officer needed to know they could trust one another to work as a team so that their coordinated efforts were done in a way that kept them safe and accomplished the task at hand.

In the hiring process, officers emphasized the importance of teamwork during the board interviews. At Rollingwood, each applicant was asked the following series of questions about teamwork during their interview: (1) What do you think are the most important qualities to be a good team member? (2) What qualities do you have that makes you a good team member? and (3) How do you maintain a good working relationship with your coworkers? Applicants' responses were usually short, vague, and focused on workplace contexts. One interviewee, for example, responded that it was important to listen, follow orders, respect the chain of command, and have good communication skills. Another interviewee said that good team members were honest, hardworking, educated, and trustworthy.

The structure of the academy further emphasized the importance of teamwork. At Rollingwood, for example, underperforming cadets were required to carry around heavy sandbags everywhere they went, a literal interpretation of one person dragging down the rest of the group. On one of my visits to the Rollingwood academy, Will—an Asian cadet in his twenties—was required to carry around six heavy sandbags for what his instructors described to me as a general "lack of effort." Will could not manage carrying the six sandbags on his own, so his classmates had to help. This obviously created resentments toward underperforming cadets and communicated to those cadets that they were a liability for and burden to the rest of the group.

The Right Reasons

Throughout the hiring process, officers continually evaluated if applicants were applying to their departments for the right reasons. The first question the board asked each applicant during their interview was "Why do you want to work in law enforcement?" Trevor, a white applicant in his late twenties, answered this question the right way during his board interview at Rollingwood. Before he entered the room, Trevor's background investigator—a white, retired officer who looked to be in his early sixties—briefed the other officers on the board: Trevor was in the Navy, had a wife and kids, had no criminal history, and only smoked weed ten times or less in high school; his parents "seem cool," and his wife "seems nice." Diane led the interview, and one other officer—a Black man in his forties—also sat on the board. "Do you have any concerns?" Diane asked the background investigator. "Nope," he replied.

After a few minutes of small talk and introductions, Diane asked Trevor why he wanted to go into law enforcement. He had been interested in law enforcement since he was a kid, he replied. When he was younger, "it was for the kind of childish reasons of wanting excitement," he explained, but as he got older, he felt that law enforcement was "really needed" and that pursuing this career was part of his "life's purpose to help others." Guiding Trevor to the acceptable story, Diane followed up on his answer by asking, "Is it a calling?" "Yes, ma'am," he replied. The board of officers nodded in recognition and moved on to the next question.

Trevor's description of police work as his life's "purpose" or a "calling" is emblematic of the kinds of responses the hiring officers were looking for when they asked this question during the board interview. The officers I met explained to me that the kind of person who should be a police officer feels a calling to protect innocent people from evil. In reality, of course, people decide to become police officers for many different reasons. Still, police officers placed a strict boundary around what kinds of motivations were either acceptable or unacceptable. Having the "right reasons" for pursuing a career in policing, according to these officers, indicated that someone was a good fit for the job and would persist through the academy and on to patrol work.

Most of the officers I met expressed this kind of "calling" for police work. For example, Joey, a twenty-nine-year-old, white, newly-minted

Rollingwood officer, told me that he pursued a career in policing after leaving the Marines because he felt "that higher calling" and wanted to protect "those who can't protect themselves." Joey "had smaller friends growing up that were getting bullied," and he "hate[ed] people that prey on other people." Chris, a forty-four-year-old white lieutenant who oversaw the hiring unit at Rollingwood, similarly told me that he pursued policing because he liked "the fact that you could actually help people." Diego, a forty-two-year-old Latino sergeant at Rollingwood's training academy, said that he "wanted something in a 'giving back' or 'helping others' field." Other officers told me that they felt a "personal calling to do something emphasizing giving back and helping people," that they wanted to "interact with the community and help people," or that they aspired to "be the person that people call when they're in need." In their explanations of why they pursued law enforcement, these officers emphasized a calling to help and defend "innocent" people.

If feeling a calling to protect the innocent was framed as the right reason for pursuing police work, then any other motivation was framed as the wrong reason. David, a Latino officer in his forties, acknowledged this binary one afternoon at Rollingwood's academy. David worked as a defensive tactics instructor at the academy, and although highly suspicious of me at the beginning of my fieldwork, he became quite candid later on. During the hours I spent with him at the academy, he talked to me about the psychology podcasts he enjoyed, his dreams for retirement, and his and his wife's efforts to adopt a child. On this afternoon, David and I stood together in the gym while the cadets learned how to escape pins on the ground. David asked if, in my research so far, I had found that the motivations for becoming a police officer differed depending on the race and gender of the officer. I replied that most officers and cadets told me that they wanted to protect or help people. David rolled his eyes. "Of course they do," he said. "They don't want to be honest," he went on, because it "doesn't sound good" to say that actually, you just really needed a job and health insurance or, honestly, you like driving fast and putting bad guys in jail. David recognized that within the institutional discourse dictating moral motivations, it "doesn't sound good," or was incorrect, to say that you wanted to be a police officer for any other reason except to protect or help others.

David pointed to two kinds of reasons for pursuing law enforcement that were considered wrong. First, officers were expected to pursue the career for reasons tied to morality. Good officers thought about policing as a calling, not just a job, and thus, pursuing this career for the pay or benefits was wrong. Second, although adrenaline, power, and violence were a part of this job, they were not supposed to be the reason why officers pursued the career.

This first kind of wrong motivation—pay and benefits—came up in my interview with Rob, a thirty-seven-year-old white defensive tactics instructor at Rollingwood's academy. During my fieldwork, Rob incessantly criticized the cadets, often complaining that they were stupid, were lazy, and lacked common sense. After my fieldwork ended, he would periodically message me to complain about the cadets in the newest class and to let me know how many of them had quit or been fired. During our interview, I asked Rob what made a cadet stand out. He explained that "mind-set" was important and, referencing unsuccessful cadets, complained, "The people that just show up 'cause they're here for some health insurance or they think it'll work for a while and they'll find something else because this city has a competitive job market, obviously not going to be in it for the right reasons." Rob explained that cadets who go into this job for the pay or benefits were not in it for the right reasons. According to this way of understanding police work, one should go into this occupation because they have a calling, a passion, or a life purpose to do so.

The second kind of wrong reason—adrenaline, power, and violence—came up during a "professionalism and ethics" class at Terryville's academy. The instructor, a white man who oversaw the narcotics unit, had been at Terryville for thirty-two years and had taught this class for the last ten. At the beginning of the class, he asked the cadets to introduce themselves: "Tell us your name, where you're from, if you have a degree, if you have any prior military or law enforcement experience, and why you want to be a police officer." After the cadets finished introducing themselves, he walked over to the whiteboard and summarized the reasons everyone gave for pursuing a career in law enforcement. "It sounds like y'all said you want to be cops because of the brotherhood"—he wrote each reason on the board, in a column, as he repeated them aloud—"and actually you all were more honest than usual, so I heard some of you say the adrenaline." He goes on, "teamwork, camaraderie, service, and I heard a few people say to be a good example or a role model that you didn't have growing up." He seemed pleased with the reasons the cadets had provided and commended the group: "Y'all joined the police department for the right reasons."

The commander then listed a few wrong reasons for entering the field. "What I didn't hear," he said, "is that you wanted to be a cop to shoot unarmed . . . ," he paused briefly, carefully selecting his next word, "I'll say minorities. Or that you wanted to beat people down. . . . I didn't hear anyone say any of those reasons." In his explanation, the commander made a direct reference to the bad apples that they were trying to eliminate during the hiring process. Good officers are not racist, and they do not use violence unnecessarily. He articulated the occupational discourse framing the right and wrong motivations for pursuing a career in law enforcement. Although he used examples that no one would actually say out loud, even if those were their motivations for entering the field, he did highlight that there were acceptable and unacceptable ways of expressing motivations for pursuing police work. The acceptable reasons, he noted, did not include a desire for power or enacting racist violence.

When applicants' explanations of why they wanted to be a police officer did not match the acceptable narrative, they were met with suspicion and accused of getting into policing for the wrong reasons. Jessica was subjected to this reaction during her board interview at Rollingwood. Jessica was one year away from the age cutoff of forty-five, had spent most of her career working in restaurants and gyms, and, at the time of her interview, was in the middle of a divorce from a current

Rollingwood officer. The board of officers spent a significant portion of the interview pressing her on why she wanted to be a police officer and, in particular, why now, in the midst of her divorce. She told the board that being an officer was something that she always wanted to do, but she got invested in her career as a chef and did not think that she and her husband, who had been an officer for fifteen years, could swing the work schedule if they were both police officers. The officers continued to press her: Why now? Why was she making this career change in the middle of her divorce with a Rollingwood officer, especially since that meant she was now becoming a "single mom"? Jessica reiterated that it would not have been possible when she was married because of her husband's schedule, and since she was about to age out of eligibility, it was now or never.

A few weeks later, I learned that Jessica had been disqualified from Rollingwood due to inconsistencies in her background history statement related to her marriage and work history. Recounting what happened, Nancy again questioned Jessica's motivations for applying. "I couldn't figure out why she wanted to be a cop now," Nancy said, again noting that, to her, it seemed like odd timing. While conducting Jessica's background investigation, Nancy spoke with Jessica's ex-husband, she told me, and asked if he thought policing was something that Jessica was "passionate" about. No, he replied, Jessica had mentioned it a few times in passing but never talked about it as a passion. Nancy determined that Jessica, who had pursued other careers and could not acceptably articulate her motivations for entering law enforcement, did not have a passion for policing. Those who did not discuss their path to policing as being fate-like, in their blood, or a calling—like Jessica—were met with skepticism and distrust.

Of course, there are norms dictating the right and wrong reasons for pursuing many different careers. Medical doctors, for example, are supposed get into medicine because they want to save lives, not because they want money and power. Sociologists are expected to pursue research careers because they have a passion for knowledge production and understanding social inequality, not because they want prestige and recognition. Scholars have noted that this emphasis on serving the community is often invoked in expressed motivations for pursuing many kinds of public work, including police work.[7]

The fact that the police have a discourse for framing motivations for pursuing police work—and one that centers on passion—is not unique. Indeed, scholars have argued that "passion" has become a dominant cultural schema characterizing the nature of work in neo-liberal economies more generally.[8] Workers are now, perhaps more than ever, expected to express feelings of passion about their jobs. In one study of hiring processes for tech workers in Silicon Valley, for example, sociologist Ilana Gershon found that employers described passion as being even more important than a potential employee's skills.[9] Having passion, these employers reasoned, meant that employees would devote themselves entirely to the work, even if it required personal sacrifice. What especially matters in the policing context, though, are the assumptions about criminality, worthiness, and human value that are embedded in this way of articulating the motivation for pursuing policing. The underlying assumptions of this motivation make a distinction between who is deserving of protection or punishment and frame police officers as the ultimate deciders of who belongs in each category.

This binary was frequently articulated by the police officers I met, such as when Joey, quoted earlier, told me that he chose to pursue police work so that he could protect vulnerable people from the bad people who "prey on" them. This binary came up in the classroom instruction at Terryville when Dylan, a white firearms instructor in his forties, warned cadets that they needed to carry their firearms in order to protect people. Sometimes, he reasoned, they would have to "take lives in order to protect others." This binary is perhaps most vividly illustrated by the American police flag, pictured in figure 2.1, which resembles a US flag but instead features black and white stars and stripes with a blue horizontal line across the middle. This blue stripe represents the police, who are the "thin blue line" standing between chaos and order, or between evil and good. According to this way of

Figure 2.1. The American police flag

seeing the world, there are innocent people, and there are bad people; and the police are meant to intervene between them. This means that the occupation is rooted in a conceptualization of criminality that is individualized and intentional (not systemic) and an understanding of people that categorizes them as either worthy or undeserving of protection.

The Right Politics

The Rollingwood cadets got their first intensive exposure to defensive tactics (DT) training at the academy during a week aptly called "DT Week." The cadets spent a full week in the gym with the DT instructors learning the basics of strikes, takedowns, and other physical movements designed to control or hurt another person. DT Week was scheduled toward the beginning of the academy, so at this point, I was just starting to build rapport with the DT instructors. On the third day of DT Week, David, a Latino officer in his forties, asked me if I brought my lunch or needed to go buy something. Yes, I replied, I brought something. He invited me to eat lunch in the back office with the instructors, so that I did not have to eat by myself in the kitchen, which I had been doing for the two days prior. I followed David out of the gym and through the locked door to the back offices, to a large wooden table set up in the middle of the DT instructors' cubicles. I sat next to Spencer, a white instructor in his thirties, and shortly after, Josh and Rob—also white instructors in their thirties—sat near me with their Subway sandwiches. A large Marines flag hung on one wall, and a wooden figurine of a Glock handgun sat atop one of the cubicles.

One of the instructors picked up the remote and turned on the TV, which was already set to Fox News. Rob defiantly announced that a staff member at the academy had anonymously complained to the command staff about the TV always playing Fox News. He did not care, he said; they were going to keep watching it anyway. That afternoon, the news anchors talked about Donald Trump's recent visit with Queen Elizabeth. Rob laughed at the story and explained to me that although he did not necessarily like Trump, he was "amused" by him. He described his sister as a "social justice warrior" and recollected that on the night Trump was elected, he was drinking and having a great time rubbing it in his sister's face. "I'm sure she loved that," I joked, and Rob laughed.

Fox News also made an appearance in Rollingwood's hiring unit, where I spent a few afternoons with Nancy as she conducted applicant background investigations. As she started to review the first applicant's packet, she turned to me and said, "I'm gonna turn on Fox News. Hope you don't mind. I just need background noise." "No worries. Your office, your rules," I said. After a pause, I asked her, "Out of curiosity, what do you like about Fox News?" She tilted her head, considering the question: "I guess I would describe myself as Republican, so I just think Fox News is less biased than some of the other news channels." After a few moments, she clarified, "Actually, I guess I would describe myself as conservative." I looked around her office as she continued to flip through paperwork and noticed a toy shaped like Donald Trump's head displayed on her bulletin board and a large Donald Trump–branded pen on her desk. Both items were easily within view of where candidates would sit, directly across from her desk, when they met with her to discuss their applications.

This conservative ethos permeated the hiring and training units in many other routine ways. Cadets made jokes about wanting to cut California out of the country. One cadet at Hudson told me that he was from California but left and came to the South because of "California politics." When I arrived at a Clarkston Police Department substation for a ride-along, three bumper stickers prominently displayed on a filing cabinet read, "EXTREMELY DEPLORABLE," "EXTREMELY RIGHT WING," and "God bless our troops. Especially our snipers."[10] Officers often referenced their membership to the National Rifle Association (NRA) and displayed Marines, Army, Navy, and Air Force flags in their offices and in the departments' gyms.

My presence at these departments—a PhD student in a sociology department at the University of Texas at Austin, sporting a gold nose ring—often served as a foil for officers and cadets. They periodically poked fun at me for being from Austin, which has a national reputation for being politically liberal. During a meeting with the sergeant who oversaw the academy at Hudson—a white man in his forties—he, seemingly out of the blue, asked me if I was a "gun nut." Feeling confused by the abrupt change of topic and pointed question, I responded, "Am I a gun nut? Um, I've shot guns. . . . But I don't own any guns." I talked about a research project I worked on previously about license-to-carry laws. The sergeant replied, "Hmm . . . you're in graduate school, you've got a nose ring. . . . You must be pretty left leaning, right?" I laughed, mostly at my own naivety in thinking that officers would not notice the way that I gave away my own politics, and confirmed that I was indeed left leaning. "What's it like for you to hang out with cops all day, then, since you're left leaning and we tend to be conservative?" he asked. I was pretty used to it, I told him: my mom's side of the family was from the South, I spent time with a lot of conservative gun owners during my last research project, and I had spoken with dozens of officers for this study. We talked about how most officers lived outside the cities they worked in, and he told me that, in his experience, most cops "may be left leaning on some issues," but they "love their guns" and are "mostly right leaning."

During the hiring process, officers did not ask explicitly about politics. In one interview, in fact, an officer interrupted an applicant midsentence when he started to say Donald Trump's name. In the exchange that followed, the interviewing officer reprimanded the interviewee, telling him, "We do not talk about politics" in these interviews. The applicant apologized and tried to explain his point: that he has avoided political topics, like talking about Trump, at work.

The recruiting and hiring officers did, however, make references to one another about how they perceived applicants' political leanings, demonstrating that they did use markers to evaluate where applicants stood politically. On one day of my observing board interviews, for example, an officer referenced the fact that most officers lived in conservative counties outside the moderate or liberal cities that they patrolled. Before the interviewee entered the large classroom at Rollingwood, the background investigator, a Latina woman in her thirties, told us that the applicant's name was Kyle, he was thirty-one, he was from the East Coast, and he had already been a cop there for four years. Before that, he worked for the Republican Party for three years. Rollingwood is a politically liberal city, so another officer on the board, also a Latina woman in her thirties, joked, "And he wants to come to here?" Laughing, the background investigator said she would just tell him to live in the counties west of the city, both of which were conservative, "where [the officers] all live." She moved on: there were no problems with his application. There was a complaint filed about him at his current department for pulling someone over "because they were Black," she said, but it was dropped. The other officers nodded, said "okay," and moved on. They did not inquire about this complaint during the interview.

Academy instructors often referenced their own political leanings in a way that assumed they shared an understanding and affiliation with everyone in the room. During a multiculturalism class at Terryville's academy, Rick discussed his conservative politics several times. Rick was white, tall, and, judging by the gray sprinkled throughout his hair and his thirty-six-year career in policing, seemed to be in his late fifties. He had a charming southern accent, dropping the *g*'s off words like "looking" or "morning," and when he lectured, he teetered from foot to foot, alternating his weight. He had reached the rank of lieutenant at Terryville and came to the academy specifically to teach this course to each incoming class.

During Rick's instruction, he described the chief's decision to assign an LGBTQ liaison as "bowing down to a politically active group," expressed dismay as to how anyone could advocate for the dismantling of the Immigration and Customs Enforcement (ICE), and mocked the city's new district attorney, who had recently announced that he would not pursue low-level drug charges. Another course at Terryville, which introduced the cadets to force options policies, happened to land on the day of midterm elections. Davis, a white instructor in his thirties, encouraged the cadets to vote. He leaned one elbow on the podium, turned his body to the side, and, smirking, said, "You're all voting for [the Republican candidate for senator], though, right?" The classroom filled with laughter. The academy's administrator, who was standing in the classroom doorway at the time, playfully noted, "You're not supposed to say anything political!" Davis went on anyway, explaining that he was voting all Republican except for a few Democratic judges he knew from testifying in their courtrooms.

Identifying with conservative politics was not a requirement to be hired at these departments, and certainly, not every police officer would identify as such. However, there was an operating assumption within the institution that officers were politically conservative, and thus, the institution itself took on a politically conservative identity. These findings are consistent with scholarship focused on police culture, which has consistently found that police officers tend to identify with conservative politics.[11] This politically conservative tendency on the part of the institution was also reflected when major US police unions—including the Fraternal Order of Police and prominent police unions in New York City and Chicago—officially endorsed Donald Trump.[12] The implications of this institutional political leaning are important for how we understand the persistence of racist police violence. Identifying with conservative politics means that, mostly, those who made it—and stayed—in the institution had a negative view of social activism, discounted marginalized groups' claims about inequality, and lacked an empathetic view toward systemic poverty and crime.

The Right Kind of Violence

During one day of fieldwork at Clarkston's academy, I stood in a large gym with Eric, a Latino defensive tactics instructor in his forties. Eric's left arm was covered in a tattoo sleeve, he had a black belt in Brazilian jiu-jitsu, and he often talked passionately about the importance of tactics training. On this particular day, as I watched the cadets run through their defensive tactics final exam, Eric expressed concern to me about cadets who had "never been in a fight." He complained about how sometimes applicants who had been in a fight but were not the "assailant" were disqualified because the record did not show that they had not initiated the fight. A lot of the military guys, he said, had been in fights, as had the guys who participated in combat sports, but otherwise, there were many cadets who had not been in a fight.

The hiring officers I met were very committed to disqualifying candidates with a history of egregious violence. For example, one day at Rollingwood's recruiting office, I asked Logan, a Black officer in his forties who worked as a background investigator, about the status of each of his investigations. Logan told me he was waiting on an email from "someone for an interesting BI [background investigation]." "What's going on with that BI?" I asked. The applicant previously worked as a police officer in Brazil, and everything was looking pretty good, Logan explained, until he talked to the applicant's ex-girlfriend, who offered information that the applicant had withheld. The applicant's ex-girlfriend told Logan that at some point during their separation, the applicant threatened to kill her, so she filed a complaint with the local police department. There were discrepancies, Logan said, between their accounts, and there was limited information available from the local police department. I asked if the applicant was going to be disqualified. Most likely, Logan said, but the sergeant had to sign off on disqualifications. In this case, and in others in which applicants demonstrated patterns of domestic violence, issuing of violent threats, or repeated disciplinary actions for using force inappropriately on the job, the institution indicated a disapproval of this behavior.

However, these departments also prioritized military veterans and preferred to hire applicants who had been in a fight before. These departments devoted a significant amount of time and resources to recruiting military veterans, and once they applied, gave them an advantage in the process. The majority of full-time recruiters and trainers at these departments were themselves veterans, and during the four months I spent with recruiters at Rollingwood, five of the thirteen career fairs they attended were at military bases. Departments in the United States, including several of those included in this study, that follow civil service processes give military veterans bonus points in the testing process, increasing their chances of getting hired.[13] Rollingwood's hiring officers told me that a few years prior, their command staff changed the age limit for applicants from forty to forty-five, specifically so that they could accommodate candidates who had recently retired from the military.

Men and women of color are overrepresented in the military, so recruiting directly from the military has been one way to demographically diversify police forces. Indeed, one recruiting officer told me that all the departments in the state were "competing over the handful of Black guys leaving the Army." Although officers of color certainly face unique obstacles in policing, the applicants of color who are successful—many of whom came from the military—fit the requirements for an ideal candidate. Often, military veterans had already mastered the habitus—or the deeply embedded dispositions that structure how we think, what we say, and what we do—required of police work and, thus, fit into the institution seamlessly.[14]

This preference for hiring veterans reveals something important about what kinds of backgrounds, experiences, and dispositions are considered a "good fit" for policing. Of course, this is partly a logistical consideration for the organization—military veterans, for instance, are already comfortable in environments where superiors shout orders at them, they know how to stand in formation and keep their uniforms in order, and they understand how to operate within a hierarchical structure. However, military veterans, according to the officers I met, were also top picks for departments because they knew how to control others, command compliance, and use violence in institutionally approved ways. It would be inaccurate to claim—and, indeed, this is not the argument I am making here—that hiring more military veterans necessarily translates to higher rates of racist police violence. Instead, I am arguing that the preference for military veterans, and the high level of institutional effort that goes into recruiting these candidates, tells us something about how departments conceptualize what constitutes a good police officer: that the skills one needs to be a soldier are directly transferable to police work and highly valued by the institution. There is also some evidence to suggest that this concerted effort to hire military veterans may indeed increase the chance of violent outcomes: studies have shown, for example, that officers with military experience are more likely to be involved in a shooting, fire their gun while on duty, and have use-of-force complaints filed against them.[15]

In addition to military experience, police departments wanted candidates who had experience fighting. During the board interviews, the hiring officers asked each applicant if they had ever been in a physical confrontation and, if so, to describe what happened. I was initially unsure if there was a correct answer to this question. With police violence so often in the news at the time, it seemed to me like this might be a trick question. But after watching several interviews and talking about the question with recruiting officers, it became clear that there was, in fact, a correct answer. The best answer an interviewee could give was that yes, they had been in a physical confrontation, but they did not initiate the fight. The hiring officers were trying to ensure that the interviewee was not reluctant to use violence when it was provoked and that, when presented with the opportunity, they would fight back.

Jason answered this question in his board interview by talking about a fight he was involved in during high school. Diane led the interview, with Nancy and Michael on each side of her taking turns asking follow-up questions. Michael asked, "Have you ever been in a physical confrontation?" Yes, Jason replied. "What happened?" Michael inquired. Jason was at a bonfire, he explained, when someone hit his friend over the head with a beer bottle. The two men started to fight, so Jason got in the middle of it. Michael clarified, "Did you break it up, or were you fighting too?" Jason shrugged, tossed his head back and forth, and conceded that he did end up throwing a few punches. Michael responded by telling Jason that he will get punched in this job, and when that happens, he cannot run away from the problem.

Applicants who had not been in a fight before were at a disadvantage when this question came up during the interview. I watched this happen during Chase's interview. Before the interview began, Chase's background investigator—Javier—provided some information about Chase: he was a forty-three-year-old white man from Pennsylvania; he had a wife who was "one of those ultrasound girls at the doctor's office," had two kids, owned a construction business with his dad, and was a "smart dude"—he had a degree in engineering and graduated with a 3.7 grade point average. Diane led the interview, but Javier and Logan also alternated asking questions.

About ten minutes into the interview, Diane asked Chase if he had ever been in a physical confrontation. Chase responded that he had been in a few verbal arguments in high school, but that was it. Repeating the usual warning, Diane told Chase that he will get punched in the face in this job and that it was important to know how he would respond. "Are you going to shy away from it or engage it? Are you going to cower up into a tiny ball?" she asked. As Chase replied that he was not a particularly aggressive person, Diane interrupted him to ask, "Can you be?" "I can be," he confirmed, trying to reassure her, "but, I mean, I can control myself. I wouldn't overrespond." Unsatisfied, Diane kept up her line of questioning, "There may be a time that you are fighting for your life. Do you think you'll be able to handle that?" "Yes, I think so," he said. Chiming in, Javier asked if he had any experience with martial arts or jiu-jitsu. No, Chase replied, he did not. At the end of the interview, Diane brought up Chase's response to this question again. She told Chase that he will get "tested" in the academy, and if "you are not ready to protect yourself, then you won't be able to protect your partner or the citizens." She suggested that he attend martial arts classes to "take a few hits," so he would know he "can take it" before the academy began, and again posed the question, "Are you going to curl up in a ball?" She emphasized that he needed to "know" how he would respond: "None of this 'I think' or 'I hope.' 'I know I can handle myself.'"

Once Chase left the room, Diane expressed unease about his response to the question about physical altercations. She was worried that he continually said that he "hoped" or that he "thinks" he could handle a fight. Javier shared Diane's concern, explaining that if Chase made it to the academy, he would be "the guy" who repeatedly had "did not engage" on his evaluation forms during scenario-based training. Diane agreed and said she thought he would "crawl into himself and disengage" if a fight presented itself. "He's gonna have to get angry," she insisted.

Although officers expressed concern about any applicant—including men—who had not been in a fight, they only explicitly brought up gender in interviews with women. Women were assumed to be less willing or able to fight than men, and thus, the hiring officers repeatedly emphasized to women that because of their gender, they would be tested in the academy and on patrol. Even when women applicants openly indicated an interest and willingness to fight, the hiring officers still emphasized the importance of standing their ground and fighting back.

During Jessica's interview process, she was repeatedly warned that she would need to prove herself capable of physically defending herself, especially as a woman. When asked about her exercise regimen in the interview, Jessica explained that she practiced jiu-jitsu, ran, lifted weights, and worked as a personal trainer. Jessica also scored in the top percentile on her physical fitness test for the department. Michael jumped in, warning Jessica that "especially being a female in the academy," the instructors were going "to push her to fight" and that she would have to "mentally wrap her head around it." Jessica responded that she had competed in jiu-jitsu and enjoyed sparring. With an air of caution, Michael inquired, "So do you enjoy that?" Later in the interview, Michael expressed concern about how Jessica would respond to someone punching her in the face, which he again said "will" happen at some point in the job. "Are you going to react or freeze?" he asked. In her reply, Jessica described herself as having an "aggressive" personality but clarified that she did not mean violent, just type A. Michael again posed the question: "How will you react when someone hits you while you are on the streets?" He held his hands up and told her not to answer the question, just to think about it. "When you have to fight for your life," he said, it is much different from the controlled environment of jiu-jitsu. The concern that the hiring officers brought up to Jessica—if she would stand her ground—was very similar to the warnings issued during Chase's interview. The important difference was that the hiring officers specifically brought up gender in Jessica's interview, telling her that because she was "female," the academy instructors would "push" her to prove that she could fight.

To be considered a good fit for policing, applicants needed to express a willingness to respond to threats of violence with violence. Recruiters pressed applicants on how they would react "when they are punched in the face" and made evaluations of their character and suitability for the job on the basis of whether they would engage the violence or "run away" from it. The recruiting officers were not necessarily wrong in their warnings—officers do sometimes get hit in the face, and their job does involve the use of physical force. However, that these departments were deeply concerned about candidates who had never engaged in violence—especially when they were women— highlights the centrality of violence to the job of policing. Importantly, what constitutes protection, violence, and aggression was, of course, rooted in racialized and gendered understandings of behavior. All applicants, though, regardless of gender and race, were expected to express a commitment to this way of understanding and enacting violence in order to be hired. This requirement for hire meant that applicants who avoided physical confrontation were considered ill suited for the job and that those who made it into the institution thought about violence as a reasonable, and necessary, response to a threat.

* * *

During the year I spent conducting fieldwork, the police officers I met often asked me if I was going to apply to their departments when I finished graduate school. Sometimes this would be a playful dig, for example, when a lieutenant at Rollingwood joked that it would be more "cost-effective" for me to just get a job there instead of conducting fieldwork. Cadets at Rollingwood earned more than double my salary as a graduate research assistant, so, laughing, I responded, "You're not wrong." Other times, officers were more serious, earnestly inquiring about my plans after graduate school and wondering why I did not want to be a police officer. I usually explained—and this was an honest, though incomplete, answer—that I did not think I would be a good police officer and that I was not sure I would make it through their hiring process. Over the course of the year, I would periodically scroll through a mental Rolodex of my friends, family members, colleagues, and acquaintances and could only identify a handful of people who might be qualified, according to the institution's parameters, to be police officers. I like to think that my social network is full of ethical, smart, reasonable, kind, hardworking people, so I felt confounded by this, wondering what exactly departments were looking for in candidates.

The police departments I studied genuinely wanted to hire good people and did not have an institutional interest in hiring applicants who were overtly racist or egregiously violent. As I have outlined in this chapter, this is not a story about police departments engaging in hiring practices that ensure that only white, violent, racist men are offered employment. The officers I met expressed a disapproval of blatantly racist behavior, and the lengthy hiring process would probably reveal a history of public participation in racist or violent practices. Police departments are not, as they once were, recruiting officers directly from patently racist, violent organizations, like slave patrols or the Ku Klux Klan.[16] And, although the unique conditions of police work may create a common occupational "personality," existing research shows that police departments are not recruiting individuals who are psychologically distinct from the general public.[17] Through my fieldwork, I instead found that a more insidious process structures departmental hiring practices in ways that reproduced and sustained the institution of policing, even as more women and men of color join police forces around the country. The problem in police hiring arises not from blatantly discriminatory hiring practices—though, to be sure, there are examples of these kinds of patterns as well—but, rather, in how departments conceptualize the "good" officer and the hiring practices that test for this.[18]

The very specific way that police officers conceptualized a good police officer has important implications for understanding patterns of racist police violence. Applicants who are honest, disciplined, responsible, and good team members, in the ways that the police define these qualities, are also comfortable with structured, hierarchical institutions, will follow commands from superiors, and are likely to feel intensely protective of their teammates (i.e., fellow officers) and the institution. Applicants who pursue this career because they feel a calling to protect the innocent from evil understand human worthiness in binary terms, in which certain people are bad and deserving of punishment and others are innocent and worthy of protection. Applicants who are politically conservative tend to have a negative view of social activism, dismiss marginalized groups' claims about inequality (especially with regard to police violence), and subscribe to an individualized, as opposed to systemic, understanding of poverty and criminality. Finally, applicants who are willing to respond to violence with violence will define avoiding or backing down from a fight as cowardly. This combination means that the candidates who make it into the institution are already likely to use force when presented with a physical threat—real or imagined—to conceptualize people who commit crimes as bad and deserving of their fate, to individualize racism, and not to take seriously activists' claims about racist police violence.

I am not suggesting that every police officer will commit racist violence. In fact, I am pushing in the opposite direction to deindividualize understandings of racism and violence. I am instead arguing that conceptualizing the good police officer in this way, and structuring the hiring practices around this construct, creates the perfect storm for institutionalized racist violence to continue. The way that police departments conceptualize good police officers, and the structures that evaluate applicants along these parameters, helps explain why attempts to scrutinize applicants more carefully or to demographically diversify departments have not led to meaningful institutional changes. Neither of these reform efforts challenge how police officers construct, and test for, suitability for police work. Doubling down on current hiring practices will exacerbate the problem, and the women and men of color who are hired by departments, despite not being white men, are deemed suitable by this white, male institution. For there to be changes to the institution, there would need to be a reconceptualization of what it means to be a good police officer, so that the candidates who then enter the academy embody a different ideal.

3   US vs. THEM

On one of my first days of fieldwork at Rollingwood's academy, I got to
the training facility early—as instructed—to spend the next ten hours
watching the cadets learn defensive tactics (DT). I called Steve, a sergeant at the academy, when I got to the campus to let him know that
I had arrived. Steve was a tall, white, forty-six-year-old Navy veteran
with eighteen years of law enforcement experience. He was friendly
and accommodating but a bit stiff and introverted. He cracked jokes
with his colleagues often, but he also avoided eye contact and displayed figurines from an assortment of science fiction and fantasy
films all over his office. Steve promptly appeared in the lobby and
made small talk as he walked me to the DT gym. The cadets were
now six months into their eight months of academy training, and this
week—called "DT Week"—was entirely devoted to developing their
tactical skills, which broadly describes moving and positioning oneself
strategically in an interaction. At the academy, "tactics" ranged from
ground fighting and grappling to ways of positioning a patrol car during a traffic stop.

Rollingwood's DT gym was large and made mostly of cement,
which created a sharp echo when someone spoke or played music.

There were three doors in the gym—one on the northeast end that connected to the staff kitchen, one on the north wall that led into the locker rooms and weight-lifting gym, and one on the southwest side that led directly outside, where a large field, the driving track, and other outdoor training facilities were located. While Steve and I made the journey from the front entrance of the academy to the northeast door of the DT gym, I asked him what the cadets had been learning lately and what they were doing today. Without elaborating, he said they were focused on ground fighting and grappling and would learn "weapon retention" and "two versus one" today. There were no instructors in the gym when Steve and I walked inside, just a dozen or so cadets stretching, warming up, and quietly talking among themselves.

At this point, I had not yet met the Rollingwood defensive tactics instructors. Each academy I studied had between one and ten instructors specifically hired to teach cadets tactics. The DT instructors were typically men in their thirties and forties, their racial and ethnic backgrounds varied, almost all were military veterans, and they usually had purple belts or higher in Brazilian jiu-jitsu. Steve pointed to the far corner of the gym to a few folding chairs and told me to have a seat there until the instructors arrived. A few cadets said good morning in a formal, studied tone as I took a seat. Aside from the air conditioner periodically clicking on and off, the gym was totally silent as I waited, anxiously wondering what kind of reception I would get from these instructors. Although it was still toward the beginning of my fieldwork, I had already gathered that there was almost a typology of personalities and life experiences characterizing officers who worked in different units. Officers in the recruiting and hiring office, for example, tended to be charismatic, funny, and welcoming. DT instructors, in contrast, were often exacting, critical, and intense.

My anxieties about the Rollingwood DT instructors turned out to be—at least for the first few days—warranted. When the instructors arrived, they stood together in the corner by a folding table about twenty feet away from me. Most of them did not greet me, make any attempt to fill me in on what was going on that day, or include me in their conversations. It was awkward and, I think, probably purposely alienating. All morning, I sat in my folding chair, jotting down notes in a small notebook, while the instructors—all men in their thirties and forties, all but one white—ignored me. If I did not know it already, their cold reaction to me made it clear that I was, in many ways, an outsider: I was a woman, a student, and a researcher, none of which were particularly welcomed categories of people.

A few days later, the DT instructors were quite candid with me about their initial suspicion and contempt about my presence. By now, they had learned that I had a friend who worked as a Rollingwood police officer. They also had a Rollingwood firearms instructor, Neil, vet me during the first few days. Neil sat next to me for most of those first two days, asking me questions about topics that ranged from my research to podcasts about astrology. These two new developments— that I had a friend who worked as a police officer and that another instructor reported back to them that I was "cool"—made it possible for me to build rapport. On the third day of DT Week, at which point the instructors had become much more friendly, Rob—a white DT instructor in his thirties—playfully recounted his reaction upon seeing me in the gym on my first day: "Yeah, I walked in and immediately: hostile. Is she media? A journalist?" David, a Latino instructor in his forties, added, "Yeah, do I need my lawyer present?" and the group all laughed. During a conversation I had with Neil, he reported that the DT instructors were initially wary of my being there. Neil explained, "You know, look, you're an outsider, right? And we don't know what your agenda is."

I knew when I started this research that the police were an insular group. Scholars who have studied the police for the past several decades often point to this insularity in their descriptions of the occupational culture of policing. Because of the potential dangers police officers face as part of their jobs, they must rely on and trust one another, leading to intense group solidarity. In the 1970s, policing researcher William Westley argued that this solidarity, and the resulting secrecy among officers, was "securely impenetrable from the outside."[1]

More recently, criminologist Bethan Loftus similarly described the police as leading "socially isolated lives" and displaying "defensive solidarity with colleagues."[2] As soon as I entered these academy spaces, I was subjected to varying degrees of this "defensive solidarity." As I spent time at these academies with officers and cadets, I learned who was allowed "in" and, perhaps more importantly, who was always considered "out."

At the academy, instructors established firm boundaries around the world of policing, subsuming cadets into the inner circle of policing and constructing a diverse cast of "others" whom the cadets would confront on patrol. These various groups of outsiders presented, according to the instructors, either a physical or institutional threat. Cadets learned to fear the unpredictable violence of "bad guys" and, in particular, those who specifically wanted to ambush and kill police officers. They also learned to be suspicious and critical of the media, activists, and the public, who instructors warned wanted to paint officers in a negative light, goad them into reacting violently on camera, and falsely accuse them of misconduct. These warnings about the public often included sexist undertones that framed women civilians as liars who accuse male police officers of sexual misconduct to get out of an arrest or get money from the city through lawsuits. Academy instructors established firm boundaries by creating and maintaining many groups of "them" that presented threats to the institution.

Learning who was considered a friend or a foe to police officers was an essential part of the socialization into state violence. This process shrank cadets' world until the only people they could relate to, rely on, or trust were other officers. They learned that they would need to navigate their new world with caution, wariness, and vigilance. Others would always be out to get them in one way or another, they were told, and they would need to protect themselves and their new family—and indeed, they did reference each other as family—from these threats.

Bad Guys

According to academy instructors, one major threat to the police were civilians who break the law or, as officers often referred to them, "bad guys." Throughout the academy, in almost every class I attended, an instructor referenced "the bad guy." During lunch, instructors reminisced about being young and eager to "catch bad guys." During defensive tactics training, instructors called the role of the person being arrested "the bad guy." In the hallway on the way to a scenario, I heard an instructor eagerly ask the cadets, "Y'all ready to shoot some bad guys?" This bad guy was ruthless and malicious, and he had a disregard for humanity. The bad "guy" was male, unpredictable, violent, and armed, and he harmed others for his own gain. Bad guys wanted to take advantage of and hurt innocent people.

Instructors sometimes used more colorful—and dehumanizing— language when describing these "bad guys," referring to them as "shit-bags," "shitheads," or "dirtbags." This came up when Dylan, the range master at Terryville, taught a class called Fundamentals of Marksman-ship. Dylan was about six foot six, and his shoulders were roughly the width of a refrigerator. When he sat across from me at the academy's kitchen table, he regularly ate two large, rare T-bone steaks for lunch. He was white and in his forties, and he often complained about his ex-wife, insisting to anyone younger than he was that they should never get married. In a presentation about shooting in low-light situations, Dylan referenced the fictional suspect featured on the Power-Point slide as a "shithead" and then, rolling his eyes, corrected himself, "Whoops, I meant person." The class laughed at his intentional slip.

Starting on the first day of the academy, instructors told the cadets that they should be afraid of bad guys and that if they let their guards down for even one second, they could be killed. During introductions on the first day of the academy at Hudson, the command staff urged cadets to take the training seriously so that they would survive patrol work. One by one, members of the command staff paced at the front of the room while they outlined their law enforcement autobiographies and gave advice about the training the cadets would undergo for the next eight months.

Commander Roger Carson was the fourth person to introduce himself to the new Hudson academy class. Roger was dressed in a formal uniform with his rank sewn neatly into the side of his suit jacket. He looked to be in his late fifties, was white, and had light-brown, wispy hair in a cropped cut. He smiled a lot and spoke in a soft tone with a slow cadence. He told the class that this was his thirty-sixth year working in law enforcement and that he was dressed up for national "Police Memorial Week," which began that day. It was unique timing, he mused, to start the academy on the first day of Police Memorial Week. Today, he said, the department would "honor our own" officers downtown at a citywide ceremony. He alerted the cadets to the "wall of honor" located in the main hallway of the academy building, where portraits hung of every officer who had died in the line of duty, along with a description of how they died. Roger encouraged the cadets to look at these portraits and to read "their stories," insisting that doing so would "keep you [the cadets] alive." The "wall of honor" at each academy—indeed, each academy I visited had one—was displayed prominently and regarded with deep reverence by officers and cadets. At Hudson, one of the many chores that cadets completed as part of their academy training included the daily dusting of those framed photos of fallen officers.

On the second day of Hudson's academy, the instructors began covering the state-mandated curriculum. The first class was titled Team Building, and Lisa, the officer who oversaw testing at Hudson's academy, taught the course material. Lisa was Black, around five foot six, and in her forties, and she had a magnetic smile. She read directly off the PowerPoint slides, lecturing about the importance of compromise, diversity, and adaptability in teamwork. Toward the beginning of the lesson, she announced that a few of the cadets in the preceding class dropped out of the academy after a Hudson officer was killed in an ambush. After this officer died, one of the cadets told Lisa that they were "not prepared to die." Eyes wide with intensity, Lisa warned, "Y'all need to start wrapping your head around it now, or you need to find a different occupation." To be a police officer, Lisa insisted, meant that someone might kill you at any moment.

The academy instructors brought these verbal warnings to life by frequently showing videos of police officers being brutally beaten and killed. The 1998 video of Laurens County Sheriff's Department Deputy Kyle Dinkheller's murder was frequently shown to convey this warning. The dash-camera footage shows Deputy Dinkheller, a young white man, pulling over Andrew Brannan, a sixty-six-year-old white man, on a country Georgia road for speeding. Brannan gets out of the car, dances around erratically, and verbally threatens the deputy repeatedly. The deputy shouts at Brannan to "GET BACK!" over and over again, but Brannan does not follow the commands. Brannan returns to his truck and retrieves a rifle, all while Dinkheller continues to shout, "GET BACK! GET OUT OF THE CAR! PUT THE GUN DOWN!" Brannan aims his gun at the deputy and shoots several times, while Dinkheller attempts to return fire. As Brannan shoots, the video captures Dinkheller's guttural, panicked screams and strained breathing as he dies at the side of his patrol car.

Each time I saw this video, sitting in a dark, still room with twenty-five to sixty cadets and officers, I dreaded the end, when I knew I would hear Dinkheller's terrified and forced last breaths. At Terryville, Kevin showed this video to the cadets during their De-escalation class. Kevin worked as the academy coordinator at Terryville, which meant he oversaw the daily operations at the academy and taught many of the courses included in the curriculum. I was in touch with Kevin frequently about the academy schedule and, over time, developed a familial fondness for him. He would often ask me how my graduate program was going, update me on how the cadets were doing, and give me suggestions of things to do in the area when I was not at the academy. Kevin was white and forty-eight years old at the time, and he had spent his career in the military and then law enforcement.

Kevin prefaced the Dinkheller video by clarifying, "Even though we're talking about de-escalation today, I'm not watering down officer safety. Do not drop your guard." He acknowledged that the cadets had actually already seen the video during their academy training but explained that "it's always good to watch these videos from time to time as a reminder." As we waited for the video to start, Hannah, the cadet who sat next to me at Terryville, leaned over and solemnly asked, "Have you seen this one?" I grimaced and responded, "Yeah, I have." We both turned back to face the front of the room, where we watched the three-minute-and-twenty-nine-second video of Dinkheller being murdered.

When the video ended, a dense silence hung in the air, and a wave of nausea gripped my stomach. A cadet turned the classroom's fluorescent lights back on. As our eyes adjusted, Kevin pointed out that Dinkheller gave Brannan thirty different commands during the interaction, with no action, and chose the wrong weapon when he initially pulled his baton. Dinkheller should have had Brannan at gun point when he did not comply with commands and acted aggressively, Kevin said, going on to insist, "If you give a command and they don't comply, you must make them do it. There has to be some use of force." The lesson here was that a failure to comply with commands required a use of force and that not adopting this approach to police work could be fatal.

Andrew Brannan's attorneys argued that he had suffered from post-traumatic stress disorder (PTSD) as a result of his time in the Vietnam War and was severely mentally ill at the time of Dinkheller's killing. Brannan was convicted of murder and, after several failed appeals, was executed by lethal injection at the Diagnostic and Classification Prison in Jackson, Georgia, in 2015.[3] This particular video is well-known throughout the world of policing. Investigative journalists have reported that the video of Dinkheller's murder has been incorporated into official training curriculums across the United States. In fact, Kyle Dinkheller's father travels to academies around the country to personally warn new officers about the dangers of not responding with enough force.[4] These kinds of graphic videos, which instructors showed over and over again, force cadets to watch people wearing uniforms very similar to theirs as they are killed, visually showing that any officer, at any time, could meet this same fate. Being "vigilant," as the instructors often described it, was an absolutely essential part of their jobs. However, this vigilance also meant that the cadets would be perpetually fearful for their lives while on duty.

Ambushes

More than just the dangers involved in officers' everyday tasks, instructors warned cadets that now, more than ever, police officers were being targeted. This warning reflects a larger, national narrative of a "war on cops," where officers feel that they are increasingly being targeted for violence because they are police officers.[5]

Paul, a Rollingwood instructor, repeatedly expressed this sentiment—that policing was becoming more dangerous—both in conversations with me and in his instruction to cadets. Paul was enthusiastic, inquisitive, and very chatty. He would often initiate conversation with me by asking about my impressions of the training so far. On days when the cadets ran through scenario-based training, I would usually alternate between watching the cadets and sitting with the instructors in the conference room, where they kept track of the cadets' progress. On one of these afternoons, Paul sat next to me and asked me if the training was what I expected it to be. I was about eight months into my fieldwork at this point but still found this question—which I was asked often by officers—to be a difficult one to answer. I really was not sure what I expected the training to look like when I began this project, and when officers asked me this question, I was never certain what kind of response they were expecting.

I explained to Paul that lately I had been finding some of the conversations I was having with officers to be even more interesting than the actual training. "That's fascinating," he noted, following up by asking what kinds of conversations I was having. I told him about a conversation I recently had with Josh, one of the DT instructors at Rollingwood, during which he suggested that I start asking officers if they would let their kids be cops. Intrigued, Paul asked me how other officers had been replying to this question. I told him that I had only asked three or four offices so far, but they mostly said no, they would not. "Would you?" I asked. Paul pondered the question for a minute and replied yes, if they wanted to, he would support their decision. He followed up by asking what reasons the other officers gave for not wanting their kids to pursue law enforcement. For the most part, I replied, they felt like the political climate right now was too volatile and that officers no longer received much community support. Paul interrupted me midreply to offer up his own theory: "It's the dangers, right?"

Paul then expressed his feeling that policing was an incredibly dangerous job. I asked Paul, "Do you think the job is more dangerous now than it used to be?" "Yes," he said, "I think so." "Compared to when?" I pressed. "What do you mean?" he asked. "Well," I explained, "you're saying policing is more dangerous now than it used to be. When was it less dangerous?" He struggled through his response, and attempting to clarify my reasoning, I added, "It seems like there was just as much, if not more, political unrest in the 1960s, which included some animosity toward law enforcement, right?" "True, there definitely was," he agreed, "but that was a movement." He elaborated, "It wasn't a feeling of hate directed specifically toward cops. If cops got in the way of a protest, then yes, there was some conflict, but cops weren't just getting ambushed because people hated them and wanted to kill them, like they are now."

The next day, Paul approached me while I stood in the gym watching the cadets go through scenarios. He silently leaned toward me to show me the screen of his cell phone. He had an article from PoliceOne.com pulled up, titled "Gunman Ambushes 2 NJ Law Enforcement Officers Sitting in Vehicle." According to the article, a man approached two Camden County Police Department detectives while they sat in their car and shot at both of them repeatedly. News articles published in the days following the shooting reported that both police officers were in plain clothes and sitting at a red light in an unmarked vehicle when two men opened fire. Both officers sustained injuries but survived, and the chief of police did not immediately identify a motive.[6] Pointing at the headline, Paul told me, "This is the kind of stuff I'm talking about. Now we have to worry about this kind of stuff." To Paul, this killing, which happened thousands of miles away, supported his argument from the day before: there were people out there who were waging war on the police, and this war was worsening.

This sense that the nature of the relationship between the public and police had changed and that, as a result, officers were at an increased risk of being ambushed also came up repeatedly in classroom instruction. Terryville cadets spent six days at an outdoor gun range learning how to use their pistols, shotguns, and rifles. Before that week of training, they spent a day in the classroom learning the basics of how firearms work and how to use them safely. Dylan, the range master, taught all the firearm-related instruction at Terryville. Each time he made the thirty-minute drive from the department's range to the academy facility, his presence emanated throughout the building. He physically took up a lot of space, the smell of the steaks he made for breakfast or lunch wafted throughout the building, and his booming voice seemed to ricochet off the walls. He usually wore green tactical pants that sagged lazily below his round belly and a long-sleeve, bright-red, moisture-wicking shirt with an all-black outline of the US flag running along one sleeve. He wore his duty belt with just his pistol, cuffs, and an extra magazine held neatly in place.

Dylan started out his instruction by explaining that there were two ways to learn a skill: through repetition or through pain. "If repetition doesn't work," he reasoned, "then you bring the pain." "You'll find out soon enough," he cryptically added. Dylan then pulled up the PowerPoint presentation titled "Fundamentals of Marksmanship." This was the instruction given to "people who suck at shooting," he explained. He clarified that any officer who did not pass their annual firearms qualifying exam (quals) had to go through this class as remediation. "If you're a police officer and you can't pass quals," he said, "there's a big problem."

To emphasize the importance of repetition and practice in developing any skill, Dylan asked the class to list some of their hobbies. He called on Hannah, asking, "What is a hobby of yours?" Sitting, arms crossed in front of her, head tall and tilted to the side, she replied, "Fishing." "How often do you go fishing?" he asked. "Fairly often, about twice a month," she responded. "Okay, so let's say about thirty-six times a year. That sound right?" "Yes, sir," she confirmed. Dylan cold-called on another cadet: "How about you, Garrett?" Without hesitation, Garrett joked, "Sleep." Dylan laughed, "All right, yeah, sleep becomes a commodity when you're out on patrol. I'm sure it was when you were in the military too." "How about you, Dan?" Dylan posed. "Watching football," Dan answered. "How often do you watch football?" Dylan followed up. "Oh, every day pretty much, except Wednesday," Dan replied. "All right," Dylan reasoned, "and let's say the season is seven months long, so that's six days a week, let's say three hundred days a year." "Yes, sir" Dan said. "Hannah," Dylan returned back to her, "how often do you shoot your firearm?" "Oh, pretty often, sir. I'd say also two to three times per month," she replied. "All right, all right," Dylan said, seemingly satisfied with her response.

Dylan then flipped to the next slide in his presentation, which included the text, "There are no time outs in deadly encounters." Dylan read the sentence off the slide and explained that when you are in a deadly force encounter, you cannot tell the person trying to kill you that you need to take a break in the middle of the gunfight. There are not any do-overs either, he added, as he switched the slide to the photo in figure 3.1.

I had already seen this photo a few times, in an assortment of contexts, during my fieldwork at police academies. The image shows a white police sport utility vehicle, with the front passenger door ajar, covered in blood. Red crime-scene tape cuts across the middle of the photo, while two law enforcement officers examine the ground around the car. The green grass, blooming trees, and sunshine beaming

Figure 3.1. Photo of Harris County sheriff's deputy ambush (Photo by Godofredo A. Vasquez, *Houston Chronicle*)

through the photo contrast sharply with the blood smeared across the length of the car and dripping out of the front seat. The photo shows the moments leading to this officer's panicked, violent death. Though Dylan did not provide the full backstory, I later looked into the event and learned that this photo shows the 2017 murder of Clinton Greenwood, the assistant chief deputy constable for Harris County Precinct 3, by William Francis Kenny. Shortly after this photo was taken, Kenny was reported to have died by suicide.[7]

Dylan asked the class what they saw in this photo, encouraging them to use the "cop eyes" they had been developing over the preceding five months. He explained that this was a chief deputy at Harris County Sheriff's Office with decades of experience in law enforcement, noting that this kind of thing could happen to any one of them at any time. As a "patrolman," he noted, you will have between 100 and 150 contacts with people in one shift. Contacts in which someone wants to kill you are rare, he said, but for this deputy, someone felt motivated enough to ambush and kill him.

Police officers do, of course, face real dangers as part of their job. Police officers are physically assaulted and killed while on duty, and the photos and videos that instructors showed in class are from real incidents. However, there is no empirical evidence to support claims that this violence has recently worsened or intensified. The available evidence instead shows that police work has actually gotten safer over time. The number of officers killed or assaulted on duty has not increased in response to the Ferguson uprisings, as some officers believe, and the number of police killings categorized as ambushes by the FBI in any given year has consistently remained between four and seventeen since 1995.[8] Academy instructors were not wrong when they told cadets that officers are sometimes killed in ambushes—they are, and it is certainly reasonable for cadets to feel fearful of this potential outcome. Importantly, though, the false narrative of a "war on cops" and the sentiment that this violence has worsened over time—and, in particular, that activist movements have made it worse—is a powerful mechanism for further intensifying an "us" and a "them" in the world of policing. The academy was structured in a way that ensured when cadets graduated and began patrol work, they believed that their job had recently become exponentially more dangerous and that they would be in physical danger at all times. This necessarily set up an adversarial and volatile institutional worldview, in which officers were trained to think of the public as a deadly threat.

The Media

At each of the academies I studied, the cadets were required to get sprayed in the face with OC (oleoresin capsicum) spray, also commonly called "pepper spray," in order to be permitted to carry it while on patrol. Having physically experienced the effects of OC spray, the instructors explained, meant that once they were on duty, new officers would understand the level of force they were using when they deployed OC spray and anticipate the physiological reactions a civilian would display afterward. This day at the academy, called "OC Spray

Day," was a highly anticipated ritual. Videos of this exercise at academies across the country are readily available on the internet, showing instructors spraying cadets in the face or eyes with OC spray, which quickly induces an intense physiological response, including screaming, crying, pacing, blindness, drooling, and nasal discharge. On OC Spray Day at Terryville, the cadets spent the morning in the classroom, where Kyle, the instructor, gave them an overview of how OC spray works and how the afternoon would run. Mostly, though, he reiterated how painful it would be and insisted that the only two things that would help the pain were cool air and time.

After lunch, Kyle separated the cadets into groups of six and announced the order in which they would complete the exercise. Everyone congregated in the parking lot, where a small obstacle course, large fans, and water stations had been set up. Each cadet picked a partner, who would help direct them through the obstacle course and monitor them afterward for any signs of an allergic reaction. Aaron, a former Marine, was first up. He stood about five feet away from Kyle, facing him head-on. As Kyle yelled, "Pepper! Pepper!" a stream of OC spray hit Aaron on his brow line, right above his eyes. "All right, open your eyes," Kyle instructed. Aaron's eyelids hesitantly fluttered open, and a second later, his entire body jolted as if he had been electrocuted. His neck spasmed, swinging his head sharply to the right, and he jumped up in the air. He groaned loudly, grimaced, and continually blinked his eyes. "Arghhhh!" he cried out. Aaron's partner directed him through the obstacle course, where he had to deliver strikes on a punching bag using his fists and then a baton, find a rubber gun on a mat and use it to issue commands to disarm his classmate, and then cuff and search them. When the instructors were satisfied, Aaron was allowed to run over to the water stations, where he furiously tried to wash the OC spray off his face. For the next hour or so, he paced back and forth along the fence sobbing while long strings of mucus hung from his nose. When an instructor tried to console him, he shouted, "It just hurts so much!" while he continued to cry.

A local reporter was visiting the academy that afternoon to write a story about the Terryville training and, specifically, about this exercise. The reporter wandered around the parking lot with a large camera, periodically cutting in to ask cadets questions. He mostly asked the cadets about how they were feeling, and no one seemed to mind him being there. The following Monday morning, however, the instructors expressed anger and frustration about the way the local news station spliced together their video segment about OC Spray Day. When I arrived at the academy that morning, I headed to the kitchen, where the instructors sat around the table drinking coffee and eating breakfast. Davis asked the other instructors if they saw the clip from the news story, and they all nodded. Davis lamented that he did not like how they edited the video and asked if anyone read the comments. Sabrina, an instructor, said she also read the comments and had to stop herself from replying to them. Davis went on to explain that he did not like the clip that they used, which showed a cadet who did not immediately feel the effects of the OC spray. The comments, he said, mostly criticized the instructors for not applying the OC spray correctly and for not training the cadets appropriately.

Kevin walked into the kitchen to join the discussion, sharing that he was planning to talk to their command staff to make sure reporters did not come back in a few weeks for TASER Day, when the cadets would each be shot with a TASER gun. "The public doesn't need to see this," he added. "They don't need to be here for this." At this point, Dylan came into the kitchen and started to cook a large hamburger patty in a frying pan on the stove. Picking up the conversation, he smirked and sarcastically jabbed, "Wait a minute, the media did a story about the police and fucked it up? And y'all are surprised?" "If it were up to me, I'd line 'em all up," he said as he imitated holding a gun and pulling the trigger with his right hand. The implication was, of course, that he would shoot them.

These instructors' reaction to their local news outlet represents a broader orientation toward the media at the academies I studied. Overwhelmingly, these officers felt that the media was out to get them and, in particular, that reporters would always misrepresent them, twist their words, and paint them in a negative light. When officers referenced the media in this way, they were mostly talking about news sources that they categorized as politically liberal or, at least, that were not explicitly friendly toward law enforcement. Fox News, for example, was not discussed as being a threat to policing but, rather, was watched in policing spaces and, for the most part, referenced positively by officers.

Academy instructors shared these sentiments with cadets during their instruction, warning that this media threat was becoming even more acute as video footage of police interactions became more easily attainable and increasingly visible through social media. During the Professionalism and Ethics course at Terryville's academy, for example, Wilson—a white instructor in his fifties—warned the class that the "media loves stories of police officers doing something wrong," adding that these stories "sell." Similarly, Kyle—the Terryville instructor who ran OC Spray Day—lamented that in news stories about the police, "we [the police] are always the bad guys, always, always, always." The story that the media wanted, instructors explained, would always cast them as the villains.

Instructors' warnings about the media were set against the 2018 backdrop of expanding social justice movements, including Black Lives Matter, and calls for the reform or abolition of the police. Instructors explained to cadets that if, as an officer, they hurt or killed a Black person in the course of their duties, the media would "make it about race" even if, according to the law, the use of force was justified. Brett, an instructor at Rollingwood, emphasized this lesson during the de-escalation course. At the time, de-escalation training was not yet mandated by the state, but many large, municipal departments had begun incorporating some version of this training into their academy. At Rollingwood, de-escalation training involved an eight-hour course titled Tactical Communications, which had been renamed from its prior title of Verbal Judo. Brett's teaching style was very matter-of-fact and at times became abrasive. He never warmed up to me, despite my knowing him for about a year, and I almost never saw him joking around with his coworkers. He was tall and white, looked to be in his forties, and had a completely bald head and sharp, pointy nose.

Brett continually reminded the cadets that they would always be on camera when they were on duty, whether through their body camera or a civilian's phone. This footage could be helpful, Brett explained, since civilians sometimes made bogus complaints. However, Brett insisted that even if the cadets were doing something reasonable in "our" eyes, the media would take the video and edit it into a ten-second clip, and the public would have a field day. To illustrate his point, Brett told the story of Officer Harvey, a fellow Rollingwood officer, who shot and killed a Black woman who was experiencing a mental health crisis and holding a "butcher knife" over another woman. Harvey arrived at the scene, Brett explained, saw the two women locked in this position, and from twenty-five feet away—he was a "good shot," Brett added—shot and killed the woman who was holding the knife. Because she was experiencing a mental health crisis and was Black, Brett reasoned, Harvey was berated by the media and the public, even though he did the "right thing." Harvey made the right decision, Brett warned, but there were still negative consequences because of the way the media described the killing. Even when you do the "right thing," Brett told the class, the media will still spin the story to make it about race.

The sense that the media—not the police—was responsible for the narrative that the police engaged in racist practices also came up in my interviews with officers. Paul, the Rollingwood instructor who showed me the headline about two New Jersey officers being ambushed, expressed this sentiment during our interview. I sat with Paul in an otherwise-empty conference room at the Rollingwood academy for just under two hours, asking him questions about his career in law enforcement, academy training, and the current political landscape around policing, among other topics. Paul did not need much prompting as an interviewee and often would take me with him to the topics he wanted to talk about.

Toward the end of the interview, I asked Paul what he thought about the current tension between the public and the police. He told me that he did not think "the tension is as high [in Rollingwood] as it is in other places." "It's there," he added, "but not like other places," like Ferguson. He immediately pivoted to explain that in his opinion, "some of that is . . . driven by people who need a job and are trying to make money. The job is like a Jesse Jackson: 'I'm gonna make a racial issue out of it because that keeps me in the spotlight. It keeps money in my pocket, and that's what I'm known for.' Or Sharpton. To me, they're just agitators." He went on to explain that "a news agency is a for-profit business" and that running stories about the police engaging in racist violence was good for business. Paul felt that this often meant that the media manipulated facts for monetary gain:

They put these sound bites out or these headlines: "Police Kill Kid" or "Kill Teen." Well, he wasn't a teen. Yes, he was killed but only because there was an attack. He drew a gun on somebody. So, the fact is true. He was eighteen or nineteen, still a teen. . . . He did die. The police did do it. But by putting that headline out there like that, it insinuates a certain thing. If—I'm gonna assume here—that most people don't read the full article or follow up with an actual case and get the facts, [so] I read the headline, "Oh, my gosh! RPD just killed another Black guy or another minority!"—or another agency or whatever. And they leave it at that. Even if the news agency puts in the actual article that "Hey, the guy pointed a gun at 'em" or they have the video and they show it. The guy's running, and he turns like this with a gun in his hand and then gets shot in the back. Well, I can still shoot you like this, and my back is to you. So, it's just a play on words. It drives and pushes activity for profit.

Paul felt frustrated by the media's descriptions of police violence. While the details included in a news story might be true, he explained, he thought that journalists purposely used inflammatory language or phrasing to fuel the narrative that the police disproportionately or unfairly used force against Black people and other people of color.

Paul's colleague Bill also placed blame on the media for the public perception that the police are racist and violent. Bill oversaw all the defensive tactics and firearms training at Rollingwood for cadets and officers. He was forty-nine years old, Black, and an Army veteran, and at the time of our interview, he had worked in law enforcement for eighteen years. I interviewed Bill almost a year into my fieldwork, so by then, I had come to expect his irritable grumblings about departmental policies and his strong opinions about most issues. I asked Bill the same question I asked Paul: What do you think about the tension between the public and the police right now? In his response, Bill complained that the media purposely created inflammatory headlines that made stories about race to "grab" attention:

> I think the media is to blame for a lot of the tension. . . . The headline says, "Cop Kills Black Male." And then the other headline says, "Cop Kills Armed White Male." What's the difference? Well, there's that extra word that's added in there: "armed." So why would they make that headline that says, "Cop Kills Black Male"? Just leave it at that? Broad like that? . . . Why would they make that headline, and then the other headline is "Cops Killed Armed White Male?" It's to grab people, and that sensationalism, and to drive that tension up, and they drive that tension up. It's better for them. And I think the media plays a large part, more today than they ever have in the history of mankind.

Bill, like Paul, explained that the media purposely crafted headlines to inflame public animosity toward the police so that they could make a profit. Both these officers framed the news media—not officers or departments or policies—as being responsible for the public belief that the police engaged in practices that disproportionately harmed Black people.

Some officers felt that the media itself was *fueling* violence between the police and the public. Steve, who oversaw the Rollingwood academy, told me he thought that the "media is trying to start some war" and that they were "pushing this whole race thing in order to make their sales." Steve warned that this kind of reporting would "lead to even further arrests in the community" and insisted that news sources should "stop putting a spin on everything." Paul similarly felt that the media "throw headlines out there" to get "activity" and "hits" on the story, which then "creates a divide."

Joey, a Rollingwood cadet I interviewed a few months after graduation, similarly thought the media was "fueling this divisive society we have now and just making that dividing line so much bigger just because of the way they're reporting stuff." When I asked for clarification, Joey explained,

> Situations are being put into the media before, or with disregard to, the full facts surrounding it. . . . The biggest one nowadays is "White Cop Kills Black Male." Like, granted, yes that happens, but it's, like, if that's all you base it on is race and cop and civilian, then yeah, it's gonna look bad. Because if every time it happens, you title "White Cop Kills Black Male," and that's the constant, like, it's always gonna look bad, as opposed to like, "cops shoot," you know, "Black male who had just killed somebody" or "was just shooting at officers" or, you know, putting the full story out.

Joey did not accuse the media of reporting false information but, rather, took issue with the way that news reports portrayed police action. The victim in a police shooting could indeed be Black, he explained, but the media made it seem as though the officer shot this person *because* they were Black. According to this worldview, an officer's actions were legitimate and fair; it was the media, not the police, that made it "about race," which then further fueled public animosity and resentment toward the police.

This narrative that the media always unfairly and negatively depicts police officers is at odds with decades of scholarship that examines the role of race in media coverage of crime-related stories. These studies use different sources of media (e.g., local television news coverage, national network news coverage, print media) in their analysis, which makes direct comparisons complicated and difficult. However, scholars have consistently found that in news media, Black people are overrepresented as perpetrators of crime and, in particular, violent crime; white people are overrepresented as victims of crime; and white people are overrepresented and Black people are underrepresented as police officers.[9]

More recently, scholars have examined if these racialized trends in news coverage hold true in cases of police shootings. The findings from these studies vary, sometimes challenging and other times supporting the perspective of officers that I have presented here. For example, in one study of news outlets' social media posts about police shootings, the authors found that official sources—in particular, police sources—are privileged in the reporting on police use of force.[10] This suggests that the police have a significant amount of influence on how police action is reported on in the news. In another study, in which the authors analyzed newspaper accounts of police killings prior to and after the highly publicized 1999 police killing of Amadou Diallo, they similarly found that news sources relied heavily on official accounts of the event, rationalizing police violence by pointing to the laws that justified their responses.[11] These two studies provide evidence suggesting that the media does not villainize the police but rather privileges police accounts of their own violence and justifies or rationalizes their actions.

Other studies paint a slightly different picture of this issue. In an analysis of written media coverage of police shootings between 2014 and 2015, for example, the authors found that while race and racism were not typically explicitly mentioned, they were implicitly discussed. Of the 364 articles analyzed, only sixty-two referenced the race of the person shot by the police. However, the authors also argue that news sources reported on police shootings differently depending on the race of the victim. They found that when the victim in a police shooting was Black, news sources were more likely to frame the officer as culpable and less likely to mention the criminal history of the victim or their possession of a weapon.[12] It is important to note, however, that these authors' period of analysis overlaps considerably with the police killing of Michael Brown in Ferguson, Missouri, in August 2014, which may have amplified explanations of police violence as being rooted in racism. In another study, the authors examined news media reports that included the phrases "police shooting" and "Black man" published during the five months following George Floyd's murder, which happened in May 2020. These authors found that during this period, news sources tended to describe these shootings as rooted in racism and police officers as responsible for the violence.[13] However, this study does not offer a point of comparison, as the authors only included in their analysis instances in which a Black man was shot by the police.

Thus, although there is some evidence to suggest that, as the officers I met insisted, the media is more sympathetic toward Black victims of police violence, there is also a large body of scholarship showing that the media disproportionately depicts Black people as violent criminals who are responsible for the violence they experience at the hands of the police.[14] And, even if the media has, at certain periods of time, reported more sympathetically toward Black victims of police shootings, this certainly does not negate the fact that the police do disproportionately harass, arrest, search, assault, and kill Black people.[15] It is harmful, and indeed dangerous, that police officers are pointing to the media, rather than themselves, as the reason why the public believes that the police are engaged in racist practices. This narrative allows officers and departments to absolve themselves of responsibility by blaming the media for manufacturing stories about racism in policing, rather than acknowledging that racist practices in policing are an empirical reality on which the news media reports.

Activists

The Multiculturalism class at Terryville's academy consisted of an eight-hour block of instruction stretched across two days. On the first day, the cadets spent the morning learning about the code of criminal procedure and then pivoted to the multiculturalism curriculum in the afternoon. Rick, a white lieutenant in his fifties, taught the course. Rick usually worked in the department's public information office but requested to teach this course each time a new class of cadets entered the academy. He began the instruction with the disclaimer that the class was dry and boring, so he would try to incorporate "war stories" that have happened at Terryville to liven it up. He also added that the course used to be called Cultural Diversity but had recently been renamed by the state licensing body to Multiculturalism.

Rick spent most of the eight hours allotted for this course discussing the current state of politics and policing. Every now and then, he would return to what seemed to be the formal curriculum, but he would usually add his own commentary about the topics. For example, when covering the PowerPoint slide about prejudice, he began by reading the definition of prejudice included on the slide and then went on to explain that there was a difference between prejudice and discrimination. Being prejudiced, he clarified, just meant that you had a "preference," which could be about a food or a color. "My prejudice," he said, "is that I like Mexican food."

Toward the end of the afternoon, right before the cadets left the classroom to begin their physical fitness training, Rick warned that they should assume that everything they do on duty is recorded. He pulled up the YouTube channel for The Battousai, a self-described "citizen journalist and video activist" specifically focused on covering "public officials" and "police officers." Rick described the man who made these videos as "goading" police officers but suggested that he had "done us [the police] a service by showing us how bad and ignorant we can look." He showed the class a video from the The Battousai YouTube channel of officers interacting with an activist to demonstrate how it should be done. In the video, the officers were calm and polite, and the interaction did not escalate in any way. Rick insisted that the cadets take note and be sure not to let activists goad them into a reaction on camera.

Throughout my fieldwork, activists were described as a major institutional threat to police departments. Officers repeatedly characterized activists as overly dramatic liberals who made illegitimate accusations about the police, did not understand or appreciate the intended function of the police, and purposefully provoked officers to capture a reaction on camera as a way to further their cause. At the time that I conducted this research, the word "activist" was most often used to refer to the Black Lives Matter movement, indicating that police officers were most concerned with activists who were organized around issues of racial injustice in policing. At the academy, instructors—like Rick—warned cadets that they would need to maintain their composure when dealing with activists so that they did not unintentionally contribute to these groups' anti-police agenda.

Cadets were required to put these warnings into action by demonstrating that they could indeed keep their composure when confronted by activists or, at minimum, by concerned civilians witnessing an arrest. At Rollingwood, the cadets spent two full weeks at the end of the academy completing role-plays of scenarios they might face on duty. The scenarios ranged from resolving a verbal argument between two people in a park to being ambushed by a civilian with an AR-15 rifle. Rollingwood patrol officers volunteered as the actors in the scenarios and the evaluators of the cadets' performance. If a cadet failed a scenario, they were required to repeat it.

During one scenario, the cadets initiated a routine traffic stop that turned into a drug-possession arrest. The cadets detained the driver, played by a male, Latino officer, and frisked him by the side of their patrol car. While they did this, a group of six other officers stood around the "suspect" getting frisked, trying to antagonize the cadets by yelling at them and recording the interaction on their cell phones. One of these officers—a white man who looked to be in his thirties—accused the officer of racially profiling his friend, shouting, "Oh, so because he's the only Mexican guy, that's why you're gonna search him? We're out here every fucking night, but we're white so you're not gonna bother us, huh? You're only gonna search the fucking Mexican guy, because you don't like Mexicans!" He went on to shout, "This wouldn't be happening if Hillary Clinton was president!" One officer held his phone with the flash on toward the cadets and yelled, "Hey, let my people go!" while another shouted that this was "police brutality." In unison, they all chanted, "Racist! Racist! Racist!" at the cadets as they continued their frisk. Another repeatedly yelled that the Latino man's rights were being violated. These imitations served both as a test of focus for the cadets and as a mockery of activists.

Although activists were, in general, not taken seriously, most of the officers I met did not dismiss *all* claims of racial injustice in policing. There were certain police killings—Eric Garner, for instance, who was killed by an NYPD officer in 2014—that solicited criticism from officers. While these officers categorized certain cases of police killings as unacceptable, they often considered them one-offs and, thus, still felt that activists' claims about racist patterns of police violence were illegitimate, despite the empirical evidence that proves otherwise.[16]

This ambivalence came up in my interview with Joey, a newly minted police officer at Rollingwood. I watched Joey go through the academy, where he stood out as one of the top cadets in his class. Within the first few weeks, his class elected him to serve as their vice president, which meant, in his own words, "if something went wrong, it was my fault." Joey's father worked as a sheriff's deputy for most of his life, and after spending some time in the Marines, Joey followed in his father's footsteps by pursuing law enforcement. I interviewed Joey at a Starbucks just north of Rollingwood about three months after he graduated. I asked Joey what he thought about the tension between the public and the police, and in his response, he began by blaming the media but then added that in certain situations, like the police killing of Eric Garner, the police officer's actions were inexcusable and a blatant violation of law: "That horrible incident in New York where the cop put some guy in a chokehold, even though chokeholds have been banned since like 1991 or '94, and you put some guy in a chokehold and the guy died, like, the cop is 100 percent at fault for that. First of all, you did something you didn't know how to do because you didn't let him go, and you did something that's been outlawed for fifteen years." Joey faulted NYPD officer Daniel Pantaleo for Eric Garner's death, pointing specifically to a lack of tactics competence and a violation of law. That officer, Joey explained, was "100 percent at fault" for Garner's death.

A few minutes later, though, when I asked Joey if he thought that there was "any legitimacy to some of the things the media says or any of the gripes that activist groups have about the police," he replied, "I mean, honestly, I would say no." He elaborated,

> They're taking one or two instances and then trying to, like, make it a stigma, when it's not. One or two instances doesn't create a pattern, especially if we're talking, like, over the entire, like—so granted, so, like, Ferguson, right? A lot of people don't know why there were actually riots in Ferguson or, like, protests, protests in Ferguson. People think it was all about Michael Brown, Michael Brown, Michael Brown, but it wasn't. So, what was happening in Ferguson was, like, cops were pulling over Black people, and you know, Black people had warrants, all that, and they would, like, give them every citation they could, knowing full well they couldn't pay for it, which would create more warrants, and then they would take them to jail. And that was, like, that was a stigma. That was happening across the department. And so that's why there were protests in Ferguson. But, like, so many people point to that Michael Brown shooting, which was 100 percent legitimate, per scientific evidence, but once again, it was like "cop killed a Black male," and that was all everyone zoned in on, not the fact that Michael Brown had just beat the crap out of the cop and then charged at him after beating the crap out of him.

Although Joey considered some instances, like the killing of Eric Garner, to be an illegitimate use of police power, he thought that these were the exception, not the rule, despite decades of scholarship that point to the systematic nature of these racist practices. Joey felt that, in general, the media, activists, and the public inaccurately and unfairly used one or two cases to make claims about larger patterns of racism in policing. He acknowledged that the Ferguson Police Department may have indeed been engaging in racially unequal practices but stood firm in his feeling that the police shooting of Michael Brown was a legitimate use of force. In his response, Joey categorized some police actions as unacceptable but maintained that regardless, the larger claims about patterns of racist use of police violence were illegitimate and either misinformed or fueled by inflammatory news reports.

Even when officers thought that activists' claims about racism in policing might be legitimate, they were still critical of the methods, strategies, or tone used by activists to advocate for their causes. This came up in my interview with Bill when he described activists, including those in the Black Lives Matter movement, as "bullies" who get others to "bow down" to their cause by threatening to label them as racists. He went on to explain, "Maybe there's genuine concern on what their cause or feelings are, rightfully so. But I think things are getting hijacked, and people are getting just bullied. . . . They've bullied their way onto the pulpit to get themselves there, to get their voice heard." In response, I asked Bill if he felt that any of the claims made by Black Lives Matter activists were legitimate. He explained that while the police were responsible for some "bad shoots," the public was too quick to judge officers' actions without adequate information:

Oh yeah, some are. But I don't think . . . [pause]. I'm just like the rest of society: if I see a bad shooting, which seems to fuel a lot of this, if I see a bad shooting, and my initial reaction is "that looks bad," I have to remind myself you're doing the same thing that society's doing. So, then I have to sit back and wait until the facts come out, delve into the facts, and then put myself in that officer's shoes and determine, Was that reasonable or not? I don't think the public's doing that. They don't . . . they do want the facts, but I think initially, we are rushing to judgment too soon, and it's never taken back. Like, once you cut a feather pillow open on a mountain top, you're not getting all those feathers back. And we're constantly doing that. We're very quick to judge people. "This guy's a sexist," "this guy's a racist," and then the facts come out, and you're like, "Woah, well, I didn't know all of that." Well, it's too late. The news cycle has already moved on. Nobody cares that this guy's been vindicated. We're on to the next headline. So, yeah, I think some things are. Again, we've—the police themselves have provided some of this ammunition for this anger. I don't think the police have done all wrong, but I think, yeah, we have provided some of that anger. There have been some bad incidents in the history of policing that, only through time and I don't know what else, society will get over it. Maybe they never will.

Bill did not absolve the police of blame, and he did feel that the police had contributed to the anger expressed by contemporary social movements advocating for racial justice. However, he was critical of activists' tone, explaining that activists had "bullied" their way into public debates about policing. He also felt that the media and the public unfairly judged police officers without full and complete information and that once someone had been labeled a "sexist" or a "racist," there was no chance of public forgiveness.

Although the majority of the instructional content and discussions about activists at these academies revolved around issues of racial justice in policing, there was also an overarching contempt toward any kind of liberal activism. Sometimes this was playfully directed toward me because I was attending graduate school in a city with a national reputation for being particularly politically liberal. Once, for example, when I returned to the Rollingwood academy after some time away back on campus to attend meetings, Rob joked, "How was your campus protest?" and followed up by asking, "How many statues did you burn down?" I played along, replying, "Just two."

Other times, instructors explicitly mocked activists during formal academy training. For example, on OC Spray Day at Terryville, Kyle showed several YouTube videos of crowds getting OC sprayed to illustrate the "physiological reaction" it solicits. He then showed pictures and videos taken at Occupy protests, including one in Denver, Colorado, and another in Portland, Oregon, when officers used OC spray on the crowds of protestors. "These people are not there to peacefully protest," Kyle explained, going on to say that the protestors were there to "fight" law enforcement and had designed their signs as weapons to resist officers. He showed a picture of officers in Portland using tear gas and OC spray on the crowd and joked, "Look, they're watering the hippies." He specifically pointed out one man in the photo who was videotaping, explaining that "these people" videotaping always try to "make us [the police] look as bad as possible." At the end of the class, Kyle showed a video of the Occupy protests in Portland in which a man being interviewed reported that officers sprayed a woman next to him with OC spray and then dragged her by her hair to arrest her. The man told the reporters that he was fearful he would be "bludgeoned" by the police at any moment. Kyle mocked the man featured in the video for several minutes. "I'm sure they told them to leave one hundred times," Kyle said. "Don't be a part of history, guy. Watch at home.... Go home in your Prius if you're so scared of being bludgeoned."

In his instruction, Kyle mocked the activists' goals and trivialized the physical effects of police responses to protests. He, for example, called spraying OC and tear gas on the crowd "watering the hippies" and thought the man featured in the video should go home in his Prius, a hybrid electric car often associated with people who are concerned with preserving the environment. Kyle also conceptualized these activists as adversaries of the police, explaining to cadets that these activists had developed weapons out of their signs to "fight" the police. Even when activist movements were not directly advocating for police reform, then, they were still considered to be an institutional threat to the police.

The Public

Terryville's eight-hour De-escalation class landed about halfway through the academy's training calendar. Kevin taught the class, reading through PowerPoint slides covering topics like impression management, active listening, and body language. Kevin began his instruction by providing some context for the topic—he explained that in the past several years, there had been a lot of talk about use of deadly force and how to de-escalate. There were "riots" and—he hesitated, trying to find the right words—"racial tension," which made de-escalation a trending topic. Although "de-escalation is nothing new," Kevin highlighted, "public perception is everything, and they perceive use of force to be out of control." "Some people, mostly older police officers, laugh at this topic," he added, "but I assure you that this is not some watered-down officer safety. This has nothing to do with dropping your guard." Throughout the class, Kevin continued to harp on this point, reminding the cadets that using de-escalation strategies should never be prioritized over officer safety. He forcefully told the class, "never second-guess yourself in the streets," and insisted that they should never worry about what an interaction will look like on camera. Instead, they should do what they were trained to do. Kevin explained that civilians do not really know what happens on the streets. "I'm not saying civilians just 'don't get it,'" he said, "but unless you've been on the streets and unless you've had your life on the line," you cannot possibly understand the situations at hand.

Kevin and his fellow instructors continually framed the public in this way, as a group of misinformed and naïve people who, at times, falsely accused them of misconduct. The public was, according to this narrative, both a nuisance and an institutional threat. Instructors often referenced the public's perception of police in their lessons, recognizing the significance of public sentiment but stipulating that the public was ignorant and easily influenced by outside forces, like the media. There was, of course, truth to some of these sentiments. Officers were certainly correct that members of the general public do not have experience working patrol, so they do not have a clear sense of what officers do on a daily basis. Arguably, though, police departments' general lack of transparency ensures that the public does not know what happens on patrol. Officers were also correct that some segments of the public do not like or support the police and that civilians do issue formal complaints about officers' conduct. However, these instructors' warnings about the public meant that cadets learned that they would, from now on, only be fully understood and supported by other officers. They learned that their worlds were now distinctly different from everyone else's and that they would need to constantly protect this new inner circle.

Many of the officers I met adopted the language of prejudice to describe what they felt was both misunderstanding and mistreatment from the public. These officers felt that there was an irony to the negative public sentiments toward the police, explaining that the sweeping generalizations made about the police amounted to the same kind of prejudice and discrimination that they had been accused of by the public. This came up in my interview with Joey, the new officer referenced in the preceding section about activists. Immediately after he brought up Eric Garner's murder, Joey went on to describe what he felt was hypocrisy in the way the public thought about the police: "When the cops are guilty, everyone thinks that all cops are like that, which I personally find very ironic. Because one of the biggest things . . . 'you're just pulling me over because I'm Black' or 'you're just doing this because I'm Black'—it's like, well, you think I'm doing that just because I'm a cop? And it goes both ways. Like, you can't, you know, say that I'm prejudiced when you are, by saying that, being prejudiced." Joey explained that when civilians claimed that all officers engaged in racist behavior, they were ironically partaking in the same kind of prejudicial behavior that elicited their reaction in the first place. If the public did not want police officers to make generalized assumptions about Black people, Joey posed, why did they feel comfortable making generalized assumptions about police officers? Joey equated racial identity with occupational identity in his comments, likening racial discrimination in policing to generalized statements about police officers. In doing this, Joey neglected both historical and contemporary power structures around race and policing and decontextualized the meaning of the word "prejudice." However, during our interview, he echoed a sentiment shared by many of his coworkers by expressing a deep frustration over what he understood to be an inconsistency, and unfairness, in treatment.

Although it is of course possible that cadets came into the academy with this way of understanding prejudice, it was certainly then emphasized in their training. This came up during the Professionalism and Ethics course at Terryville. Wilson, a white instructor in his fifties, had taught this class for over ten years, although he worked full-time as the commander overseeing the narcotics unit. Wilson was tall and had short, gray hair, thin lips, and a long, oval-shaped face. He was dressed in his formal uniform, which was not typical for academy instructors, who usually wore khaki cargos and an athletic, moisture-wicking shirt. He addressed this in his introduction, explaining that because he worked in narcotics, he was usually dressed in plain clothes, but he felt it was important to dress in full uniform when teaching this class. His voice was dry, and though he seemed knowledgeable, he was not engaging or funny.

We spent about half an hour reading through Terryville's code of ethics. Wilson called on a different cadet to read through each paragraph of the long, dry text. "We have a duty to protect everyone and to respect everyone's constitutional rights," one cadet read aloud. "The code of ethics applies to your private life as well; you are expected to conduct yourself ethically off duty," another cadet read to the class. At this point, Wilson tangentially pivoted from the text to talk about stereotypes, telling the cadets that they had chosen the "only" job in which it was apparently okay to be stereotyped. "You aren't allowed to stereotype Black people or Asian people or women," he said contemptuously, "but it's okay to stereotype us. So, because of what one person did, you all like to beat people, you're all power hungry." He told the class the story of meeting his wife as an example. When they first met, she said she did not like dating cops because they were all "players." "That's not fair," he replied. "That's the same as me saying that you're some way because you're Hispanic." In his example, Wilson conceptualized policing as a racial or gender identity within the context of prejudicial belief systems and accused the public—including his wife—of holding inaccurate, unfair, and damaging stereotypes of police officers. Just like Joey, Wilson described a frustrated confusion about why stereotypes against racial minorities and/or women were considered unacceptable but stereotypes about police officers were generally accepted.

In this same vein, academy instructors warned cadets that inevitably, at some point in their career, a civilian would falsely accuse them of misconduct. Brett brought this up during his de-escalation instruction at Rollingwood, insisting that being professional, communicating effectively, and attempting not to use force—all tenets of de-escalation—were good for officers because they would reduce the likelihood of their getting formal complaints, criminal charges, or sued civilly. If you work as a cop for long enough, Brett explained to the class, you will get sued. To illustrate, Brett and Paul both recounted times when they were sued during their careers, concluding that the civilians' claims were groundless and absurd. Paul lamented the intense stress of his lawsuit, which dragged out for eighteen months while he was trying to buy a house. The instructors added that neither one of them was found to have committed any crimes or policy violations.

This warning about, and dismissal of, being sued as an officer came up again at Terryville during the Force Options class. Davis, who taught the course, assured the cadets not to "worry about being sued" for excessive force. "It's probably gonna happen at some point in your career," he added. He then described when he got sued for excessive force, insisting, "I didn't even touch her." He and his partner arrested a woman, he explained, who then tried to swallow the drugs she was holding. Davis clarified that he was not forceful with her because he knew it would not look good on camera, so he pulled her cheeks open to try to prevent her from swallowing the drugs, but she did anyway. She head-butted his partner, he told us, and his partner reacted by smacking her, resulting in her head hitting their patrol car hard enough to break her nose. Sometimes, Davis clarified, people bring lawsuits against the department hoping that the city will just settle the case. These people are just looking for easy money, he explained, since they know the city will probably settle to avoid the expense of going to trial.

The training officers at these academies were correct in their assertion that the cadets would probably not experience negative consequences stemming from citizen complaints. Although there is a lot of variation between departments in the number of civilian complaints issued against officers, there are some consistent trends in the content, context, and outcomes of these complaints.[17] Overwhelmingly, civilian complaints are not sustained, which means there is little to no consequence for the officers involved. In one study of civilian complaints across eight cities, the authors found that only 11 percent of issued complaints were sustained. These percentages were even lower when isolated to complaints of improper force, for which only 2 percent were sustained across all eight agencies in the analysis.[18] In a study of civilian complaints issued in Chicago between 1988 and 2020, the authors found that just 3 percent of civilian complaints of improper force resulted in any kind of disciplining of the officer involved.[19] These findings are consistent with national reports released by the US Department of Justice, which, for example, document that across all large US state and local law enforcement agencies, only 8 percent of the twenty-six thousand complaints issued against officers for improper force in 2002 were sustained.[20] Importantly, there is a racial disparity in the complaint process, in which Black civilians spend more time than other groups on the complaint process and are much less likely to have their complaint sustained.[21]

Some instructors' warnings about civilian complaints were also rooted in underlying sexist logics, in which men instructors cautioned men cadets that women civilians would falsely accuse them of sexual misconduct, abuse, or assault. This came up in Rollingwood's tactics training, when the cadets learned how to conduct frisks and searches. Most departments have specific policies dictating how invasive a search can be on the basis of the gender of the officer and of the civilian. At Rollingwood, men officers were allowed to frisk women but not search them. Conducting a frisk was considered appropriate if an officer believed that someone may be armed and involved the officer touching someone, over their clothing, to check for weapons. A full search—which involved turning out pockets, taking off shoes, and shaking out clothing—could not be conducted until after an arrest had been made. At each department, regardless of whether men officers were allowed to search women, there were rules dictating how the officer touched and inspected "sensitive areas," which included the groin, butt, and breasts. This also applied to women officers searching men's "sensitive areas," though instructors did not spend nearly as much time discussing this scenario.

The Rollingwood cadets spent a full day practicing searching one another. At the end of the day, their instructors asked if they had any questions. Largely, the cadets' questions focused on the specifics of how men can or should frisk women. One man in the class asked for clarification on how to frisk a woman wearing a skirt or dress. Another man asked whether he would be allowed to pull a woman's sports bra away from her body and shake it to let weapons drop out. In answering these questions, the instructors repeatedly reminded the cadets that everything would be on camera, so as long as you frisk within policy, no one would be able to accuse you of harassment or assault. In this case, they explained, the body cameras were your "best friend." The concern here was that women civilians would create false stories or misinterpret men officers' touch as sexually invasive, not that men officers may actually inappropriately touch women's bodies while on duty.

This anxiety around men officers being accused of harassing or assaulting women while on patrol also came up when cadets were put through scenarios during their training. In one scenario at Rollingwood, the cadets were required to make a traffic stop, run the driver's and passenger's names through dispatch to check for warrants, and, upon finding out that the driver had a warrant, arrest and search her. The cadets were supposed to find the gun she had in her shorts and the small bag of drugs hidden in the side of her sports bra. One cadet—the class president, a South Asian man in his twenties—lifted the officer's shirt completely up to her neck, exposing her bra to the pair of cadets and the two officers evaluating the scenario. When the instructors asked during their debrief why he did this, he explained that he wanted to make sure his entire search was captured on his body camera to avoid any complaints. To ease his own anxiety about being falsely accused of sexual misconduct, the cadet exposed this woman's entire bra and stomach in the process of frisking her. The concern, again, was that he would be falsely accused, not that this woman's body would be exposed publicly and on camera.

Police sexual misconduct is notoriously difficult to track in any systematic way. Police departments do not make this information readily available, and people subjected to misconduct may be hesitant to report it to formal institutions. Scholars have had to go around formal systems to study police sexual misconduct, using court filings, arrest records, media reports, or surveys of officers. The findings from these studies suggest that police sexual misconduct—which includes a range of activities, like consensual sex on duty, initiating a traffic stop to get a "better look" at the driver, completing an inappropriate and/or unnecessary search, calling victims of crimes unnecessarily after a contact, or sexual assault/rape—is not uncommon.[22] In one study, the authors examined newspaper articles and court records of US police officers who were arrested for one or more sex-related crimes between 2005 and 2007. In just that three-year period, they found 548 arrest cases, 118 of which were identified as cases of rape and 236 of which involved a victim who was less than eighteen years of age.[23] Again, these were just the cases that resulted in an arrest of the officer involved, suggesting that many more instances of misconduct occurred and went unreported. Confirming these findings, police officers themselves report that sexual misconduct is common, and national leadership organizations, like the International Association of Chiefs of Police, have identified police sexual misconduct as a problem in their field.[24] At the academy, though, this issue was not taken seriously. Instead, instructors taught cadets how to be sure they would not be falsely accused of sexual misconduct, assuming that these complaints were not legitimate and were women's way of manipulating their contact with officers in their favor.

It makes sense to prepare cadets for the civilian complaint process, as this will probably be a part of their careers as police officers. Cadets should know that civilians have the right to file complaints and that officers can be sued for using force even when they believe their actions were within departmental policy. However, the tenor of this instruction was entirely dismissive of civilian complaints, painting them as groundless, frivolous, and inconvenient, rather than as an important system of checks and balances for an institution that has been granted to right to use state-sanctioned force. By doing so, the public became a necessary liability and burden that officers must handle, rather than the human beings whom they have been tasked with serving for the rest of their careers.

* * *

Police officers often say that their social circles are almost entirely made up of other officers. They spend their days at work together, exercise at the department's gym facilities together, grab drinks and eat together on the weekends, and go to each other's homes for birthday parties and barbeques. Some of this, of course, is about proximity. As other scholars have noted, though, policing is a particularly insular occupational group, one defined by an intense suspicion of others and a high level of group solidarity.[25] There are many possible reasons for this, including officers' exposure to danger as part of their daily duties, their experience of intense supervisory scrutiny, and the nature of shift work. However, this insularity and camaraderie among officers are also established by drawing firm boundaries not only around the circle of insiders but, perhaps more importantly, around the many groups of outsiders who present a threat to the institution.

The academy training brought cadets into the inner world of policing, transforming them from civilians to police officers. As they learned in the academy, part of being an insider was protecting themselves and the institution from outside threats. Cadets learned that these threats endangered both their own and the larger institution's survival. Bad guys, instructors warned, would use violence unpredictably and viciously for their own benefit, harming innocent civilians and specifically targeting police officers. Consistent with other scholarship, the officers in this study shared a belief that this violence toward police officers had escalated recently and that now, more than ever, officers needed to remain vigilant against anti-police attackers.[26]

Cadets were also encouraged to be wary of several institutional threats, most notably the media, activists, and the general public. The media, instructors warned, intentionally twisted stories about the police to portray them negatively for their own profit. Some officers blamed the media for public resentments toward the police, specifically those related to racism. Although the media may report accurate information, these officers explained, it had purposely created a false narrative that there were racist patterns in policing. At times, officers held the media responsible for violence between the police and the public and expressed concern that news reports would further intensify this violence. These officers similarly felt that activists had used one or two instances of racism and/or violence to make claims about racist patterns in policing. Even when officers categorized specific police killings, like that of Eric Garner, as inexcusable, they still felt that these were the exception, not the rule, and that activist movements had "bullied" their way into public conversations on false pretenses.

Lastly, instructors warned cadets that the public would never understand their jobs, would resent and unfairly judge them, and would falsely accuse them of misconduct. These anxieties about accusations of misconduct were rooted in deeply sexist conceptions of women and sexual violence: men cadets were warned that women would falsely accuse them of sexual misconduct. The public, even when it did not present a physical threat to officers, was primarily framed as a mass of ungrateful, misinformed, manipulative, lying people who would constantly create obstacles to officers doing their jobs.

The academy training socialized cadets into the new world they would occupy once they graduated and began working patrol. In this world, bad guys lurked around every corner; anti-police attackers could pop up anywhere to ambush officers; the media intentionally fabricated damaging narratives about the police for profit; activists goaded officers into reactions to further their anti-police agendas; and the public, at best, expressed no gratitude for officers' sacrifices to protect them and, at worst, discriminated against officers and falsely accused them of misconduct.

As I have pointed out throughout this chapter, these beliefs are not wholly unreasonable or unsubstantiated. Police officers are indeed ambushed and killed every year in the United States; most mainstream media sources are designed within a capitalist system that strives for profit; and civilians do file complaints against officers. However, even within this reality, decades of research show that the police department, as an institution, is very well protected. Policing is safer now than it has ever been, the media tends to privilege police accounts of their use of force, civilian complaints are very rarely sustained and almost never result in the disciplining of officers, and the police continue to engage in sexual misconduct while researchers struggle to even quantify the rates of these incidents.

Cadets are taught that these groups should be thought of as outsiders. This process fosters a constant sense of danger and insecurity, making these cadets feel deeply protective and defensive from the outset. If everyone is out to get you, in one form or another, it becomes easy to legitimize violent responses and dismiss any criticism. For example, within this frame, the possibility that the police may, in fact, participate in patterns of racist enforcement is swiftly dismissed as a targeted attack against the police by the liberal media. This worldview makes the institution incredibly durable and resistant to any kind of change or reform, making it an essential component of the socialization of state violence.

4 POLICE WORK AS WARFARE, OFFICERS AS WARRIORS

Toward the end of Terryville's academy, the cadets spent three days in a course titled Force Options. The curriculum for this course outlined what case law, the code of criminal procedure, and departmental policies dictated about their ability to use force, what level of force was appropriate, and how to articulate their actions in a report. On the last day, they completed three different scenarios to get hands-on experience applying the information they had learned in the classroom. Kevin took the lead on teaching this course, periodically weaving in his own perspectives or experiences throughout the sometimes-dry material. On the first morning, Kevin got caught up at city hall downtown, so Davis filled in for about twenty minutes. Davis did not want to get started on the material without Kevin, so he stood at the front of the classroom, one arm leaning on the podium, running an informal question-and-answer session for the class. The cadets mostly asked questions about the gear they would wear on duty, for example, inquiring about what kind of bulletproof vests they would be issued and whether they should have earpieces with their radios.

Kevin rushed into the classroom around 8:20 a.m., out of breath and a bit frazzled. He jumped right into the Force Options curriculum, pulling up the PowerPoint presentation and starting his lecture. The first PowerPoint slide that he showed featured a quotation credited to Heraclitus, a sixth-century BCE Greek philosopher: "Out of every one hundred men, ten shouldn't even be there, eighty are just targets, nine are the real fighters, and we are lucky to have them, for they make the battle. Ah, but the one, one is a warrior, and he will bring the others back." "What does this mean to you?" Kevin asked the class. One cadet talked about the importance of bravery. Another said that not everyone is cut out for this job. Kevin nodded at the cadets' responses and added that being a police officer meant that you are a warrior: you are one of the few who goes into battle and does what it takes to win the war. Kevin emphasized that this job is a "calling" and that not everyone can do it, adding, "Not everyone is a warrior."

Kevin asked the class, "When do you start becoming a warrior?" One cadet answered, "Through training." Another explained, "When you develop the mentality." And a third responded, "Once you have something worth protecting." Kevin affirmed the last response, nodding and adding, "purpose." Kevin then pressed each of his index fingers into his temples and told the class, "It's between your two ears. It's a mind-set. It is who you are. This is who you are." "When you're out on the streets," he said, referencing patrol work, "and it'll probably happen in your first week, you'll have to use force. And you will have already made decisions about who you are before you get to that call. You'll have already decided that you're going home tonight. He might be a bad guy who is six four, but you've decided that you are a warrior and a guardian and that you are going to win this fight no matter what it takes, and it may take deadly force." He told the class that they needed to make the "mental shift" to decide that they are "this person," the kind of person willing to do whatever it takes to survive.

Kevin continued to emphasize the binary concept of the warrior-guardian, explaining to the cadets that a warrior-guardian does not serve for his own cause. He suggested that the cadets were now public servants, explaining that on one call, they might get out of their patrol car to high-five some kids playing basketball, and on the very next call, "you're whippin' someone's ass" or "defending someone." He repeated a phrase he used just a few minutes earlier, reminding the class that they had to decide that they are "this person." Kevin then played a video that featured a montage of police officers being killed, while a man's voice delivered a speech in the background about brotherhood and healing as a team. Some of the officers featured in the video were shot, while others were beaten or hit by cars. At the end of the video, the man narrating said, "Either we heal together, or we die as individuals."

The way that Kevin characterized the role of police, as being both warriors and guardians, represents a larger, long-standing debate about law enforcement, crime, and danger. The images of the warrior and the guardian—and the tension between them—have been invoked in US policing for decades. The "officer friendly" programs of the 1960s, for example, were implemented during the same decade as President Nixon's War on Poverty. Although the enemy in these political wars shifted over time from poverty to crime to drugs to terror, they all similarly enabled aggressive surveillance and policing in communities of color, particularly in Black neighborhoods.[1] The most recent iteration of this binary conceptualizes police officers as both warriors fighting criminals and guardians protecting the innocent.

Framing the job tasks as warfare and officers as warriors reflects a traditional, highly masculinized image of the crime-fighting officer running toward danger and putting bad guys in jail.[2] This way of thinking about the role of the police and their relationship to the public has implications for the way the police do their jobs. Law professor Seth Stoughton, a former officer himself, explains that by thinking of themselves as warriors, officers "are locked in intermittent and unpredictable combat with unknown but highly lethal enemies." As a result, officers "learn to treat every individual they interact with as an armed threat and every situation as a deadly force encounter in the making."[3] This kind of warrior imagery is also a prominent component of privately run police training workshops organized around the country. David Grossman, a well-known instructor at these workshops, calls his philosophy "killology" and encourages officers to master the use of violence in an unpredictable and dangerous world.[4] Although Grossman's policing philosophy may seem extreme, this way of seeing the world does not just belong to him or to instructors like him. Scholars studying police departments around the country have consistently found that officers are socialized to emphasize, and to some degree mythologize, danger and death in police work.[5]

The warrior and the guardian were referenced repeatedly throughout my fieldwork, usually as a set of binary images that were distinct from, and contrasted with, each other. Sociologist Jennifer Carlson explains that, unlike the warrior, the guardian officer "emphasizes a moral obligation to protect innocent lives, grounding police work not in dominating, but in protecting others."[6] The conception of the police officer as the protector of the weak, vulnerable, and/or innocent has long been a staple in policing rhetoric and imagery. Norman Rockwell's iconic 1958 painting *Runaway*, for example, reflects this image. The painting features a white, male officer and young, white boy sitting together at a lunch counter. The officer is leaning over toward the boy, and the boy is glancing up at the officer adoringly, while a sack of his belongings sits below him, suggesting that he has run away from home. The shift toward community policing in the 1970s and 1980s also reflected this guardian image. Through increased foot patrols, community substations, and neighborhood watches, community policing promised better, more meaningful interactions between officers and civilians and a shared responsibility for community issues, including crime control.[7] This approach framed police work as problem solving and encouraged citizen involvement and oversight, challenging the traditional masculine, dominating, crime-fighting image of policing.[8]

Although the warrior and the guardian constructs are usually presented in opposition to each other, both reflect an investment in masculinized performances that are rooted in systems of patriarchy, heterosexuality, and white supremacy. The images of the warrior and

guardian are flip sides of the same coin: the warrior reflects a dominating masculinity, which creates the need for a guardian to perform
protective masculinity. This way of conceptualizing the guardian, or
the "good" man as a foil for the "bad" man, has been used to justify
all kinds of violent practices. For example, in war, state actors use the
image of aggressive, violent (i.e., bad) men to necessitate the protection of women and children by good men. Political theorist Iris
Marion Young explains this process, whereby "good men can only
appear in their goodness if we assume that lurking outside the warm
familial walls are aggressors who wish to attack them. . . . The protector must therefore take all precautions against these threats."[9] In the
United States, white men—including police officers—who carry guns
in their everyday lives explain this practice by pointing to the threat
of racialized others and their moral imperative to protect innocent
lives (which, in effect, means women and children).[10] Men—again,
especially white men—invest and engage in violent fantasies through
video games, film, and role-plays to protect their version of America
from the threat of women, racial minorities, and liberals.[11] The role
that women play in this narrative—as vulnerable innocents who need
men's protection—is highlighted in the privileging, and historically the
requirement, of heterosexuality in the US military.[12] In each of these
cases, men contextualize their violent practices within a frame of economic decline, liberal threats, crime, and terrorism to construct ver-
sions of masculinity that depend on notions of innocence, sacrifice,
and protection.

Earlier in this book, I described the world of policing that instructors established at the academy for new cadets. This world is full of
adversaries who constantly threaten officers' physical safety and the
institution's well-being. In this chapter, I explain where police officers fit into this world. As Kevin explained to the cadets during his
instruction, they needed to be ready for "battle." Although Kevin and
other academy instructors referenced the image of the warrior and
the guardian, in practice, the academy taught cadets that to be guardians, they must be warriors. In other words, cadets learned that they

must use violence in their efforts to protect the innocent. This way of approaching the police role meant that new officers conceptualized their relationship with the public as a war. To survive this war, cadets needed to learn how to identify their enemy and be willing and able to adopt a warrior approach to the world. This way of seeing the world, and their role in it, was once again an integral part of their socialization of state violence.

Importantly, these institutional accomplishments drew heavily on gendered and racialized conceptions of threat, innocence, and violence, in which Black people—in particular, Black men—were framed as the enemy. Consequently, cadets who were not white men faced unique dilemmas in trying to adopt their role as warriors. Although this process required extra work for cadets who did not embody the conventional image of the white, male, masculine warrior-guardian, these lessons were taught to all cadets, regardless of gender and race.

Profiling Bad Guys

The state-mandated Multiculturalism class at Terryville included learning the definitions of words like "ethnicity," "stereotype," "prejudice," and "discrimination." After reading the state-approved definitions of these words off the PowerPoint slide, Rick, the instructor, typically added his own elaborations and stories. Rick defined the word "stereotype," for example, and then told the story of when he was in the academy almost forty years ago and his class of cadets was given a group counseling session because they frequently made race-related jokes and were told that they needed to stop. He insisted that the whole class participated in these jokes, regardless of their race and ethnicity, and explained that they "had a ball doing it." He then played a few clips from the 1970s show *All in the Family*, one of which was titled "The C**ns are Coming!" A cadet sitting in the row ahead of me turned around and, eyes wide, said to the back row, "Do you see the name of the clip?" referring to the anti-Black racial slur included in the title. Hannah, who sat next to me, commented, "Dan is dying."

I glanced over to the other side of the classroom to see Dan, the only Black cadet in the class, laughing. The clip showed Archie, the protagonist of the show, complaining to his wife about Black people moving into the neighborhood. Rick then played another clip in which Archie lamented about a neighbor selling his house to "the Jews," only to find out that the neighbor sold it to a Black Baptist couple, much to his dismay. Rick did not provide any extended conversation about these clips, nor did he address the explicit racism and antisemitism included in the footage. Instead, he simply mused that humor is often used in talking about race and stereotypes and that good comedy usually had some truth to it.

Rick then moved on to talk about the concept of discrimination. He first provided a definition of "discrimination," which he explained was "acting on your prejudices." He said that he hoped that individuals who discriminate are eliminated in the hiring process at the department and that "people like this don't need to be here." Following a frustrated sigh, he told the class that although he thinks discrimination is bad, he "struggles with" the discussion around profiling, warning that, as a cop, "if you don't know how to profile, you need to learn." Rick immediately added, "We do not racially profile," but he said they do profile based on "body language, appearance, and mannerisms." "If you can't profile someone who wants to hurt or kill you," he explained, "that's a problem." Racial profiling, he said, is a form of discrimination, and they "don't do that." They do not profile based on "skin color, gender, or language," he clarified, "but if they look like a burglar, then that's good profiling."

Rick's instruction echoed a larger skill that cadets were taught at the academy: how to profile bad guys. Although, as I described in chapter 3, academy instructors warned that any interaction could be dangerous and that an ambush could happen at any moment, they did not express an equal fear of everyone. Instructors taught cadets whom to fear and how to identify dangerous people and situations, insisting that cadets learn how to identify bad guys by profiling behavior and appearance. This lesson taught cadets what bad guys looked like, what kind of clothing they wore, what kinds of cars they drove, and how they moved their bodies when they were going to initiate an attack. To survive patrol work, cadets were taught that they must learn how to identify threats. Although instructors officially told the cadets that they should never conceptualize these threats in relation to race, they unofficially trained cadets to use markers of race, income, and gender to distinguish who should trigger their suspicion.

One major component of profiling bad guys was learning to identify body movements and behavior that were considered suspicious and/or dangerous. Officers were most concerned with hand placement and what were called "pre-attack indicators," which signaled that someone was going to initiate a physical attack. In the De-escalation class at Terryville, for example, Kevin told the class that someone's use of space and hand placement were clues that they were hiding something, especially weapons or drugs. During the lecture, Kevin hovered over a cadet's left shoulder and said, "See, I'm in his personal space, so already he is pulling away from me, trying to give himself more space since he's uncomfortable." Despite the fact that this cadet was, presumably, not hiding guns or drugs at that moment, Kevin told the class that if someone is giving themselves more space—like this cadet did—they might have a "gun or dope or something." Someone's body placement and use of space provide a lot of information, he explained.

Kevin clarified that if a person walks away from him as soon as he arrives on a scene, this means that they do not want to be around him and, thus, are probably hiding something. To illustrate, he asked two cadets to come to the front of the class and approach him from either side. Kevin turned his body so that he was positioned perpendicular to the two cadets and placed his hand over his pocket. "This could tell us something," he said, referencing his hand placement. He drew a comparison between his body positioning and a child trying to hide a piece of candy. This emphasis on hand placement was ubiquitous and repeatedly invoked in warnings about officer safety at these police academies. In the classroom that Kevin taught in, for example, a poster on the wall showed a man with his hand behind his back, holding a pistol. Large text overlayed the photo, reading, "WATCH THE HANDS: The hand you can't see is the hand that could be holding a weapon that will kill you." The consequence of not constantly being aware of someone's hand placement was clear: someone could kill you.

Instructors also warned cadets to watch for indicators that someone was going to attack them. Instructors explained that if someone swings their arms back and forth in front of their chest, tosses their head from side to side, jumps up and down, or, especially, announces, "I'm not going to jail," they were probably going to throw a punch or try to run away. Instructors emphasized the ability to discern intention—whether it was lying, hiding something, or initiating violence—from the body and encouraged cadets to always, without question, trust their gut. Kevin told the class, "Always listen to your hunches." If someone is "exhibiting awkward behavior, they have furtive movements, or they are sweating," he explained, "we cannot dismiss these red flags in our job." Kevin warned, "If your subconscious is telling you that someone needs to go into cuffs, you need to put them in cuffs." "Maybe the guy in front of you has a bad leg," Kevin went on, "and that's why he's walking strangely. Or maybe he has a gun, and he's going to shoot a cop so that he doesn't have to go back to jail. Do not ever question your instinct, because it's what will keep you alive." Cadets were taught that their lives depended on their ability to discern intention from body language and to always err on the side of suspicion.

Who was considered suspicious or dangerous depended heavily on their race and gender. Officially, the cadets were told that in no situation should they racially profile. During a lecture on the code of criminal procedure, for example, Sabrina, a white instructor in her thirties, derisively asked the class, "Can we racially profile?" An exaggerated and obvious "no" filled the room. "No," Sabrina confirmed, "don't do it." Just as Rick explained in his instruction during the Multiculturalism class, however, instructors did encourage cadets to profile "criminality." Without explicitly pointing to skin color, the instructors talked about clothing, body language, gang affiliation, and criminality to frame people of color—and, in particular, Black and brown men—as being dangerous and violent. This was not about race, they said, but about criminality and the propensity for targeted violence. You do not question, detain, pull over, or arrest someone based on their race, instructors told cadets. You do these things, instructors explained, on the basis of what people are wearing, their gait, what kind of car they are driving, whether they belong in this neighborhood at this time of day or night, if they walk away when you arrive on scene, if they avoid eye contact with you, or if they touch their pockets, among other things.

This talk of criminal profiling instead of racial profiling came up at Rollingwood when the cadets learned how to conduct frisks and searches. Tyler, a white defensive tactics instructor in his thirties, explained that the only reason to frisk someone was because you believe they have a dangerous weapon. Tyler was stoic and, apart from just a few moments over my year of fieldwork, was totally unapproachable. He stood with his feet far outside hip width, his hips swayed forward slightly, arms crossed in front of him, with a toothpick sticking out the side of his mouth. During this day of fieldwork, he explained that the cadets did not need to frisk every person they meet while on duty. He gave an example to illustrate his point: If you stop a woman for jaywalking while she is trying to cross the street in a hurry to get her two kids to school, you probably do not need to frisk her. You should just give her the citation and move along. However, if you are in an area of town like the southeast part of the city (where most of Rollingwood's Black and Latino/a population lives), where you know there is a high crime rate and gang presence, and you stop a man for jaywalking who is wearing red sweats and a red hat, then you should frisk him. You should "key in on what [you] know" in making that decision, he explained.

Tyler thus identified what kinds of people pose a threat to officers. A mother taking her kids to school is not a threat. Importantly, he did not mention in what part of town this woman lived or what she was wearing. In the second example, a man, who lived in the Black and Latino/a part of the city and was wearing red sweats and a red hat, is a threat. Implied in this definition of criminality is that the threatening person is himself Black or Latino.

This framing of criminality was also dependent on local context and geography. For example, Terryville was located closer to the US-Mexico border than were the other three departments I studied, which shaped conceptions of race, crime, and threat. This regional specificity was illustrated clearly during the Multiculturalism class at Terryville, when Rick tangentially brought up his opinions about immigration policies. Earlier that day, he expressed dismay as to why anyone would advocate for eliminating the US Immigration and Customs Enforcement (ICE) and insisted that police officers have a duty to enforce all laws, including federal laws. Before we broke for lunch, Rick told the class, "You can tell by appearance if someone is an illegal alien." "Not from their skin color," he clarified, "but from what they're wearing or how they're behaving." He went on: If an officer initiates contact with someone because they think that person is an "illegal alien," then that is racial profiling. But, if the officer stops the person because they suspect criminal behavior, then that is good police work. No one in the room acknowledged the xenophobic phrase Rick used in his description of immigrants, which rolled off Rick's tongue in a way that seemed habitual. Rick also barely disguised his conflation of race, nationality, and criminality, explaining to cadets that the only characteristic that was off-limits as a direct justification for stopping someone was skin color but that their "appearance" could indicate if someone was an undocumented immigrant and/or engaging in criminal behavior.

During the training focused on profiling, instructors drew on different, sometimes contradictory, narratives about race and racism in policing. The official curriculum, as Sabrina articulated in her lecture, denounced racial profiling of any kind. Sabrina insisted that racial profiling was against departmental policy and would not be tolerated. Although Sabrina framed the concept of racial profiling as a discrete, individual, conscious choice, she explicitly recognized the existence of race and the potential for racism in police decision-making. The discursive strategies used to frame race and racism shifted, however, with Rick, who acknowledged the existence of race and racial profiling but denied that police officers engaged in racial profiling. Instead, he insisted, officers used cues, like body language, appearance, and mannerisms—which essentially amounted to someone's embodiment, necessarily invoking race—to profile "criminality." According to this narrative, race exists, but officers look for the potential for criminality on the basis of gestures, clothing, body language, and location, not race. The narrative shifted again with Tyler, who never explicitly mentioned race or racism but used thinly veiled racially coded language to justify racial profiling through the guise of criminality and threat.

Race scholars have theorized about these kinds of discursive maneuvers, whereby white people and institutions selectively recognize, ignore, or deny race and racism in ways that sustain systems of white supremacy and racial domination. Sociologist and race scholar Eduardo Bonilla-Silva explains that color-blind ideologies about race emerged as part of a post-civil-rights-era "new racism."[13] Color-blind ideology provides a way for people (mostly white) to create "'raceless' explanations for all sorts of race-related affairs."[14] Rick and Tyler, for example, pointed to several characteristics of a person that, within a color-blind discourse, are unrelated to race to explain why the police might stop or frisk them. Tyler did not even say the word "race" in his fictional example of deciding to frisk someone, even though race was very clearly invoked in other ways, specifically through naming the part of town that this person was in and the clothing that this person was wearing. Both officers essentially denied that race informed officer decision-making and instead pointed to "criminality" as the explaining factor.

However, these officers did sometimes talk about race and, at times, acknowledged the potential for racism in policing. There was not an utter denial that race might matter; there was instead a denial that police officers, knowingly or not, systematically engaged in racist patterns of policing. Philosopher Charles W. Mills's theory of white ignorance provides a way of understanding how this kind of ignorance, whether in bad faith or not, works to sustain racial hierarchy.[15] Mills explains that in the US context, social and political life is organized by a racial contract that denies full personhood to nonwhite people by exploiting "their bodies, land, and resources" and denying "equal socioeconomic opportunities to them."[16] This racial contract, he argues, is sustained in part by an epistemology of ignorance, which produces "the ironic outcome that whites will in general be unable to understand the world they themselves have made."[17] White ignorance protects a racial hierarchy that benefits white people and white interests.

Sociologist Jennifer Mueller builds on Mills's work by arguing that white supremacy is sustained not just by denial but also by a willful, intentional, and strategic white ignorance. According to Mueller, racial ignorance persists because white people are committed to this epistemology of ignorance, which she defines as "a way of knowing oriented toward evading, mystifying, and obscuring the reality of racism to produce (mis)understandings useful for domination."[18] Even when presented with empirical information that demonstrates racial inequality, white people will engage in cognitive gymnastics to maintain their worldview that racism does not exist and that race is not salient. Importantly, white people and institutions can draw on this epistemology of ignorance when color-blind ideology fails: when they must see race, they can at least deny racism.

The academy instruction operated within an epistemology of ignorance: cadets learned when they could and could not invoke race, and in what ways, during the course of their duties. It is impossible for police officers to deny the existence of race. For example, officers describe people by their race, gender, height, and weight, among other identifying features, when they are on patrol. They cannot, as color-blind ideology would dictate, say that they "do not see race." Instead, cadets received a toolkit of strategies at the academy that enabled them to "see" race but rewrite the narrative claiming that race informs police decision-making. Instructors drew heavily on an epistemology of ignorance to pretend, knowingly or not, that they were invoking raceless, objective, value-neutral images and explanations in their instruction on profiling "bad guys." Police officers do not profile based on race, cadets learned; police officers simply profile criminality.

However, conceptions of criminality are inextricably linked to race in the US context, where images of Black criminality have been used to justify the subjugation and domination of Black people.[19] This equating of Blackness with criminality has its roots in colonialism and slavery and deeply shapes today's criminal legal system, politics, popular media, and indeed, social science research as well.[20] These images are so ingrained in the US imagination that, as criminologist Melissa H. Barlow argues, "talking about crime is talking about race": "discourse about crime" is "a coded form of discourse about race."[21] Relying on the seemingly unrelated concept of criminality allowed the academy instructors to continue to invoke race without doing so explicitly and strategically worked to protect and sustain this institution's racist practices.

Importantly, although instructors told cadets that police officers did not systematically engage in racial profiling, decades of scholarship suggests otherwise. It is nearly impossible to evaluate on a large scale whether police stops are racially motivated; that is, researchers cannot ask officers if each of their stops included in an analysis were racially motivated, and of course, even if they could, officers may not know or may not be honest. As I have explained in this chapter, we know that officers describe their suspicion within a frame of "criminality" instead of race. However, existing research consistently shows that Black and Latino drivers are more likely to be stopped by the police, a pattern that is even more pronounced when the analysis is isolated to include only investigatory stops, as opposed to stops resulting from traffic violations.[22] In a study of traffic stops in the Kansas City metropolitan area, for example, Charles Epp, Steven Maynard-Moody, and Donald Haider-Markel found that Black drivers were 2.7 times more likely than white drivers to be pulled over as part of an investigatory stop. These scholars point out that the racial disparities they found in their study were not necessarily a result of individual officers' explicit racial biases but, rather, part of institutional practices that "grow from and reproduce negative racial stereotypes."[23] Clearly, then, these strategic maneuvers in which cadets are taught to profile criminality, not race, can still result in racist outcomes.

* * *

I interviewed Bill almost a year into my fieldwork in his office at the Rollingwood firing range. Bill was Black, forty-nine years old, and of average height. Bill started his career in the Army—his father spent twenty-three years in the Army before him—and after eight years of service, he left to pursue law enforcement, first with the Border Patrol and then with Rollingwood Police Department. After over a decade of working in patrol and SWAT units, he moved over to the training side of things, taking a job as the sergeant supervising all "learned skills," which included defensive tactics and firearms. When I first met him, he was very hard to read, but over time, I found that he was both stern and playful. He often complained about departmental policies or coworkers and cadets whom he perceived did not work hard, but he also frequently cracked jokes and teased other officers.

At the end of our two-hour interview, after I had finished asking all of my questions, Bill smiled earnestly and asked, "How'd I do?" I laughed and told him he did great, which was true; he engaged thoughtfully and provided detailed examples, which interviewers always appreciate. "Really?" he asked. "So I'm not gonna have Black Lives Matter come knocking down my door, right?" I was taken aback by his comment and unsure of how to respond. All I could come up with in the moment was, "I don't think so." Bill then told me he had a group of other Black officers—all sergeants, he added—who talk about "this stuff" together and that sometimes it gets heated. Some of them, he explained, think that "the institution is racist, but I disagree." Bill shared that it was "tough being a Black cop." "In what ways?" I probed. Bill told me about being on scenes where he was accused of showing favoritism to Black people or, alternatively, of not showing enough sympathy toward Black people. "I mean, jeez," he went on, "I had to work security when the Klan marched in Rollingwood. And I did my damn job. I didn't like it, but I did my job, because my job is to protect their freedoms. But man, that was hard." Bill went on to talk about the tension involved in being both Black and a police officer, explaining that he felt like he was not viewed as a person by other Black people when he had his uniform on; he was only seen as an officer. That was hard, he said, "because it's like, c'mon man, I still get followed at Whole Foods just like you do when I'm not in uniform."

Bill was uniquely positioned within the policing institution. As a police officer, he was an agent of the state. As a Black man, he was part of a community that has been, and continues to be, subjected to narratives that equate Blackness with criminality. For Bill and other Black officers I met in the field, this made it more complicated for them to fully take on the role of the warrior officer. They were, within this framework, both the warrior and the enemy. The Black officers I met tried to navigate this maze, which constantly put them in a bind. They expressed an investment in this white, male institution, often justifying policing practices in communities of color and defending high-profile police shootings of Black men. At the same time, though, they also described instances when they were subjected to racist policing practices themselves.

In many ways, the narratives that Black officers drew on to explain police actions mirrored those presented at the academy, reflecting their investment in the institution's worldview. Many of the Black officers I met pointed to crime, class, or suspicious activity, rather than race, in their framing of police surveillance and violence in communities of color and, in particular, in Black neighborhoods. This came up during my interview with Robert, a biracial (white and Black) police officer at Clarkston with twenty-eight years of law enforcement experience. As I spoke with Robert over the phone while he drove home from work, I asked him what he thought about the recent news stories covering tensions between the police and communities of color. In his response, he described anti-police sentiments without ever actually using the word "race," instead using ostensibly race-neutral concepts like crime rates and neighborhoods: "Most people in certain areas of certain neighborhoods, they don't like policing because, in most cases, police officers are in the poor-income neighborhoods. In most low-income areas, you do have more crime. Wherever you have more crime, you're gonna have a certain type of police order. Do you let people run ragged, or do you enforce the law more so than other places?

In places that's really enforced laws, you're gonna have a movement of retaliation towards people that don't wanna respect police." Despite my including race in the question, Robert pivoted to talk about crime rates, income, and neighborhood context. He aligned himself with the institutional narrative, which points to seemingly race-neutral characteristics to explain why the police are concentrated in certain neighborhoods, without ever explicitly mentioning race.

In my interview with Tricia, she similarly pointed to criminality and community resentment, not race, to explain police action in Black communities. Tricia was Black, was twenty-eight years old, and had just graduated from Rollingwood's academy six months before our interview. She and I sat together in a Starbucks in downtown Rollingwood for two hours talking about her decision to pursue law enforcement, her experiences at the academy, and her impressions of patrol work so far. We talked about the role of demographic diversity in policing for a while, and Tricia explained that having a diverse police force made it easier to handle different kinds of people. Having Black officers, she said, meant that Black citizens could not accuse them of racism with the same level of credibility, and it helped the department build rapport with Black communities: "When you're dealing with Black people, it's like, 'Oh, that white female officer did something.' But when you have a Black female saying like, 'Dude, don't even try it,' then you could also build a different rapport when you could come to the same level: 'I'm also Black, so I know what you understand.'" Tricia then gave an example of a recent interaction she had on patrol with a Black adolescent boy:

I told this thirteen-year-old, "Don't play a victim of society. Don't do this." . . . He was like, "Yeah, but I don't see a lot of Black cops, so when I'm hanging out with my friends, and there's these white officers just driving around looking at us 'cause we're Black kids in this neighborhood." I'm like, "I understand. I get where you're coming from, but I also didn't play victim. I also went over there and greeted those officers and said, 'Hey, I live over here. What's up?' I spoke to them." I said,

"Don't sit here and look at the news and think that every officer is that [way]. . . . They know that something's going on, and that's why they're canvassing this area. It's not because of you. Sometimes they may be looking at you, but that's not always the case."

Throughout the interview, Tricia illustrated the tensions of being both Black and a police officer. She discussed being able to build rapport with Black civilians, explained that it was helpful for Black kids to see Black officers, and then recounted encouraging a Black adolescent not to "play victim." In her explanation to this boy, she pointed to crime, rather than race, as the reason why officers may be surveilling his neighborhood. She rejected his experience of being watched by white officers because he and his friends were Black and instead told him that the officers were probably canvassing the area—meaning, looking for someone who committed a crime—pointing to crime, rather than race, as the rationale for policing practices in Black communities.

The investment in this framing of criminality also came up in my conversations with Black officers about the recent police shootings of Black people that had captured the nation's attention. Black officers, in very similar ways to their white peers, emphasized the law in these discussions. Almost always taking on the perspective of the officer in these scenarios, the officers I met explained that given the context, and the law and policies dictating officers' authorities, these shootings were usually reasonable. According to these accounts, it was not about race; rather, it was about the perceived threat to the officer. These officers' accounts were not necessarily inaccurate; use-of-force policies typically dictate that officers are able to use "objectively reasonable force" in carrying out their duties, a concept that can be traced back to the US Supreme Court's decision in *Graham v. Connor*. What qualifies as being "objectively reasonable" depends on multiple factors, including the severity of the crime being committed, if the subject is attempting to flee, and most importantly, the officers' perception of threat to themselves and others. These policies are written in ways that provide officers with discretion and protect the institution from claims of excessive force, which is evidenced in the ways that officers—including Black officers—used them in justifying shootings of Black people.

This reliance on the concept of reasonableness came up in my interview with Bill, the Rollingwood sergeant who oversaw tactical and firearms training. As we talked about Black Lives Matter, I asked Bill if he thought any of the criticisms being lodged against the police were legitimate. In his response, he described how he, as a police officer, evaluated police shootings:

> Oh yeah, some are. But I don't think . . . [pause]. Some are [pause]. And I'm just like the rest of society. If I see a bad shooting, which seems to fuel a lot of this, if I see a bad shooting, and my initial reaction is, "That looks bad," I have to remind myself, "You're doing the same thing that society's doing." So then I have to sit back and wait until the facts come out, delve into the facts, and then put myself in that officer's shoes and determine, Was that reasonable or not? . . . I think the shooting of the officers in Dallas, so that's fueled by Black Lives Matter in retaliation for an incident that happened in Baton Rouge [Alton Sterling], right? So, Baton Rouge happens, and other incidents, and then the march in Dallas, [when] one person . . . takes it upon himself to kill five officers. How many of those people that were marching that day [for Black Lives Matter in Dallas] know that those officers were cleared in Baton Rouge? And after looking at the facts, if I were in those shoes of those officers, I would have shot that guy too.

Bill drew on his experience as an officer to determine whether a shooting was reasonable and/or justified. In the case of Alton Sterling's killing, he suggested that had he been in that officer's shoes, he would have done the same thing.

Phillip similarly relied on use-of-force policies in explaining how he interpreted police shootings. Phillip was Black, was fifty-eight years old, and had thirty-four years of law enforcement experience, mostly at Fairview Sheriff's Office. I asked Phillip how he thought policing had changed since he started, and he replied that he felt like the "brotherhood" of policing was not as strong anymore and that public scrutiny had intensified. He described the dangers of police work and expressed frustration about what he felt was the public's lack of understanding and appreciation of officers' sacrifices. "Each one of us," he elaborated, "even though we are a police officer, when we leave our house, we really don't know if we're coming back again to that house. When we leave our family, we don't know if we're coming back. We pray that we come back." He went on to explain how the law shapes police decision-making:

> Anything can happen out there [on patrol]. . . . If it comes to a thing where you exhibit a firearm or a deadly weapon, we are authorized to use deadly force. . . . Everybody sits back and they say, "Well, he should've did this. He should've done that." That's all armchair quarterbacking. . . . I talked [about this] at my church. We were on a symposium one time, and I happened to be one of the speakers on there because this was when the big thing about "Don't shoot," Black Lives Matter, and all that type of thing. . . . The way that I dealt with them is with the law. That's our governing body is the law. . . . 'Cause everybody ain't gonna like the way you handle a certain situation. . . . We had the Black Lives Matter, then you had Police Lives Matter, All Lives Matter. I'm a Black American, and I happen to be a police officer. All lives matter, Black, white, whatever. Everybody's lives matter. I think that we should get away from these distinctions or whatever. . . . Now we've had situations where Black males have been killed. There are maybe one or two, I may have said, "Yeah, that was an unjustified shooting."

Phillip criticized the public in their judgments of officers' actions. He talked about the law as an indisputable source of justification, explaining that police officers are allowed to act in this way and, thus, that the behavior is acceptable. He also invoked a color-blind discourse, expressing a wish to end "distinctions" around race and aligning himself with "All Lives Matter" messaging. However, he also told me that at least "one or two" police shootings of Black men have, in fact, been unjustified.

At the same time that the Black officers I met explained patterns of racist policing practices by pointing to the law and the dangers they faced on the job, they also recounted experiences of being racially profiled, pulled over, and handled forcefully by the police. At multiple points in my interview with Bill, he brought up being profiled or subjected to racial discrimination by police officers. At the very beginning of the interview, I asked respondents if they remembered the first time in their life that they interacted with a police officer. When I asked Bill this question, he recounted being fourteen years old, when he and a friend "made a homemade firework" that injured his friend's hand. "We both ran home, and then next thing I know, the police are knocking on my door," he said. "I told 'em the whole story," Bill recalled, "and they laughed, and that was the end of that. So that one sticks out as like the very first interaction. And then after that, not all of them were good." I followed up by asking what happened during one of the not-so-good interactions he referenced, and he told me the following story:

> I was on my way to Germany. I was in the Army then, and a buddy was driving me to Newark airport, and I was in my class A uniform. . . . A state trooper pulled us over, and the reason he pulled us over was for making furtive movements on the turnpike. Not until I got into law enforcement did I know there's no such thing—that wasn't PC [probable cause] or reasonable suspicion. . . . But, backing up, there was a lot of snow on the ground, mixed with salt and all that crap. His car was covered in grime, and the trooper wanted to search the car, and he put us both on the hood of the car, even though I was in my dress greens [Army uniform]. And he left us on the hood of the car, with our arms spread, while he searched the car. He didn't find anything, let us go, and then I got to the Newark airport, and it looked like I had been rolling around in the mud in my dress uniform, and I was really pissed. I'll never forget that day. I don't hold it against the state police, per se. It's

that trooper. . . . Knowing what I know now, I know why he stopped us: just because it was two Black guys. . . . He automatically assumed that we were transporting drugs, so he searched my car and then left me with a filthy uniform. I was embarrassed.

Bill recounted being racially profiled by this officer, who, he said, assumed that he and his friend were transporting drugs. He expressed anger and embarrassment but explained that he blamed the individual officer, not the state police generally. Despite repeated negative experiences with officers, including ones that he described as being racially motivated, Bill still used an individualized frame to explain the officer's behavior.

Tricia similarly framed prior negative experiences with police officers as an individual, rather than institutional, problem. When I asked Tricia if she felt comfortable around officers while growing up, she told me that she "didn't have any issues" and suggested that "when you treat officers with respect, they give the same respect back." Later in the interview, though, she told me about being pulled over repeatedly by a white officer while she was in high school:

I had an officer who would stop me every day from school and give me a ticket, and there was no reason whatsoever. I found out he was one of my classmates' dads. His son called me the n-word, and I cursed him out. Then I guess he told his dad who I was, and I got tickets every day. I was like, "You're abusing your power 'cause I know your son told you." It was after cheerleading practice. I'm like, "There's no reason why you should be stopping me every day. Out of all these people who leave, all these other cars, and you stop me every day."

Tricia described this experience as being clearly racially motivated, highlighting that her being stopped daily by this white officer was because she was a Black girl who resisted racial degradation by a white boy. However, after telling this story, Tricia contextualized this experience within law enforcement generally, explaining that she did not have any other issues, and because she had family members working as officers, she knew that this was not how officers were supposed to act and, thus, was the exception, not the rule.

Scholars who study the experiences of Black police officers have analyzed this tension in institutional position within the frames of double consciousness or the outsider within.[24] W. E. B. Du Bois described double consciousness as the "two-ness" that Black people in the United States experience, or the "sense of always looking at one's self through the eyes of others."[25] In the US context, Black people are forced to manage potentially antagonistic identities to maintain their own sense of self while seeing themselves from outside, white perspectives. Social theorist Patricia Hill Collins's concept of the outsider within considers how this tension operates for Black women specifically. Collins defines the outsider within as a situational identity "attached to specific histories of social injustice."[26] Both approaches highlight the negotiations inherent to occupying two potentially conflicting social positions. For Black police officers, this means negotiating their position as being both Black and "blue," which is made uniquely complicated for Black women officers. Echoing the findings presented in this section of the book, other scholars have also found that Black officers report being stopped, harassed, and assaulted when out of uniform.[27] In its most extreme form, Black officers are disproportionately likely to be mistaken for a suspect and killed by a fellow officer.[28]

This experience of being both the enforcer and target of racialized law enforcement is present in other contexts, for example, for Latino/a Border Patrol officers. Although the historical contexts and relationships with the state differ, Black police officers and Latino/a Border Patrol agents have in common that they work for institutions that systematically oppress and dominate communities to which they belong. Scholars have highlighted that Latino/a Border Patrol agents also take on their institution's racial ideologies in the carrying out of their duties by identifying themselves as first and foremost citizens, institutional insiders, or soldiers fighting to secure their nation's border.[29] Latino/a Border Patrol agents, in similar ways to their non-Latino coworkers, adopt the racial ideologies of the institution, which conflate Latino identity with criminality, insecurity, and threat.[30] This prior work and the research I present in this book show just how strong institutions are in the shaping and maintaining of racialized ideologies, whether it is in the context of the Border Patrol or municipal police departments.

Although the data I present in this book cannot shed light on the actions of Black officers while on patrol, they do show that, despite being subjected to racist policing themselves, the Black officers I interviewed drew on institutional frameworks that point to the potential for criminality or violence, rather than race, in explanations of racist patterns of policing. This way of conceptualizing threat, criminality, and, ultimately, the "enemy" was an essential part of adopting the warrior role in policing and, thus, being socialized into state violence. For Black officers, this meant navigating the complex process of aligning themselves with a worldview rooted in anti-Blackness and racism.

Whatever It Takes

Toward the end of every interview, I asked each officer what they thought the police's role was in the United States. When I asked Paul this question, he laughed, perhaps at the scale of the question or maybe because this was the central topic of contentious public debate at the time. In his response, Paul described what he felt was a discrepancy between what the public wanted the police to be (the guardian) versus what the police needed to be (the warrior):

> I know the public right now is thinking only two things, "guardian" or "warrior." Through the majority of my career, I've not thought of either one. There was no definition of it. I'm here to help people, and some people need to be physically helped. I never looked at it as a warrior. Culture changes. The department changes. The pendulum swings. Sometimes the police get really scrutinized and tightened on what they're able to do, and then sometimes in history, it's gone the other way. I think right now it's probably a pendulum swing towards they're

trying to do more restriction for the police. And somebody has come up with this "warrior-guardian."

Paul felt that the warrior-guardian concept was a buzzword that just pandered to the public. He went on to explain that no matter what the conversation was around these concepts, the police still needed to be "warriors":

> If you wanna use those terms, you have to have both and each. I think what the city wants right now is just the guardian, . . . but you have to have the warrior. The guardian comes across in, How do you interact with people? How do you talk to people? The willingness to help people and go out of your way to help. Whereas the warrior is that I have skill sets that I need for survival that without, then I jeopardize myself. And if I do that, why am I doing this job? If I have no warrior skill sets, then the city is jeopardizing the entire police force. If that happens, then the criminal element will take over, and you'll have cities like Chicago or Philadelphia or whatnot.

Paul then elaborated that the warrior skill set and mentality were vital for officer survival, emphasizing the dangers inherent to the job:

> It's a dangerous job. You gotta have people that can handle the danger. You have to have people with skill sets that can fight and shoot and control a scene. But, at the same time, you have to have the guy, or person, that can interact with people and do it in a way that is pure service. But you cannot take the warrior out, the officer's safety. Because I have a family to go home to. Right? I have obligations and duties. . . . My first priority is to myself and family. . . . I have to take care of myself. I have to keep myself safe. And then after that, I can help other people.

Ultimately, Paul said, being a warrior was necessary to make it home to his family at the end of a shift. Being a guardian, he explained, was helpful for policing, but being a warrior was a requirement for the safety of officers and the public alike. Without this, he said, cities could descend into criminal chaos, citing Chicago and Philadelphia as examples.

This sense that officers needed to have a warrior approach to their work was repeatedly invoked in the academy training. The warrior approach to policing meant that officers needed to be willing to do whatever it took to make it home at the end of their shifts, including using violence. Cadets learned that a warrior is wary of every person they meet, always prepared for violence, prepared to stand their ground and fight back, and willing do whatever it takes to win a fight. Adopting this warrior approach, instructors insisted, was an essential part of cadets' transition to seeing and moving through the world as police officers.

At different points in their academy training, cadets completed exercises that emphasized the importance of adopting a warrior's mentality. During Terryville's Force Options class, for example, Kevin led a discussion about the role of killing and dying in police work. The Force Options class included instruction on the relevant procedure, case law, and departmental policies that dictated officers' ability to use force. On the first day of the course, Kevin asked the class, "What's the difference between killing and murder?" Cadets gave varied responses, but the common thread throughout each was whether there was a "need" to do it. When you "need" to do it, it is killing, they explained; when you did not "need" to do it, it is murder. It is a matter of whether it is justified, one cadet said. Another cadet explained that it is dependent on the presence of malice.

Kevin flipped to a PowerPoint slide with the title, "Facing Death and Dying." Kevin began reading off the slide, asking the class, "Have you faced the fact that you may have to take someone's life" in this job? Collin raised his hand and replied that yes, he had, and if the decision was between another person or himself dying, it was going to be the other person. Jake responded next, explaining that according to his faith, "killing is wrong"—he caught himself, "well, murder is wrong"—and that when he joined the academy, he had to revisit his faith to determine if he would feel okay with killing someone. There is killing in the Bible to protect others, he reasoned, and since as a police officer, he would only be killing someone to protect others, he came to terms with it. Ryan's reply was more candid: "Sometimes killing is necessary. Sometimes something's gotta give."

Kevin followed up by asking the class, "What made you think you could do it?" Andrea answered first: she had come to the decision because she knew that a person could go and kill someone else, a potentiality that she could not stomach. Hannah echoed Collin's prior response by explaining, "It's me or them, and I'm gonna go home. It is what it is." Dan shared with the class that when he had thought about it, he pictured his son. If someone was trying to hurt his son, he added, "I'd take someone's life in a heartbeat." Kevin nodded and affirmed Dan: "You have a purpose." Kevin wrapped up this part of the discussion by insisting, "You've been purposed with this job, you may have to kill someone, and you have to be okay with that."

Kevin then read the text off the next part of the slide: "Have you faced the fact that you could be killed?" Chase raised his hand and said he understood that this risk came with the job; he wanted to help people and protect them from bad guys, and bad guys are going to have weapons, he concluded. Michael, who was only twenty years old at the time, said he figured he was going to die either way at some point, and he would rather die doing something worthwhile, like police work. Kevin seemed satisfied with the cadets' responses and reiterated that "these are really important questions" to be considering as they began their careers in policing. He asked the class if anyone had ever been to a police officer's funeral. A few people raised their hands. It will "knock you off your feet," Kevin remarked. They would get a much better sense of the "greater thin blue line of all [their] brothers and sisters" at a police funeral, he added, and they would feel gratitude, humility, and brotherly love.

The two questions that Kevin posed to the class—about killing and about dying—were listed on the same PowerPoint slide, in relationship with each other. The thought processes that the cadets described reflected an all-or-nothing way of understanding lethal decisions in police work. Cadets explained that they were okay with killing because it was necessary both for their own safety and for the greater good. By putting these questions next to each other, and in conversation with each other, Kevin's instruction communicated that being okay with the possibility of killing another person was necessary to survive police work. Kevin tied this to their "purpose" as officers and explained that as part of this purpose, killing could be required. This willingness to do whatever it takes to survive—as Hannah said, it was either her or them—was an essential part of aligning themselves with the warrior mentality to police work.

This warrior approach to policing was present in formal instruction but also became ubiquitous in the academy setting. At Terryville, one cadet's pass code to his phone was "kill." When a cadet told me about this, she lightheartedly added, "Not his birthday or l-o-v-e or his mom's birth year, just k-i-l-l." At Rollingwood, a large sign covering one of the walls in the gym read, "THE MORE YOU SWEAT IN HERE, THE LESS YOU BLEED OUT THERE." The podium in the classroom at Rollingwood featured a plaque that read, "Only The Strong Survive." During morning formation at Rollingwood, the class president read the names of any officers who were killed on duty—anywhere in the country—the day before. Flags for every branch of the military hung in the academy gyms, and officers who volunteered as actors during scenario-based training wore T-shirts and hats featuring military branches and gun brands. The necessity of violence, and the framework of a war, filled this space.

Throughout the cadets' training, they were encouraged to adopt a warrior approach to policing, which necessarily meant being willing to do whatever it took to make it home at the end of a shift. When instructors talked about doing "whatever it takes," they meant using violence. Cadets learned that their survival depended on their alignment with this mentality and that a failure to do so could cost them their lives.

* * *

The images of the warrior and the guardian are both rooted in masculinist ideas about using violence to protect the innocent, who, in the context of war, are conceptualized as women and children. Women officers were expected to act as warriors on patrol—and indeed, the women cadets and officers I met embraced this worldview—but this masculine institution positioned women impossibly within the warrior-guardian framework. Women cadets and officers explained that they needed to work harder than men to prove themselves as warriors. This was made difficult by the fact that their men classmates "took it easy" on them during tactics training by not exerting their full strength during fights and, once on patrol, by men officers' paternalistic desire to protect women officers. When women overcame this barrier and performed violence better than men, they were subjected to informal discipline. Women cadets and officers were stuck in a maze, in which they had to navigate dizzying expectations to be both protected and protectors.

The women cadets and officers I met explained that they felt the need, as women, to prove themselves in both physical fitness and defensive tactics training. Scholars who study many different fields have found that women working in male-dominated occupations often feel that they are treated as "tokens," or as representatives for their entire gender.[31] The women cadets and officers I met expressed anxieties that echoed those reported in previous scholarship about tokens in the workplace generally and women in policing specifically.[32] These officers did not want to be considered liabilities, especially as women. They explained that performing badly reflected poorly on all women officers.

This sense that women needed to work harder than men came up on the second day of Terryville's academy, when the two women instructors there—Faith and Sabrina—pulled all the women cadets into a separate room to have "a talk." Faith worked as the physical training (PT) instructor at Terryville, a role I rarely saw filled by a woman. She was Filipina, looked to be in her forties, and was just over five feet tall. She almost always wore the typical instructor outfit—a bright-red Terryville-branded, moisture-wicking shirt with khaki tactical pants—with her thick, black hair pulled back into a neat, tight bun. Her shoulders slumped forward slightly, and her movements were stiff but confident. Sabrina worked as Terryville's field training officer (FTO) coordinator, which was a somewhat peripheral role to direct academy work. Once the cadets graduated, she would be responsible for assigning each of them to an officer who would supervise them on patrol for several months. Sabrina was around five foot five and had light-brown hair with a few gray hairs rebelliously poking out of her otherwise-neat bun. She wore thick-rimmed black glasses and coral lipstick, which popped against her fair skin. Her voice had a deep tone to it, and she took large steps when she walked, her shoulders moving with her.

On that afternoon, the instructors let the class know that they would be separated by gender—man and woman were the only two choices offered—for instruction specific to their respective group. Faith and Sabrina, who were the only two women on staff at the academy, led the women cadets into the smaller classroom. The men cadets, who made up most of the class, stayed behind in the large classroom with Kevin, Davis, and Caleb. I decided to join the women cadets for this section of instruction, and for the next hour, Faith and Sabrina covered a range of topics: they showed the class how to arrange their hair in a proper bun, warned them not to engage in sexual or romantic relationships with fellow cadets or other officers, and commiserated about the difficulties of being a woman officer. Faith concluded by warning the cadets that "as a woman, you have to work twice as hard to be taken seriously" in this job.

It became difficult, though, for women to prove themselves as physically strong and capable of fighting within the warrior-guardian construct, which dictates that men ought to protect women. This translated into men "taking it easy" on women during defensive tactics training and expressing a feeling of obligation to protect their women colleagues while on patrol. Sociologist Susan Martin has noted that this protective dynamic in police work is both gendered and racialized: white women, especially those who are considered attractive by their male colleagues, are more likely to be protected by men from the dangers of patrol work. Martin explains that white men officers expect that both Black and white women will be liabilities on patrol, but they draw on racialized stereotypes to conceptualize white women as "pets" or "mothers," while considering Black women to be "lazy."[33] Black women do report, however, that their male counterparts act in paternalistic ways toward them while on patrol, for example, trying to shield them from having to enter a strip club in response to a 911 call.[34]

This first scenario—in which men cadets "take it easy" on their women classmates—played out at Terryville during tactics training. The cadets were always assigned a partner for tactics training at Terryville, though these partners shifted from week to week. At this point in the academy, there was an odd number of cadets, which meant that whenever I was at the academy, I got paired up with whoever was the solo cadet that week. On one day of tactics training, I was paired up with Marcus, a six foot three, 200-pound, military veteran in his twenties. For context, I am five foot three, weighed 125 pounds at the time, and have no prior military or tactical experience. During lunch, one of the cadets realized that I was paired with Marcus and made a joke about it, assuring me that Marcus would "go easy on me." Craig, another cadet, quickly replied, "Nuh uh, I already got in trouble for doing that. We're not supposed to go easy on the girls!" Throughout the day, I heard women cadets complain several times about men cadets "taking it easy" on them during tactics training. Rachel, for example, told me that she liked getting paired up with Haley because she still went "hard on her," so she did not have to worry about a "guy going too easy" on her.

I experienced this gendered dynamic myself during defensive tactics training. One afternoon, I was partnered up with Collin. Collin was about five foot ten, white, in his thirties, and thin but strong. He had many tattoos and a delicate Southern California intonation in his speech. That afternoon, the instructors taught us how to physically stop someone who was aggressively approaching you. Per the instructions, Collin and I took turns playing the role of the aggressor and the officer. Dozens of times, I quickly and forcefully walked toward Collin. As soon as I got within arm's length, he threw his hand up and hit the middle of my forehead with the meaty part of his lower palm.

Collin repeatedly apologized as he did this and told me he would go lighter next time. Each time he apologized, I insisted that it was fine, that it did not hurt, and that he should complete the exercise as it was designed. By the end of the hour, I had a red mark in the middle of my forehead, and Collin again apologized. The next day, Collin told me that when he got home from the academy, he told his wife that he felt bad for hitting "a girl" in the head a bunch of times. He said his wife made fun of him for "hitting a girl" and told him that he should have taken it easy on me. Within the warrior-guardian framework, men are not supposed to hit women; they are supposed to protect them. In this situation, Collin was required to hit me, a woman smaller in stature than he was with almost no experience fighting. Collin's discomfort with his hitting me highlights the discordance that arises for men when they must fight women.

Men officers described feeling especially protective over their women colleagues while on patrol, pointing explicitly to gender in these conversations. At Clarkston, while watching the cadets go through tactics drills, I talked with Brad and Alex about a variety of topics, including a discussion about women in policing. Brad oversaw the tactical training at Clarkston and was very friendly and accommodating of my research. He was tall, white, and muscular, looked to be in his forties, and had a deep, booming voice with a slight southern accent. He asked me what my research was about, and I replied that I was interested in how departments were working to recruit more women and racial minority officers and how they trained cadets in tactics. He latched onto the part about women and began talking about several women cadets and officers.

During the conversation, Brad illustrated the complexity of this gendered maze. First, he pointed out a "female cadet" who performed poorly that afternoon during a grappling drill with her instructor. "You saw that, right?" he asked me. "Yeah," I said, "she wasn't doing much." Invoking the way that one's woman's performance reflects on all women, he then told me about a "badass" woman officer he knew who performed better in tactics than a lot of men in her academy class.

Whenever he told her about "shit like that," referencing women cadets who do not perform well in tactics, "it really pisses her off." Within the framework of tokens, this makes sense: if a woman cadet performs poorly in tactics, that contributes to the idea that all women are incompetent fighters and, thus, incapable of being police officers.

Brad then articulated the sense that women officers needed to work harder to prove themselves, while simultaneously illustrating the way that men make this difficult by insisting on protecting women. He told me about a woman officer named Catherine who worked patrol with him years ago. He prefaced the story by saying that she was "really beautiful." His eyes widened, and he repeated himself: "like, really beautiful." Because she was a woman and also beautiful, he said, he thought that Catherine felt the need to "really prove herself" tactically. "I was raised a certain way," he said, and on their first day as partners, he opened the passenger door of their patrol car for her. In response, he told me, she laughed and sternly told him not to do it again. On one of their first days working together, he recalled, he got into a physical struggle with someone, and "out of nowhere," Catherine slid across the hood of their car, tackled them, and got the man into cuffs. "I was like, 'Hell yeah, girl! Now that is badass!'" he added. Brad and Alex then talked about how "pissed off" they felt on patrol when someone would hit a woman officer, more so, they noted, than if a male partner got hit. Alex recounted a time when his partner, a fifty-something-year-old woman, got punched in the face on patrol. "Man, that pissed me off so bad!" he said. When on patrol, then, women can prove themselves tactically—like Catherine did—but they must overcome the obstacle of men's insistence on treating them in gendered ways, including engaging in a protective masculinity.

When women outperformed men tactically, though, they were subjected to disciplining comments. Haley, a cadet at Terryville, experienced this disciplining during her tactics training. Haley was in her twenties, white, blond, and remarkably strong, consistently lifting more weight than any of the women—and several men—in her class during their workouts. She was very kind and warm and always cheered on her classmates. She had spent years training in boxing and, as a result, completed the academy tactics training with relative ease. Haley was so tough, in fact, that no one even noticed when she broke her leg during tactics training later in the academy—she just sat along with the rest of her class during the debrief, silently, until Davis noticed that she was periodically wincing in pain.

During one day of tactics training, the instructors taught the class how to get out of several types of choke holds. Davis called on Haley and a male cadet to come to the front of the class so that they could demonstrate. As Haley walked to the front of the gym, her classmates let out a loud "Oooooooh," communicating sympathy toward her partner. As soon as Haley put her partner into a bar-arm choke hold, the class erupted into a chorus of "Oooooh!" and "Oh shit!" Haley furrowed her brows, tightened her eyes, and swung her head to look at her classmates. Haley glanced at Davis and, in an irritable tone, asked, "What? Was I not supposed to do it that hard?" "No, no," Davis replied, "you're fine. They're just giving you a hard time." I never saw the class have this reaction when a man overpowered another man during tactics training, and, thus, it was highly specific to a woman overpowering a man. The reaction was both disciplining to Haley and her partner—a woman should not overpower a man, and a man certainly should not allow himself to be overpowered by a woman. Women like Haley were supposed to perform the tactics competently but not better than men. When they performed better than men, they took on the role of the warrior and the guardian, negating the need for men to act as protectors or, even worse, rendering men as the receivers of protection by women.

Historically, one justification for excluding women from patrol was because they were considered incapable of carrying out the physical tasks of police work, especially the use of violence. Once women were permitted to work as patrol officers, they still faced difficulty accommodating the conflicting expectations and norms of being a woman and being a police officer. In Susan Martin's seminal work on women police officers in the 1980s, she found that women officers had to choose to either be a POLICEwoman or a policewOMAN, picking one role over the other.[35] Either option, however, came with risks of being criticized and undermined by their colleagues. Those who emphasized their identity as police officers reproduced forms of traditional masculinity and were often labeled with homophobic slurs by their coworkers. On the other hand, those who emphasized their identity as women needed to enact deference to their male colleagues and were labeled "pansy police" and, as such, not taken seriously.

I did not witness any cadet or instructor use homophobic slurs to describe women who outperformed men in tactics. This does not mean that women cadets and officers do not experience this kind of treatment or that lesbian, bi, and queer women officers are not subjected to homophobic language or behavior. Existing research does show that lesbian officers are often hesitant to disclose their sexual identities to their coworkers for fear of negative consequences, and they do report experiencing unequal treatment at work.[36] That women were not necessarily having homophobic slurs lodged at them, however, does not mean that they were not subjected to gendered disciplining of their behavior. I found that women officers were positioned within this institution in a way that made it nearly impossible for them to prove themselves competent without stepping on men's toes.

The warrior-guardian construct created gendered dilemmas for women officers, who did not quite fit into this framework. The women cadets and officers I met explained that they had to work twice as hard to be taken seriously in this masculine institution. To prove themselves, though, women had to overcome men's insistence on protecting them. When women outperformed men, taking on the role as protectors or aggressors, they were disciplined. Women officers were placed in a bind, then, in which they could never quite get it right. They must simultaneously perform well so as not to be considered a liability, overcome men's insistence on protecting them, but still allow men to fulfill their role as protectors by not outperforming them.

* * *

The warrior-guardian binary reflects a long debate about what the role of the police ought to be. Are the police there to fight crime and combat evil, to build relationships and serve the community, or both? Trends in police reform efforts reveal the contention in this debate. The push for community policing, an approach that emphasizes problem solving and civilian involvement, attempts to reconceptualize officers as public servants rather than crime fighters. Although these constructs are often discursively framed in opposition to the other or as separate concepts, in officers' training, the warrior role encapsulated the guardian role.

At the academy, cadets learned that their role in this dangerous and unpredictable world was to be warriors. To be a warrior, instructors told them, they must learn how to identify their enemy and be willing to do whatever it takes to make it home at the end of their shift. Their survival, instructors insisted, depended on their ability to develop and invest in this approach to their work. Identifying their enemies, they were taught, required that cadets always remain suspicious and learn to discern intention and threat through indicators like body movements, hand placement, eye contact, clothing, and location in the city. Although instructors insisted that cadets never profile based on race, they instructed cadets to profile criminality, which relied on deeply entrenched associations between race, gender, criminality, and violence. Despite decades of scholarship that shows the persistence of racial disparities in police stops, these academy instructors maintained that racial profiling was not a problem and that if cadets did not learn to profile based on criminality, they could not do the job.

The cadets were also told that to survive, they must adopt a warrior approach to policing. Instructors warned that while on patrol, cadets needed to be wary of everyone they met, constantly prepared for violence, and willing to use violence. Their number-one priority, they learned, was making it home at the end of the night to their families. If that meant that they had to kill someone while on duty, then so be it; that is what warriors do. It was okay, cadets were told, and indeed encouraged, to be polite when possible, but ultimately, the warrior skill set and mentality were the necessary parts of police work.

Learning to align themselves with this ideology was more complicated for cadets who did not fit neatly within the white, masculine, heterosexual framework that supports warrior imagery and narratives. The warrior-guardian construct positions white men as the protectors of white women and children from men of color, especially Black men. Black officers, then, especially but not exclusively Black men, had to contend with their institutions' framing of Black people as threatening and criminal. The Black officers I met described experiences of being racially profiled by police officers but nonetheless expressed a commitment to the accepted institutional narratives that pointed to crime rates, income, neighborhood context, or the law in explaining racial inequality in policing outcomes.

The warrior-guardian framework did not have a place for women police officers, who, as women, were supposed to be the protected, not the protectors. Echoing findings of women working in other male-dominated occupations, the women officers I met explained that they had to work twice as hard to prove themselves as capable. However, they were restricted from doing so by men officers who insisted on taking on a protective role, either by protecting women from physical threats or by disciplining women who took on the role of a protector of men. This dynamic may be more salient for white women, who are conventionally understood as being frail and vulnerable. However, Black, white, and Latina women cadets and officers expressed frustrations around this positioning. Women of color, though, must contend with being subjected to both racism and sexism in ways that white women do not.

The use of the word "warrior" implies that there is a war. If there is a war, then there is an enemy, and violence must be used to defeat them. The academy training at these departments emphasized this way of thinking about the relationship between the police and the public. The police were on one side of this war, and bad guys were on the

other. Being a police officer meant that they must parse out which civilians were bad guys. Instructors emphasized the very high stakes of
this identification process: if they made a mistake and did not correctly
identify a bad guy, they could be attacked and/or killed. Warriors do
whatever is necessary to eliminate the threat and make it home each
night, which necessarily requires violence.

5   TRAINING FOR WAR

With just two weeks left in the academy, the Clarkston cadets spent a full day completing the "redman" exercise. All the academies I studied had some version of this ritual, which required cadets to go through a series of stations to demonstrate a mastery of defensive tactics skills. The term "redman" referred to a large, padded, usually red training suit that an instructor wore as protection from injuries while cadets used their batons, expandable batons, and other weapons to fight them. When I entered the defensive tactics gym that morning around 6:00 a.m., everything was set up for the day, with orange cones, weighted dummies, blue mats, duty belts, fake batons, temporary walls, and weighted bags arranged into different stations.

When it was time to get started, the instructors turned off the overhead lights, flipped on flashing blue and red police lights, and played loud, mostly rap, music. The instructors explained to me that this was supposed to create stress and overwhelming sensory stimulation to expose the cadets to the challenges of remaining focused in distracting environments. The cadets were required to get through six stations to pass this exercise. First, the cadet would enter the gym and get onto their back on a blue mat in the middle of the room. Either another cadet or an instructor would then mount them, straddling them around their hips, to test the cadet's ability to escape the mount. When the evaluating instructor was satisfied with the cadet's maneuvers, they would blow their whistle for the cadet to move to the next station.

At the next station, an instructor directed the cadet to respond to a "suspect" (played by an officer) running on foot. An instructor standing across the gym would shout, "Hey, he's over here! He just stole from me!" while he pointed at another instructor about ten feet away, who then took off running. The cadet was expected to chase after the instructor, yelling commands for him to stop running. The cadet pursued the "suspect" as they ran outside of the gym, around the courtyard, and back into the doors on the far end of the building. An instructor standing outside those doors would then tell the cadet that there was another suspect inside. The cadet needed to then draw their (fake) pistol and do a "threshold evaluation," carefully clearing the corner. An instructor would be standing there, with his back pressed against the walls and his arms extended out with a pistol aimed at the cadet. The instructor would then immediately take off running.

The cadet then needed to maneuver around three temporary walls, each one taller than the next, to find the "suspect." They had to carefully approach each wall, pistol drawn, and clear the other side of the wall. The "suspect" stood on the other side of one wall. The cadet needed to spot him and immediately yell commands for him to stand up with his arms in the air. At the end of this station, an instructor handed the cadet a fake baton, and another instructor, dressed in a redman suit, pushed the cadet, prompting the cadet to respond with the baton. The cadet was expected to immediately deliver baton strikes on their instructor. After enough "effective strikes," the instructor in the redman suit took a knee, marking the end of the fight.

Next, the cadet was guided by an instructor to the stairwell leading up to the free-weights area of the gym. The cadet was handed a fifty-pound weighted bag and told to go up and down the stairs two times and then subsequently drag a weighted human-shaped dummy through a pathway on the gym floor outlined by orange cones. If they did not complete this exercise in the allotted time, they needed to do it again. At this point, most of the cadets gasped for air, unable to catch their breath. Dripping sweat, they moved on to the next station, where they put on protective head gear, picked up a fake baton, and fought another one of their instructors. The instructor gradually escalated their level of aggression and, by the end of the fight, attempted to take the cadet's firearm from out of their holster (and often succeeded in doing so). At this station, one cadet abruptly stopped fighting and extended his arms straight out in front of him. Several instructors rushed around him, and from a distance, I could see that his wrist was entirely disfigured. "Lights!" an instructor shouted, and the fluorescent bulbs hanging from the ceiling clicked on. Eric, one of Clarkston's defensive tactics instructors, commented, "Oh, we've got a bleeder." Another instructor responded, "No, I think we have a breaker." The cadet left the gym, presumably to be shuttled off to a doctor.

Finally, the cadets ran into a room at the back of the gym to conduct a search and arrest of one of their classmates. The instructors expected the cadets to push through their exhaustion and recenter their focus to conduct a comprehensive search. Their classmate had fake weapons planted on their body, and the cadet conducting the search needed to find them and then correctly apply handcuffs.

At the end of the day, the instructors debriefed the cadets, giving them feedback on what they did well and where they could improve. The instructors concluded the debrief by outlining the cadets' homework assignment for that evening. Since every one of the cadets used force—these stations were designed for this to be true—each cadet had to complete a use-of-force report that night. Once they graduated and started working patrol, this would be the form they filled out after using force on duty. One of the instructors asked the class, "Who got their gun taken from them?" A handful of cadets raised their hands. "Okay," he said, "for all those who got your gun taken, you have to write your own obituary. If you don't know what that is, look it up. Write about everyone you're leaving behind and the whole thing." This exercise emphasized to the cadets the very high stakes of mastering the tactical skills taught at the academy and put into sharp focus the cost, to both them and their family, if they failed to do so.

Through these exercises, the academy training taught cadets how to physically embody the role of the warrior by using their bodies to control, incapacitate, and hurt other people.[1] Being a warrior was not just an ideological approach but also an embodied practice. The academy instructors taught the cadets how to use their posture, uniform, and voice to compel compliance, their bodies to control another person's movement, and their weapons to incapacitate, injure, and kill someone. They practiced, over and over again, until they looked, sounded, moved, and fought like police officers.

Police officers are a literal embodiment of state power, and during their training, cadets were taught how to interact with the world with an assumption of possession. When a police officer walks onto a scene, they own the space. When they speak, you listen. When they ask you a question, you answer. When they give a command, you comply. If you do not, they can physically force you to comply; and if you resist their physical manipulations or try to harm them, they have the authority to escalate the violence above and beyond yours to subdue, injure, or kill you. Through hours of tactics training, the cadets learned to embody the warrior, marking their physical transformation from civilian to officer.

Practice Makes Perfect

About two months into Terryville's academy, I spent the afternoon in the defensive tactics (DT) gym, practicing giving commands and applying handcuffs. When we entered the gym, Davis, the instructor, yelled, "Up top!" and we all scurried to remove our shoes and huddle around him. A few weeks prior, we had learned how to handcuff starting with the bottom ring, and on this day, we were learning how to start with the top ring. Davis picked a cadet to help him demonstrate. He reminded us to make sure the cuffs were arranged correctly in the duty belt, so that when we pulled them out, we could manipulate them easily. Throughout his instruction, Davis's voice was congenial and familiar. He was not laughing or smiling, but his tone and volume were relaxed.

When Davis began demonstrating the commands, his voice instantly and dramatically changed. The volume of his voice tripled in magnitude, the tone deepened, the warmth evaporated, and a threatening harshness encased each word. "Turn around for me," he instructed. The cadet turned around. "Arms behind your back, palms up," he said. The cadet did as he was told. Davis continued, "Spread your feet. Bend over at the waist." The cadet obeyed the commands, and Davis handcuffed him. I had spent dozens of hours with Davis, often chatting and joking around. Once, during a warm-up for a long run in over one-hundred-degree heat, he teased, "Hey, if you get tired on the run"—he then paused as if he were going to tell me to take it easy—"then suck it up and keep running!" "Oh, okay, great advice. Thanks, Davis!" I replied, laughing. Each time, then, when his voice and demeanor rapidly changed, I felt disoriented and nervous. Even though I knew Davis, when he gave commands like this, I felt scared of him.

Learning how to give commands was the first step in the cadets' tactical training. Throughout their six to eight months at the academy, they spent hours learning how to contort their voices and position their bodies to communicate authority and exert physical force on other people. Learning these skills took practice. Through this practice, cadets made not just the ideological and moral transition from civilian to officer but also the embodied transformation. Through movement and the use of their bodies, cadets learned to embody the idea of the warrior.

Just like at Terryville, the Rollingwood cadets began developing these skills by first focusing on issuing commands. Rob, the Rollingwood instructor of this training, was white, blond, and in his thirties. He sported a mustache and the usual defensive tactics instructor outfit: khaki pants or black shorts with a red Rollingwood-branded athletic shirt. Rob was always very chatty and opinioned, eagerly sharing funny stories with me about his son in one moment and then harshly criticizing the cadet class in the next. His cubicle at the academy was filled with wooden figurines of an assortment of guns, and he once told me he would "die" if he had to go a year without shooting a gun.

During this portion of instruction, Rob used another instructor to demonstrate how to give commands. Rob bemoaned to the class that increasingly, some officers were being "too polite" and were "making requests instead of demands." He imitated this, his voice soft and unsure, hands delicately clasped together at his waist, standing about ten feet away from the "suspect": "Um, excuse me, sir. Could you please turn around?" His voice returned to normal, though tinged with frustration, as he told the class, "Don't do that. You don't need to be rude, but you need to be stern. You need to let this person know that you are in charge and that you have authority."

First, he said, you tell someone to turn around. His voice became louder and more rigid as he demonstrated: "Sir, turn around for me. Spread your feet." He explained that these first few commands also serve as a "compliance test." He went on, "Is this person doing what I'm telling them to do? Do they seem like they are going to be compliant?" Rob continued with the commands: "Put your hands behind your back, toward the sound of my voice." The instructor playing the "suspect" in the demonstration put his hands to his sides, palms facing Rob, and lifted them up, against his shoulder's normal range of motion. "Widen your feet more," Rob instructed, adding that usually when you tell someone to spread their feet, they will stand about hip distance apart, where it is comfortable. You do not want them to be comfortable, he told us; you want to put them at a "tactical disadvantage." Rob insisted that the cadets "need to be confident," explaining that their safety depended on their ability to communicate authority through their voice: "If you are not confident or you give someone too much time to think while you consider your options, that could up their predator drive."

After the demonstration, Rob instructed the cadets to pair up, spread out, and practice commands. They arranged themselves into two lines of nine, and immediately, a disjointed chorus of commands echoed throughout the gym. The cadets were supposed to give just three commands, in this order: "turn around," "spread your feet," "put your hands behind your back toward the sound of my voice." Then, the cadets needed to "offset," taking a few steps back and to the side so that their partner's hands were in their line of sight. The cadets fumbled over the commands. Several continually gave the commands in the wrong order, shaking their heads and tensing their lips when they realized that they had done it incorrectly. One cadet repeatedly yelled, "Spread your legs," instead of "Spread your feet," until Rob, trying to conceal his laughter about the sexual nature of the phrase, shouted, "Don't say 'legs.' That doesn't sound right." The cadet again yelled, "Spread your legs," during the exercise, then shook his head side to side, paused, and, correcting himself, yelled, "Feet!"

The cadets' ability to give commands was evaluated during scenario-based training. Scenario-based training, which usually began a few months into the academy, tested cadets' ability to apply classroom and tactical skills to law enforcement scenarios. Their instructors designed the scenarios, officers at the department volunteered as "actors," and officers (either their instructors or officers volunteering) evaluated their performance. Cadets always had their duty belts for these scenarios, including their handcuffs and a fake rubber pistol. If they decided to use their gun, they would shout "bang bang" to indicate that they had fired their weapon.

At Terryville, the cadets' first scenario-based training came directly after their classroom and tactics instruction about the mechanics of arrest. Before each scenario began, the instructors briefed the cadets on what information they had from dispatch about the scene. In one of the scenarios, the instructors told the cadets that they had just made the first arrest of their career and were stopping at a gas station—for the scenario, this was just the academy gym—with their partner for a celebratory coffee. When they entered the gym, there were two teenage Latino boys in civilian clothing standing together in a corner. These two teenage volunteers were a part of Terryville's Police Explorer Program, an organization that offers fourteen- to twenty-year-olds who are interested in pursuing law enforcement exposure to the field. The two boys shook hands, one of them dropped a small plastic bag, they split up, and then they left the building. The cadets were supposed to do the following: articulate their suspicion, notice that one of the boys was from a BOLO ("be on the lookout" sheet) they were shown earlier that day, talk to them, ask for consent to pat them down, find the concealed gun and brass knuckles on one of them, and arrest him. After making the arrest, they were supposed to investigate the small bag that one of the boys dropped, which they would then learn was full of cocaine. When Carmen, a Latina cadet in her twenties, and her partner, Dan, a white cadet in his twenties, ran through this scenario, the instructors expressed concern about their tactics, specifically criticizing Carmen for not using a "command voice." Kevin, their instructor, spent several minutes telling Carmen that she needed to work on her command presence. Echoing Rob's warning at Rollingwood, Kevin advised, "Otherwise, people will take advantage of you."

Eventually, through repeated practice, these commands became second nature to the cadets, even in stressful situations. At each academy I studied, the cadets were required to pass a defensive tactics final exam. The specifics of the exam varied slightly among departments but in general involved a multistation tactical obstacle course. As I described in the opening of this chapter, at Clarkston's academy, part of this obstacle course included a station where cadets needed to "clear" a hallway, guns drawn, to make sure no one was hiding behind the corners. A "suspect" sat on the other side of a low wall at the end of the hallway, hiding from view. The first cadet to run through the scenario, a white woman in her twenties, did everything correctly, according to her instructor. With her (fake) pistol drawn the whole time, she carefully approached the wall and noticed the suspect. She shouted commands for him to get up with his hands in the air, backed away from him, and found partial cover behind one of the walls. Following her commands, he stood up. She continued with her commands: "Lift the collar of your shirt up with your right hand!" When the suspect did this, a (fake) pistol tucked into his waistline became visible. Next, she shouted, "Turn around slowly until I tell you to stop." He turned around in a circle slowly. "Stop!" she yelled once he completed a full circle. She yelled for the suspect to slowly climb over the wall, get down on one knee, then on both knees, then lower himself onto the ground, onto his stomach, and put his hands out to his sides. Once he was on the ground, body sprawled out, she handcuffed him, cleared his weapon, and put the gun in her pocket.[2]

Although cadets were taught to begin with verbal commands, they were repeatedly warned that words would not always work. If someone does not follow verbal commands, the instructors explained, then physical force is necessary. This warning came up at Terryville's academy during the De-escalation class. After showing the dash-cam footage of Andrew Brannan killing Deputy Kyle Dinkheller, Kevin told the class, "If you give a command and they don't comply, you must make them do it. There has to be some use of force."[3] When he was in the academy over a decade ago, Kevin explained, he was taught to abide by the phrase "ask, tell, make." To illustrate, he showed how he would ask, then tell, then make someone sit down on a curb: "I'd start out by asking nicely: 'Hey, man, could you just sit down over here, please?'" If they do not sit, he said, then he might ask them one more time, to make sure that they understood and heard him. Now, he explains, "they are not complying, so I might raise my voice at this point and tell them [his voice became louder and deeper], 'All right, man, I already asked you two times to sit down, so now I'm telling you, sit down on the fucking curb.'" If the person still will not sit down on the curb, he said, "then now I'm going to need to go hands on and make them sit on the curb, or I'm going to put them in cuffs and temporarily detain them, because they are now refusing to comply with my commands." "Especially with suspects who do not give a shit," he explained, "they will not take you seriously if you don't enforce your commands." If not followed, commands act as a promise of force. Instructors warned early on that mastering a command voice communicates authority and, ultimately, is necessary for officer safety.

Physical Control

During one of the first weeks of tactics training at Terryville, I got paired up with Sabrina, a Latina cadet in her twenties, to practice handcuffing and searching. She gave me commands but had not quite mastered them yet, so she hesitated, fumbled over her words, spoke softly, and nervously laughed. "Ma'am, please turn around and put your hands behind your back," she instructed. I turned around and put my hands behind my back. She forcefully grabbed my left wrist with her right hand, clasped my left shoulder with her left hand, and pressed me against the wall. She pushed her weight into me, so that that my entire chest and the right side of my face were flat against the concrete wall. "Spread your feet for me, ma'am," she said. She kicked the inside arch of each one of my feet, forcing them to awkwardly slide out to my sides, widening my stance. My weight was now unstable, which was the goal—Sabrina had been taught to "put me at a disadvantage" while she searched me. Sabrina kneaded her hands along my legs and arms, ran her thumb around my waistband, and pulled at and shook the elastic band of my sports bra so that anything I could be hiding there would fall to the ground. While she did all of this, Sabrina repeatedly apologized to me. Touching other people in this way was both dominating and intimate, and without any practice, it felt uncomfortable for both of us.

Once cadets learned how to issue verbal commands, they moved on to learn how to control someone's body through physical touch. The level of physical contact involved in academy training was a unique part of this job, and the initial awkwardness that Sabrina and I felt highlighted the central role of touch in police work. The amount of physical contact at the academy was so substantial, in fact, that at Rollingwood, the instructors required that the cadets wear long sleeves and pants to prevent the spread of staph infections. In their previous academy class, a dozen cadets contracted staph infections, so the concern was not unwarranted.

After many hours of practice, the cadets became skilled in the kind of controlling and invasive touch that was required to frisk and search someone. At Clarkston, the cadets demonstrated their mastery of searching during their defensive tactics final. The final exam required the cadets to chase a "suspect" and fight two of their instructors individually before arresting and searching a classmate. For part of the day, I sat in a chair next to Nikki, a Latina instructor in her thirties, in a small room on the far end of the gym watching the cadets complete this search and arrest station. A blue mat was laid out on the floor, and a clear, plastic bucket full of fake weapons sat on a nearby shelf. Nikki evaluated each cadet's search, taking notes on her clipboard. Before each cadet entered the room, Nikki instructed the cadet who would be searched to plant several fake weapons on their body. When the cadet being tested entered the room, they found their classmate standing on the blue mat and were told by Nikki to give commands, get their classmate in cuffs, and search them for weapons.

The first cadet I watched was a tall Black man who looked to be in his twenties. Droplets of sweat fell from his bald head down his face and off his chin, in quick succession, landing either on his classmate, who lay on the floor in cuffs, or in a puddle on the blue mat. He issued commands to get his classmate up off the ground: "roll over," "get up onto one knee," "lean back," "put your weight on your heels," "get onto both knees," "cross your legs at the ankle." The cadet being searched winced as his body was contorted in awkward, unnatural positions. Once the classmate was positioned on both knees, ankles crossed, with his hands behind his back, the cadet conducting the search pressed one foot down onto the soles of his classmate's boots, grasped the cuffs securing his classmate's wrists with one hand, and conducted the search with the other. He kneaded his hand on the outside of his classmate's pockets, turned out each pocket, shook each pant leg and the belt line, took off the belt, pressed his hand along the belt, took off the classmate's shoes and knocked them on the ground, pressed his fingers between each toe, peeled down the socks, and glided his palm around each leg, up to the groin, the belt line, chest, back, and arms.

The cadet conducting the search looked physically exhausted and frazzled. He mumbled under his breath, expressing doubt about being able to find the planted weapons. Nikki told him to slow down, take a few deep breaths, and "take care of business." Though he expressed uncertainty about finding the planted weapons, there was no visible or vocalized discomfort or apprehension—from anyone—about his touching his classmate in this way. The cadet had pushed his full weight onto his classmate's ankles, forcefully pulled his classmate's arms behind his back, removed items of clothing, and pressed his hands over his classmate's entire body with ease. The concern that this cadet expressed was about his own safety, not about the well-being of his classmate. Each cadet whom I watched conduct a search that day did so with a level of confidence and fluidity that had to be learned through practice.

Hurting

After learning how to control other people's bodies, the cadets moved on to mastering tactics that are designed to hurt people. This shift in intention came up during one day of tactical training at Rollingwood, when an instructor told a cadet that, at a certain point, he needed "to transition from arrest to damage." The phrase "doing damage" came up repeatedly during my fieldwork and described a physical response intended to hurt, injure, or kill the other person. During a physical interaction, the cadets were told, their goal should, at some point, move from merely controlling to hurting.

At Terryville, the cadets started by learning how to use "pain compliance" techniques. The instructors explained that these skills were important because issuing pain can coerce compliance with commands. Although many departments no longer teach pressure points— mostly, it seems, due to ineffectiveness, rather than ethical qualms—at Terryville, we spent an afternoon practicing finding and pressing into points on each other's bodies to elicit pain. The instructors first handed out a worksheet with an image of a person's silhouette in a fighting stance, hands up protecting their face and feet splayed apart. Fourteen pressure points were marked around the silhouette, starting as high as behind the ear all the way down to the calf. After going over the worksheet, we headed to the gym, paired up, and spent three and a half hours practicing the fourteen different pressure points on one another. These pressure points—sometimes referred to as pressure point control tactics (PPCT)—were developed as part of a training course by Human Factor Science, a company that provides training curricula and courses to law enforcement, military, and other first responders.

Once we were in the gym, we started off with the behind-the-ear pressure point. Davis talked us through it as he demonstrated on a cadet. He asked one of the cadets to come to the front of the gym, get on their knees, and sit up straight. He told us to maintain a tactical stance behind our partner, one foot slightly behind the other with our body pressed against their back. He went on: cup their chin with your left hand, hit the side of their head with your right palm, so that their head is pressed into your forearm and bicep—"like you're holding a football," he said—and push their head into your chest and arm, securing it. For a pressure point to be effective, he explained, we needed to have counterpressure. Once we immobilized their head, we should ball up our right fist, extend our right thumb, find the soft spot between their jawline and ear, and press directly in and then up, keeping our elbow down so that we could push with some force. As he demonstrated, the cadet's eyes tightened shut, their lips stiffened, and they flinched. When it starts to hurt, Davis explained, we should tap our chest a few times or tap our partner's leg to let them know.

Hannah and I were paired up for the day. I opted to go first, kneeling and clasping my hands together. I felt Hannah's body press against my back, and I could sense her apprehension, as she barely put any pressure against me. She cupped my chin, gently pressed the side of my head into her forearm, and tried to find the pressure point between my jaw and ear. She pressed in and up, and although I certainly felt pressure, I did not feel pain. Caleb, a Latino instructor in his forties, walked down our row to check everyone's progress. Caleb was around five foot ten, had dark-brown hair with a slight receding hairline, and was very muscular—his body was shaped like a V, his shoulders significantly broader than his lower half. Toward the beginning of the academy, he was quite tough on the cadets, telling them once, for example, that if they did not think he was an asshole by the end of the academy, then he had not done his job. As he made his way around the gym, Hannah and I asked him if we were doing the exercise correctly since I was not grimacing in pain like everyone else. He very naturally and comfortably walked behind me, cupped my chin, forcefully pushed my head into his forearm, and easily found the pressure point, digging into a soft spot under my jaw. A sharp, piercing pain shot up my neck. My eyes pinned shut, and I tapped out. "Ooooh," I said. "Yep, that worked." Hannah tried it again, with his guidance on where to press, and got it right.

Hannah and I moved through each of the different pressure points together. When we got to the "brachial plexus origin," we each used our thumbs to press into the meaty portion of the other's neck. Still in the same position as before, with Hannah's head secured in my left arm—like a football, as Davis had suggested—I pressed along the long muscle stretching from her jaw to her clavicle, trying to find the sensitive spot. I pressed in with my thumb and saw her eyes squint shut. I released the pressure, asking, "That hurt?" "Yep, you got it," she confirmed. Then, Hannah practiced this one on me. This one hurt in a deeper way than the previous two since this spot on the body was embedded in the muscle, rather than between bone and tissue. Feeling pain, in this case, meant that we could move on to the next pressure point and felt more like a checklist of tasks than an afternoon of hurting each other. Each pressure point felt slightly different in its level of discomfort, pain, and physiological reactions, like watering eyes, briefly blacking out, falling, or involuntarily releasing the arms or legs.

After we practiced the "brachial plexus origin" point on each other, Davis instructed us to line up in our rows, all on our knees, side by side. Because we had been working just on touch pressure, he said, he and Caleb were now going to demonstrate what it feels like to use a strike with this pressure point. Davis told the class that he has knocked someone out by striking them in the brachial with his forearm, so it can be very effective. Laughing, Davis recounted feeling very scared when the man he was fighting collapsed to the ground unconscious after he used a brachial strike. His voice high-pitched and breathy, he said, "Oh my god, did I kill this guy? Are those the death snores? What the fuck?" "The first time you knock someone out on duty," he explained, "it's really scary."

While we lined up, all on our knees, I glanced around the room. Carmen and I met eyes, and we both frowned, worried about how this was going to feel. When Caleb got to me, he stopped and said, "I'm not gonna do you, Sam." Surprised, I replied, "What? Why?" Laughter filled the room, and he asked, "Do you want me to?" "Yeah!" I replied, still committed to feeling what the cadets felt in training. "All right," he replied hesitantly. He rubbed the right side of my neck, explaining that he was going to hit that meaty part with his forearm. "Okay," I said. I felt his forearm slam into the side of my neck, and my whole body folded in half, over my right hip. My vision went black for a moment, and I let out an "Ooooof!" Again, the room filled with laughter. "You good?" Caleb asked. It took me a second to recover, but I replied, "Oh yeah, I'm fine!" Caleb continued down the line of cadets. A few cadets just shut their eyes, keeping their hands clasped together, maintaining complete composure, while others completely collapsed to the ground. By the end of the day, I was sore in a unique way; very specific parts of my body—mostly crevices between bone and tissue or soft spots where muscles meld together—ached.

Throughout the next several months, the cadets learned how to strike, kick, take down, disarm, and use a baton against their classmates. After dozens of hours of practice, they were tested on these skills in their defensive tactics final. The details of this exercise varied slightly among departments, but the general structure was the same at each one. The cadets started out by doing calisthenics for several minutes so that they began the exam out of breath. This "oxygen deprivation," as the instructors called it, was meant to make the test more difficult and to replicate "real life," when they may have to fight someone while out of breath after a foot pursuit. After a few minutes of exercises, the cadets were then put through an obstacle course, including some combination of clearing a room with their firearm drawn, delivering baton strikes to an instructor in a redman suit, boxing an instructor, getting out of a hold while ground fighting, and usually at the end of the test, making an arrest, which included giving commands, getting the person in handcuffs, and searching them without missing any planted weapons.

The cadets tended to have the most trouble at the grappling station—where they fought an instructor who usually had a purple or black belt in Brazilian jiu-jitsu—and at the baton strike station. At Clarkston's academy, after cadets had grappled an instructor, run laps around a "robbery suspect," conducted a "threshold evaluation" where they carefully cleared a corner with their weapon drawn, delivered baton strikes to an instructor in a redman suit, run up and down a flight of stairs with a fifty-pound bag on their back, and dragged a human-shaped dummy across the room, they then put on headgear, grabbed a baton, and entered the ring with an instructor. Almost a dozen instructors and cadets held up pads in a circle around the mat, while the instructor in the ring alternated his level of aggression to evaluate the cadets' ability to use the correct amount of force. The instructor started out by just pushing the cadet, then escalated to punching and then trying to take the gun out of their duty belt. In the middle of the exercise, one cadet, who was completely soaked in sweat, took off his protective headgear, limped over to the trash can, and vomited. Another cadet clumsily teetered back and forth on her feet, on the verge of losing consciousness. When she got pushed down by the instructor, she lay there, halfheartedly covering her face, unable to get up. The instructors around the mat yelled at her, "GET UP! COME ON! DO SOMETHING!" The instructors talked about her afterward—in an exacerbated tone, one asked the other, "Did you see her? She didn't do shit. She just laid there [sic]."

Most of the cadets, however, mastered these skills and passed their defensive tactics final. At Rollingwood, the cadets' tactics final was very similar to Clarkston's exam. In the gym, the overhead lights were shut off, police lights flashed from the center of the room, and the loud riff of guitars and jarring pitch of heavy metal vocals echoed off the cement walls. The instructors explained to me that the lights and music were meant to generate "sensory overstimulation," inducing stress and creating distraction. The cadets warmed up by delivering strikes to a punching bag and completing a series of calisthenics. Then, they moved through stations that tested their skills in grappling, boxing, delivering baton strikes, and conducting a search.

At the first station, the cadets entered the grappling ring, an instructor shouted, "FRONT LEANING!" and, doing as they were told, the cadets dropped into a plank position. One of the instructors instructed the cadet to do ten push-ups and to count them out loud. While that instructor gave those directions, another instructor crouched down, maintaining eye contact with the cadet while he leaped from right to left. As the instructor hopped around, he repeatedly turned a shock knife (a fake knife that issues shocks) on and off, making it light up with white light and buzz loudly with electricity. Another one or two instructors also knelt to the cadet's level, surrounding the group, pounding loudly on the mat with their fists. When the cadet began the push-ups—down, up, "ONE!"; down, up, "TWO!"; down, up, "THREE!"—an instructor, who was hidden from the cadet's view, tackled them from the side. The cadets were supposed to use the techniques they had been taught—shrimping, hip bridges, elbow strikes, framing with your knees—to get out from underneath their instructor.

Most of the time, the instructors, who were far more skilled than the cadets, ended up on top of the cadet, with a high mount, legs tucked underneath the cadet's armpits and groin against their chest, putting their full weight and force into controlling the cadet's body. Gordon, a middle-aged, muscular, white man, was the first cadet to complete the exam. David, a Latino tactics instructor in his forties, leaned over to tell me that at forty-one years old, Gordon was the oldest cadet in the class but that he was "in awesome shape" and had "done really well with DT." At that point, I was only a few months into my fieldwork, so I could not quite tell whether the cadets were doing well. I did not yet have the knowledge to determine who was in control of the fight. To me, it looked like Nick, the instructor, choked Gordon for a full minute. After Gordon completed the grappling station, I asked David how he did. He said that Gordon did great, adding that if the cadets used the techniques that they had been taught, as Gordon had, the instructor fighting them would let up.

That these tactics were designed to hurt another person was emphasized by the fact that cadets were often injured during their defensive tactics training. These injuries ranged in severity, from minor strains to broken bones. Haley, for example, broke her leg during one afternoon of defensive tactics training. Haley was in her twenties, white, and blond. She had trained for years in boxing and, as a result, was highly skilled in both physical fitness and defensive tactics training. That afternoon, the instructors taught the cadets several different "takedowns," which involved tactical strategies to get another person on the ground and into handcuffs.

For the last takedown of the day, the instructors split us into groups of three, where one of us played the "suspect" and the other two played the role of officers. I got paired up with Jackson and Matt. I was much smaller than Jackson and Matt in stature, and I was also outskilled: Matt had already worked as a police officer for years at another agency before joining Terryville, so these tactics were not necessarily new for him. In this exercise, the person playing the "suspect" was instructed to start out on their hands and knees and resist arrest, moving and flailing around as much as possible, while the two officers—one assigned to each half of the body—maintained control and got the person in handcuffs. One cadet took on the top half of the "suspect's" body, wrapping one arm over the their shoulder and the other around their waist, clasped together in a cable grip. While yelling commands, the first cadet tried to press all their body weight onto the "suspect" so that they fell to the ground and were unable to move. While the first cadet did this, their partner would pull the "suspect's" legs out from under them by their ankles and try to wrap them up with their own legs, sitting on them and crossing their own legs at their ankles. This second cadet was also supposed to press down onto the "suspect's" hips, while keeping their legs entangled, to get their body pressed on the ground, while their partner started to try to cuff them.

I started out playing the "suspect," so I got situated on my hands and knees on the blue mat. As instructed, Jackson wrapped his arms around my chest and gripped his hands together, while Matt pulled my legs out from underneath me and pressed down onto my lower half. It was almost comical how easy it was for the two of them to get me to stop resisting. With all my energy, I tried to get out of their grip, but I could not manage it. Jackson inadvertently started to choke me with his forearm, so I adjusted my position to breathe, all the while trying to wiggle my way out of their holds. We cycled through, each taking a turn in each of the assigned roles. By the end of the day, I had a large bruise on my left hand, on my left calf, and on my inner thigh, and my entire body hurt from the afternoon of exercises.

At the end of the exercise, Davis shouted, "Up top!" and we all scurried to the middle of the gym and sat in a large circle around him. Haley, however, crawled on her hands and knees to the middle of the gym. At the time, I thought she was just winded or sore, as I was. A few seconds into Davis's debrief, his eyes caught Haley, and he asked if she was okay. She pushed out an unconvincing "yes," so he asked again. This time, she did not say anything, and her eyes welled up. "Can two of you take Haley to Kevin's office, please?" Davis instructed. The next day, Haley showed up to the academy on crutches and reported that she had broken her leg. Unfortunately, this meant that she was no longer eligible to graduate with her class and would have to complete the remaining training with the next class.

With some exceptions, most cadets did not come into the academy already knowing how to control and hurt another person's body using these techniques.[4] Through countless repetitions, they learned how to contort their voices to communicate authority, touch others in invasive and controlling ways, and use their bodies to hurt other people. The cadets made mistakes throughout their training, highlighting how these embodiments and skills are, in fact, learned. By the end of their training, though, most cadets mastered these skills and began to hold themselves and interact with others as police officers.

Killing

The cadets spent one or two weeks learning how to use firearms, focusing mostly on pistols but also incorporating rifles and shotguns. At Terryville, this training segment began in the classroom, where Dylan spent the afternoon teaching firearms basics. Dylan pulled up the PowerPoint presentation on the projector, the title of which read, "Fundamentals of Marksmanship." This was the instruction they gave "people who suck at shooting," Dylan explained. He clarified that any officer who fails their annual firearms qualifying exam was required to take this class. Dylan clicked to the next slide and read the text aloud: "There are no time-outs in a deadly encounter." When you are in a deadly force encounter, he elaborated, you cannot tell the person trying to kill you that you need a break to take a few breaths. There are not any do-overs either, he added.

The next slide included the question, "Why is marksmanship important?" with a list of four items underneath: (1) consistency, (2) accuracy, (3) speed, and (4) survivability. The last item—survivability—Dylan explained, referred to being consistent, accurate, and fast under stress, all of which were necessary to survive a deadly force encounter. Dylan emphasized the importance of all four of these components of marksmanship, explaining that speed and accuracy are equally vital. If you are an accurate shooter, he went on, but you are slow, your opponent may shoot you first. You need to be somewhere in the middle on these two, Dylan said, where you fire accurate enough rounds faster than your opponent. That is how you win a gunfight, Dylan concluded, by being first and hitting the most. "If you aren't training to be faster *with* accuracy, you are not training to win a deadly force encounter," Dylan warned.

The rest of the cadets' firearms training focused on these primary principles, practicing repeatedly to ensure that even in the most stressful situations—which, by definition, would be the only scenarios when they would use their firearms—they could shoot accurately and quickly. The goal here, their instructors reminded them, was to "win" the gunfight, which almost certainly meant killing the other person. Of course, the instructors did not encourage cadets to draw their firearms for no reason, nor did they take deadly force encounters lightly. They did, however, repeatedly remind the cadets that if they did not master these skills, their lives were on the line.

Aside from speed, accuracy, and consistency, the instructors also instilled in the cadets the importance of aiming for the "center of mass," which referred to the trunk of someone's body, including their chest, back, and stomach. This concept came up in my interview with Phillip, a fifty-eight-year-old Black retired deputy at Fairview Sheriff's Office. Before he retired, Phillip had worked in law enforcement for thirty-four years. I asked Phillip how he thought policing had changed since he started over three decades ago. In his response, Phillip talked about a fading sense of "brotherhood" between officers and an intensified scrutiny from the public, especially about police-involved shootings. Referring to public reactions to police shootings, Phillip explained, "You're gonna question, 'He [the police officer] didn't have to shoot him [a civilian].' Well, I've even heard people say, 'Well, why didn't he shoot him in the leg?' That's not what we were trained to do. You know what our training is? Our training is to shoot center of mass. What center of mass? That's the largest portion of a person. . . . It's too hard for me to try to hit you in the leg. You're moving or whatever. You shoot for the largest portion." As Phillip described, cadets were trained to aim for the center of a person's body, not the arms or legs, which might be less lethal. The reason for this, as Phillip explained, is to increase their odds of shooting the person they are aiming at and, ultimately, to "win" the gunfight.

Cadets were also instructed to keep shooting until the other person completely fell to the ground. During Terryville's firearms training, Dylan reviewed what was called the "post-engagement checklist" multiple times. They went over this in the classroom and then practiced it later that night at the firearms range. If you have been in a shooting,

Dylan said, you need to do the following, in this order. First, track your "threat" to the ground and find cover. On the range, he elaborated, the targets you will be shooting at do not fall to the ground. In real life, Dylan went on, if you shoot someone, they are not going to stand still; they will run or fall or keep coming at you, so you need to keep shooting until they are on the ground and no longer moving. Next, Dylan said, do a weapon check. Do you need to top off (i.e., fill the magazine with bullets)? Is your weapon functioning? This step will break your tunnel vision and get you back on the task at hand, he said. Third, reload your gun if needed. Lastly, if the shooting occurs at night, scan your surroundings with your handheld flashlight: look left, right, and behind you. He added that they should use a flashlight, not the light mounted onto their pistols, to avoid scanning potentially innocent people with a loaded weapon. Maybe the person you just shot "is a shithead. Maybe his head is now a canoe, brains all over," Dylan said, "but maybe his four-year-old kid isn't, or maybe the guy just walking in his neighborhood isn't."

Later that day, the cadets practiced shooting in "low light" situations. Once the sun set, the cadets went out to the range and practiced several different ways to hold a flashlight while shooting. Each time they shot, the instructors told them to practice the full "post-engagement checklist." After you shoot, Dylan instructed, follow your target to the ground, do a weapon check, and scan the area. Just a few minutes into practicing, Dylan shouted at the cadets for "getting lazy" with their scan of the area and insisted that they should not just go through the motions; they needed to actually look around them. Later, Dylan criticized the cadets' shooting speed, instructing them to shoot faster, reminding them, "Just because its night doesn't mean shitheads take any longer to shoot you." The stakes of this training, the instructors continually warned, were unimaginably high: this was a skill, they warned, that officers' lives literally depended on.

The cadets were tested on these skills at the firearms range but also during scenario-based training. The firearms range was the only place where cadets ever shot their real guns, but their ability to draw their pistol and make the decision to shoot was still tested in other contexts using rubber or "simunition" pistols, which are guns that use nonlethal ammunition. At Rollingwood, the cadets completed two full weeks of scenario-based training toward the end of the academy. On the eighth day of this training, the cadets were put through several back-to-back use-of-force scenarios, running from one station to the next, having to respond to each with what the instructors believed was the appropriate amount of force. At one of these stations, the cadets were told by an instructor to run outside to the back of the gym and around the corner, where a role-player in civilian clothes would be pointing to the other end of the building and telling them to hurry because there was someone there trying to kill a woman with a knife. Once the cadet rounded the corner, they would see a person lying on the ground while another person held a knife over their body. The person with the knife would then start imitating a stabbing motion, yelling, "Die, bitch!" The instructors had set up a barrier so that the cadets were forced to shoot at the "target" from eighteen feet away, not any closer. I asked Omar, one of the instructors, why they had set up this barrier. He explained that the longer you take to shoot, which would include any time it takes to get closer to the person, the more time the person would have to stab the woman lying on the ground. You cannot wait until you have a better shot, he said; you just have to take the shot.

Once the scenario was over, the instructors debriefed each cadet, giving them feedback on what went wrong and ways to improve. Most of the cadets took the shot as soon as they rounded the corner, but some of them did not. In the latter case, Scott, the instructor evaluating the scenario, posed, "Can you shoot from eighteen feet?" Some of the cadets paused, unsure of what they should say, while others just replied, "Yes." "You've practiced from twenty-five feet at the range, right?" Scott pressed. The longer you take trying to get a better shot, Scott explained to them, the more times that guy stabs that woman; so as soon as you see that happening, you stop moving and take the shot. Scott sharply criticized cadets who did not draw their pistol before they rounded the corner while approaching the scenario. "What intel do you have?" he would shout as they ran. "That there is a knife, sir!" or "that someone is trying to kill someone!" the cadets would reply. "So, where the FUCK is your gun?!" Scott would scream.

That cadets were trained to use their guns to prevent a murder in progress or to defend themselves against someone shooting at them is arguably reasonable. However, this training, which required that cadets draw swiftly, shoot quickly, aim for center of mass, and continue to shoot until the person dropped to the ground, creates ample opportunity for lethal errors. This was most vividly illustrated by a conversation I had with Omar about a scenario that the Rollingwood academy used to have cadets go through as part of their training. I stood with Omar for over an hour while we watched cadets, one by one, go through the stabbing scenario. Omar looked to be in his mid-forties, was average height, and was Puerto Rican. Before pursuing law enforcement, he had served in the Army for seven years, but he left once he got promoted to captain. Omar told me that when he was in the Rollingwood academy, fourteen years prior, he remembered going through similar stations as part of the scenario-based training. In that version, though, the last station was a routine traffic stop. When Omar completed this training, he had just responded to multiple lethal force scenarios, he explained, so he was amped up by the time he got to this last station. The person sitting in the driver's seat quickly extended her arm out of the car window to show her driver's license. He thought she was pulling out a weapon, he said, so he shot her. Although his instructors did not teach Omar to shoot unarmed civilians during traffic stops, his body was trained to react in this way, leading to potentially lethal consequences for civilians.

Where's Your Gun?

Two weeks into the academy, and with only one afternoon of basic tactics training under their belts, the Terryville cadets were each put into a boxing ring with a semiprofessional fighter for three, one-minute rounds. I first learned of this ritual—called "Fight Day"—when

I attended Terryville's Multiculturalism and Introduction to Defensive Tactics courses. I got to the academy early on that Tuesday morning and sat with the instructors while they ate breakfast around a wooden table in the small kitchen near the back of the building.

Kevin walked into the kitchen after inspecting the cadets' uniforms during morning formation and outlined the schedule for the day. He told me that he was surprised I did not want to be here on Thursday. "What's happening on Thursday?" I asked. Caleb jumped in: "That's when they learn how to box." Dylan laughed: "Well, it's really more like a supervised beating." On Thursday, Caleb explained, they would go to a boxing gym and put each cadet in the ring with officers who fight competitively. There was no way for the cadets to win, he said. What they were testing, Caleb explained, was whether the cadets had the will to "not give up" and stay in the fight. Some of the cadets had "never thrown a punch," he said, eyes wide with concern, so they needed to experience getting hit and not running away from it.

On Wednesday, when Caleb introduced the exercise to the cadets, he repeated this same explanation, telling the class, "The point of Thursday is to show that you have the will to live, that you won't give up in a fight. There's no second place in a fight on the street," he warned, "so you gotta get up and give it your all." Through this ritual, the instructors were not testing skill or technique; the cadets had received virtually no training yet. Rather, they were requiring that the new cadets, especially those who had "never thrown a punch," showed the instructors that they would use violence when the institution required it.

I was not able to make it to Fight Day, but when I returned to the academy the following week, the cadets were still fixated on the ritual. The cadets eagerly told me, often without prompting, how they did in the ring the previous week. Hannah, a white cadet in her twenties, hardly remembered any of it—it felt like she blacked out, she said—but she knew that in the first couple of seconds in the first round, her previously injured knee got tweaked again. Andrew, a Latino cadet in his early twenties, woke up the next morning with a bloodshot red eye.

He must have popped a blood vessel one of the times he got punched, he reasoned. During defensive tactics that afternoon, I watched Aaron, a Latino cadet and ex-Marine in his twenties, grimace in pain, grabbing at his ribs, while he attempted to do push-ups. I asked him about it later, and he said he popped two ribs out of place during Fight Day. The referee called time, he told me, so he dropped his arms, and his opponent was able to get in one more rib shot. Limping and wincing and unable to fully see, the cadets expressed pride in what these injuries illustrated: they did not give up, they did not stay down, and they tried their best. They proved to their instructors that they were willing to fight.

A similar exercise happened a few weeks into Rollingwood's academy, during the first day of the cadets' defensive tactics training. Previously called "Fight Day," the command staff had recently renamed this ritual "Will to Win Day." One by one, each cadet ran around the track outside, entered the gym, jumped rope for a minute, and punched a bag for two minutes. Once they were warmed up, an instructor pointed toward the ring and yelled at them to put on headgear and get in. For the next three minutes, an instructor boxed each cadet, delivering strikes mostly to their chest, stomach, back, and arms.

As one cadet—a tall, skinny, blond man with large, round, blue eyes—walked into the ring, Jason, a white instructor in his thirties, lamented, "Guys like that make me fucking nervous. . . . I can see white around his entire eyeball, he's so scared." About two minutes in, the cadet stumbled backward and keeled over, his head following his shoulders downward, stepwise, like it was detached. The cadet looked like he was going to vomit a few times during the three minutes, contracting his stomach forward and his eyelids flimsily threatening to shut. Expressing fear, cowering away, or not eagerly engaging the fight all resulted in instructors chastising cadets. At one point, the instructor fighting the cadet—who was basically chasing after him in the ring—slammed his gloves together and yelled, "DON'T FUCKING APOLOGIZE! LET'S GO!" When a few of the other cadets struggled, either balling up in a corner, trying to run away from the instructor, or standing still, arms down at their sides, the instructors shouted from outside the ring: "Do something! Don't just stand there!" "We have enough slugs in this department. We don't need another one!"

This exercise illustrated an important mechanism whereby the cadets learned to embody the warrior: through the institutional disciplining of their performances of violence. The instructors berated, humiliated, and physically punished cadets when they did not issue commands, search effectively, or stand their ground in a fight. Throughout the academy, the instructors tested cadets on both their willingness and their ability to engage in violence. Instructors expressed extreme frustration and engaged in intense displays of anger when cadets performed poorly on these tests, often shouting, cursing, and lodging insults, all publicly. These theatrical and passionate reactions disciplined cadets into enacting violence willingly and competently on behalf of the institution.

This intolerance for, and disciplining of, any display of either unwillingness or inability to fight also came up during the cadets' tactics and scenario-based training. Importantly, cadets were more harshly punished for using too little, rather than too much, force. This inconsistency in the disciplining of violence was illustrated by two separate tactics drills at Rollingwood. The first happened during one afternoon of tactics training, when the instructors taught the cadets how to disarm someone with a weapon. At the end of the day, the instructors paired up the cadets and told half of them to grab either a fake weapon or a miscellaneous, innocuous item. The cadets playing the role of the officer did not know that some of the items were not weapons. The cadet with the hidden item was told to make furtive movements—like avoiding eye contact, turning around, or touching their pockets—to suggest that they might be armed, and the "officer" was supposed to notice this and disarm them. The cadets playing the officer all assumed that their partner was armed and, in most of the pairs, yelled, "Bang, bang!" within a few seconds, indicating that they had taken the shot. Tricia's partner pulled a black sharpie out from her pocket, and mistaking it for a weapon, Tricia shot her. During the debrief, Tricia explained that her partner's hands were tucked under her shirt, so she could not tell if her partner was armed. Another cadet pulled a fake yellow crack pipe out of his pocket. His partner shot him and, realizing her mistake, pressed her hand on her heart and dropped her jaw open.

After the exercise, Josh, one of the Rollingwood tactics instructors, debriefed the class. Josh was tall, in his thirties, and white, with cropped blond hair. He was a former Marine and had a tattoo sleeve covering the length of one arm. Josh had a reputation among the cadets as being especially harsh, and indeed, I saw this dynamic play out on multiple occasions during the academy: he often screamed at the cadets to get their "sacks" off the ground while doing push-ups and frequently delivered long, impassioned speeches about officer safety. After most of the cadets playing the officer in this exercise shot their unarmed partners, Josh explained that this was a "familiar problem" that officers face, acknowledging the difficulty in determining if someone is armed and acting appropriately. The instructors were not visibly angry about the cadets' performance, and they did not punish the class.

In sharp contrast, the instructors became enraged when cadets did not use force at all, or did not use enough force, during their tactics and scenario training. This was most vividly illustrated during the defensive tactics final at Rollingwood, when several instructors gathered around the grappling ring and screamed at the cadets for either not fighting back or not using their weapon. The academy staff often talked to me about Lila, a cadet who had a PhD, specifically bringing up her degree when discussing her poor performance at the academy. The point of this, I think, was to let me know that even people with high levels of education—like me—may not have what it takes to get through the academy. Lila did not do well on the defensive tactics final, repeatedly failing the grappling station. The instructors assigned Lila to fight Spencer, a white instructor in his thirties. Spencer stood around five foot nine and had a completely shaved head with arms covered in tattoos. He had a thick New York accent, loved heavy metal music, and often talked about his support of gun rights and general discontent with the police union. During Lila's fight, she ended up on her back, with Spencer mounted on top of her, constraining her body with his legs, continually hitting her in the head. While in this position, Spencer looked around at the other instructors, indicating his frustration. He was not even trying, his facial expression told the group, and he was still winning the fight by a landslide. From the sidelines, the instructors threw their hands in the air and screamed at Lila, "FUCKING DO SOMETHING! GET OUT OF THAT POSITION! YOU'RE JUST TAKING PUNCHES!" After lunch, I went to the bathroom and saw Lila packing up her locker. I asked the instructors about it, and they confirmed that she had been fired. She barely passed her driving test, did poorly in her firearms training, and now failed her tactics final, all of which were grounds for termination.

During the grappling station of the defensive tactics final, the instructors often grabbed the (fake) gun out of the cadet's holster and threw it across the ring. This tested the cadet's ability to retain their weapon during a fight. Sometimes the cadets noticed, but most of the time, they did not. Whenever the cadet got out from underneath the instructor, the other instructors yelled, "WHERE'S YOUR GUN?!" Eyes wide, arms out, and fingers spread, the cadets whipped their heads back and forth, scanning the mat for their gun. When they spotted it, they ran toward it, picked it up, and aimed at the instructor. Some of them yelled, "Bang bang," indicating that they took the shot. Others yelled, "Put your hands up!" or another similar command. Three of the cadets picked up the gun, reholstered it, and reengaged in the fight. One of the times this happened, Spencer threw his face guard in the air, splayed his arms out wide, tilted his head completely back, and exclaimed, "WHAT THE FUCK!"

After the exam, the instructors debriefed the exercise. Josh told the class that they did not use the techniques he taught them, and they did not shoot. "How many of you lost your gun?" he asked. Everyone raised their hand. "How many of you knew you lost your gun?" Most of the cadets raised their hand. "Why didn't you shoot?" he asked. The class remained silent. "Why didn't you shoot?" he asked again. Silence. The frustration in his voice intensified: "Seriously, why didn't you shoot? I need to know for training purposes." One cadet said he wanted to give the person a chance to comply with his commands. Another said he used unnecessary lethal force in other scenarios, so he was wary to use it here. "It's you or him or her," Josh said, "and we want it to be you. You just fought someone on the ground for two minutes, basically being smothered. They took your weapon. Why would you not shoot them?" Josh relayed an important message to the cadets: if someone threatens your life, do not give them an opportunity to change their behavior.

* * *

Often, the disciplining that was reliant on verbal humiliation at the academy was rooted in sexism: women cadets, or the abstract threat of femininity, were used as a foil against which men's performances were evaluated. Other scholars have pointed to the ways that "cop culture" relies on performances of masculinity that often degrade femininity.[5] Within the academy context, men instructors berated men cadets when women outperformed them, using feelings of emasculation to motivate them to perform strength and violence better. When instructors did not use women cadets as literal comparisons, they instead lobbed gendered insults at men who displayed any physical vulnerability or fear.

I experienced this dynamic myself at Hudson during the first workout session of the academy, referred to as the "Breakout Workout." During the first three days of the academy, cadets and instructors frequently brought up this workout, hyping it up as an important first step in training. Instructors told us about cadets vomiting, fainting, and needing oxygen during the workout and warned us to "get ready for" it. On the first afternoon, I mentioned to Andrew, the cadet I sat next to in the classroom, that I was nervous about the Breakout Workout. Andrew, a white Army veteran in his thirties, replied that he was excited for it and that he "loves that kind of shit." "Can you do a push-up?" he asked me, smirking. Andrew and I had developed a playful, humorous relationship in the first few days of the academy, but despite our established dynamic, his question—and his tone—irritated and insulted me. He was mocking me, and I knew it was because I was a small woman. I barely turned my head in his direction and glared at him out of the corner of my eye. "Yes," I responded, maintaining my glance, "I can do several." At lunch on the second day, a cadet in the most senior class at the academy gave me and another cadet the advice to just "get through it" and told us that "only one cadet from" her class "puked."

On the third afternoon of the academy, our instructor directed us to go to the locker room, change out, and meet in the gym. For the next two hours, in one-hundred-degree heat, we ran laps around the parking lot and did push-ups, bear crawls, sit-ups, mountain climbers, and squats, all as punishment for infractions—either not following directions or not doing something in unison—that the instructors had kept track of over the preceding three days. Several cadets vomited, others collapsed, and one received oxygen. For the entire two hours, we had an audience. The entire training staff, including sergeants and lieutenants, and several cadets from more senior classes spectated. Officers who worked patrol, and therefore had no other reason to be at the academy, attended to witness our suffering. Each time we ran a lap outside and came back into the gym, we passed by a large group of officers, instructors, and sergeants yelling at us to move faster. Out of an awkward, probably gendered habit, I smiled at the instructors as I ran past them. Although I thought I was being polite, I did not realize what my smile communicated until the sergeant, a white military veteran in his forties, forcefully shouted at me, "GRAD STUDENT, YOU AREN'T WORKING HARD ENOUGH IF YOU'RE SMILING!"

About an hour and a half into the workout, I was winded but getting through it comfortably. Others, including many men, were not. The sergeant used me as a point of comparison to embarrass the class, yelling, "DO NOT LET THE GRAD STUDENT, WHO DOESN'T EVEN HAVE TO BE HERE, SHOW YOU UP!" When I returned to the academy the next week, several cadets told me that the sergeant was "talking shit" about me on Monday, when I was not there. They told me that he said I was "giggling" throughout the workout. Although the sergeant's reaction and comments highlighted my being an outsider to the institution (i.e., calling me "grad student"), they were also dependent on my being a woman. He used my outperforming men, in a masculine institution, in a task that men ought to be good at, to embarrass the cadets into performing better.

This use of women as foils also came up at Clarkston during a day of firearms training. I spent the day at the indoor firing range, where the cadets completed their qualifying exams for shooting. Kurt, a white firearms instructor in his fifties, led the cadets through the exams. There were too many cadets in the class to all complete the exam at once, so groups of about a dozen cadets came into the range, completed the exam, and then left to make way for the next group. After the first group shot, two of the instructors came into the command booth, where I was sitting. One of them said that the two women cadets, who were standing next to each other on the far-right end of the line, were "lighting it up," meaning shooting well. He said he made fun of the men cadets who were not shooting as well, apparently telling them, "Maybe they [the women cadets] can shoot for you, and you can drive for them." The room full of firearms instructors—all men—broke into laughter.

At times, this kind of gendered disciplining did not require an actual woman but, rather, just the specter of femininity. Sociologist and gender scholar C. J. Pascoe examined this gendered dynamic in a high school, where boys constantly tried to dodge and then displace the label of "f*g" onto other boys.[6] Being labeled a f*g, Pascoe explains, could result from a range of behaviors, including expressing emotion or warmth or demonstrating a lack of physical strength. In the police academy setting, men cadets risked being disciplined when they displayed any sign of physical weakness or fear, in ways that women did not.

This came up at Terryville on TASER Day, when each cadet was required to be shot in the back with a TASER gun. The purpose of this exercise, according to the instructors, was for cadets to fully understand the TASER's level of force. The cadets headed to the gym, where the administrative assistant stood with a hat filled with scraps of paper, each with a cadet's name written on it. She explained that the order would be determined by whose name she picked out of the hat next. The cadets lined up against the far wall of the gym while the instructors finished setting up. Caleb stood in the middle of the gym with his TASER gun holstered on his duty belt while he opened a new box of TASER cartridges, which is the piece of equipment holding the two prongs that shoot out of a TASER gun. Caleb gave a quick rundown on how the morning would go: when it was their turn, each cadet would stand in the middle of the gym, about ten feet from Caleb, facing away from him. Each cadet would be helped by two of their classmates, who would hold their arm on either side and slowly lower them to the ground when they were shot. The TASER prongs would deliver an electric current through their bodies for five seconds. After the five seconds, the two classmates holding the cadet would apply basic first aid. One would pull the probes out of their back, and the other would swab the two entry points with alcohol wipes and put bandages over the small wounds.

When his name was called, Anthony, the largest cadet in the class—who was six foot three and weighed around 250 pounds—apprehensively walked to the center of the room and nervously looked back to the line of cadets standing along the wall. He avoided standing in the spot that the instructor had designated, walking around it for over a minute. "Come on, Ant!" the class yelled, cheering him on. "You got this!" He continued to look back at the line of cadets along the wall, his hands forcefully shaking. He raised up his fist to cover his mouth as he started to gag. "Are you going to throw up?" one of the instructors asked flatly, carelessly kicking a trash can closer to him. "I think so," Anthony said, his large body subtly convulsing. His classmates encouraged him to take some deep breaths, and he finally stood in the correct spot, with two cadets grasping each of his arms. Still, while he stood there, he continued to glance behind him, where the instructor holding the TASER stood. "Stop looking behind you," Davis, his instructor, shouted at him. "Anthony, STOP LOOKING BEHIND YOU!" Davis yelled again, his finger pointing toward the back wall, where Anthony was supposed to be facing. Anthony continued to nervously look backward. Davis's voice became steeped with anger, and, as he pointed at the door, he shouted, "Anthony, do you want to quit? You can fucking quit right now if you want to." "No sir," Anthony replied, still shaking. "Then fucking face the wall and get this done. You're making us look bad," Davis complained. "I don't usually get mad," he said to another officer, "but damn." All of this was video recorded, and in the afternoon, we went back to the classroom to watch the videos of every cadet in the class being shot with the TASER. When we got to Anthony's video, the instructors mocked him, one saying, "Well, we don't have thirty minutes to rewatch you shitting your pants," and everyone laughed.

Months later, at Terryville's graduation, the instructors again made fun of Anthony for his trepidation on TASER Day. A few hours before the ceremony, Davis gave each cadet two TASER cartridges and told them to test their TASER gun and then load a cartridge. The cadets all pointed their TASER guns at the ceiling and pulled the trigger. A loud, deafening buzz filled the room. Smiling, Davis turned to Anthony and sarcastically asked, "You gonna be okay?" Dylan, the firearms instructor, slapped Anthony on the back and, making fun of him, asked, "Hey, man, do you need peer support?" The room erupted into laughter. Anthony's display of fear, which conflicted with the masculinized performances required in policing, was disciplined repeatedly, for months after the incident. Despite, or perhaps even because of, his large size and muscular build, Anthony's brief lapse in a performance of fearlessness and strength in the face of extreme pain was considered unacceptable.

De-escalation Is Nothing New

In each of the interviews I conducted, I asked the respondent how police work had changed since they started the job. Bill, the forty-nine-year-old Black sergeant who supervised tactics training at Rollingwood, had worked in law enforcement for almost two decades.

When I asked him this question, he immediately brought up de-escalation. "In some ways," he said, "I think the officers are better. They're more willing to try to talk to people as opposed to before." He went on, "That key word 'de-escalation,' which has always been there—a new word pops up, and people jump all over it as if it's just been discovered. Or 'Hey, here's this novel idea. Let's ask cops to de-escalate.' Well, police have been de-escalating the entire time; since the very first foot patrol, cops de-escalate, so it's nothing new."

Michael, a white lieutenant in his fifties at the Rollingwood academy, similarly felt that de-escalation simply described existing policing strategies. During a day of scenario-based training at Rollingwood, Michael pointedly asked me what exactly I was studying. I replied that I wanted to learn how officers were trained to use force and to de-escalate. He immediately retorted that "de-escalation" was "just a buzzword." Sporting a smug grin, Michael added, "A sociologist probably came up with the word." He explained that police officers had "been doing this [de-escalating]" forever, that it was just called "being a good cop." In response, I asked, "So you don't think the training has changed at all?" "No!" he replied. "We've always been doing this. It hasn't changed. It's just a buzzword."

As Bill and Michael suggested, as I was conducting fieldwork, the public was demanding that the police learn to verbally "de-escalate" situations in the hopes that these strategies would limit the use of physical force. In the public imagination, de-escalation strategies offered a different, gentler, way for officers to do their jobs. In practice, however, the de-escalation training that I observed did not, in any way, challenge, contradict, or contest the warrior approach to policing. Consistent with the rest of the cadets' tactics training, they were taught never to prioritize de-escalation over officer safety. Doing so, instructors warned, could cost them their lives.

There was not a singular, clear definition of "de-escalation" within the policing circles I studied or, arguably, in public conversations about policing. There was no prescriptive list of behaviors, actions, or tasks that constituted de-escalation. The inherent vagueness of the concept lends itself to being defined in many ways by people with different, sometimes opposing, perspectives. Echoing Bill's and Michael's sentiments, the officers I met felt that de-escalation was a buzzword that described already-established policing strategies. De-escalation, they explained, was nothing new or innovative.

In academy trainers' instruction to cadets, they defined "de-escalation" as a way of initiating contact with a civilian respectfully and politely. At Terryville, Kevin explained to cadets that "the point of de-escalation is how [officers] start an interaction." Kevin clarified that de-escalation techniques created pathways for effective communication and provided ways for officers to defuse people who were worked up. Approaching a situation calmly and politely, instructors explained, had multiple benefits for officers: it made it easier for them to collect information, ensured compliance from civilians, and, ultimately, bolstered officer safety. Kevin articulated this lesson in his introduction to the De-escalation class at Terryville, telling cadets that it was very important to have "the favor and support from [the] community": "That's how we get things done." "Cops can't have eyes everywhere," he elaborated, "so we need the community to help us gather information." Being polite during interactions, he explained, made the community more cooperative with the police and, by extension, made officers' jobs easier.

Instructors also insisted that being polite and respectful bolstered officer safety. Officer safety was, in fact, conceptualized as integral to the goal of de-escalation. On the handout that Rollingwood instructors gave cadets at the beginning of the De-escalation class, the first subheading on the first page read, "Part I: Professionalism, 1. Goals of this course: A. Officer Safety." This message was communicated again later in the class, when Brett, one of the Rollingwood instructors, showed a video of a man shooting himself in the head while in police custody. After playing the video, Brett speculated about potential alternative endings to the incident. The video showed an older Latino man in a police interview room as an officer hands him a bottle of water. As soon as the officer leaves the room, the man pulls a gun out of his pants, presses the barrel against his head, and fires a shot into his skull. Officers immediately rush into the room, panicked and cursing—"Oh fuck," "Holy shit," "What the fuck"—and bemoan that the man was not patted down before he entered the station. When the video ended, Brett posed the question of what would have happened if the officer had treated this man disrespectfully. He would have shot the cop, Brett surmised, and probably a lot of the other cops at the station. Brett suggested that the officers' polite demeanor probably saved their lives. If they had not treated this man with respect, he implied, he would have killed the officers at the station that day.

Instructors' encouragement of de-escalation was often immediately contradicted by warnings about the dangers of attempting de-escalation strategies. Instructors insisted that, even when using de-escalation techniques, cadets must always maintain their warrior mentality. Cadets should approach a situation politely, instructors explained, but they should never drop their guard, always anticipate violence, and constantly remain cautious. This came up at Rollingwood when the instructors showed a video during the De-escalation class of several different law enforcement professionals talking about the importance of communicating before using physical force. One man featured in the video recounted an experience with his first field training officer (FTO).[7] His FTO told him to take out a one-dollar bill and asked him, "What's in the eagle's hands?" The one-dollar bill features an eagle with an olive branch in one set of talons and thirteen arrows in the other, the man in the video explains, signifying peace and war. His FTO told him to be like the American eagle: to extend an olive branch to someone first but to always have a plan to kill them.

Instructors issued a similar warning during Terryville's De-escalation class. About an hour into the class, Kevin flipped to a slide showing statistics outlining how many police officers die in the line of duty.[8] Repeating an oft-used mantra in policing, he reminded the class that their number-one goal "is going home each night." Kevin then flipped to a slide showing a picture of General James Mattis. The following text was overlaid on the photo: "Be polite. Be professional. But have a plan to kill everybody you meet." Kevin acknowledged the intensity of the quotation by asking the class, "What do you think a civilian would think of this if they just walked into the room right now and saw this without any context?" The cadets all laughed. "Right, exactly," Kevin responded. "How would they react?" One cadet called out, "Appalled." Another noted, "They wouldn't get it." Kevin asked the class, "What does this quotation mean?" One cadet raised her hand and suggested that it meant to expect the best from people but to know that "it could turn bad." Yes, Kevin confirmed, "every call should start out polite and professional, but it could end up like that," he said, pointing to the last line of the quotation, suggesting that even if an interaction initially seems safe, you may end up killing someone. Kevin again warned, "Even though we're talking about de-escalation today, I'm not watering down officer safety. Do not ever drop your guard." Kevin suggested that police officers should be "polite" and "professional" but reminded the cadets of the always-present potential for violence and urged them to be prepared for it.

Relatedly, throughout cadets' training, instructors insisted that de-escalation strategies should never be used in the place of physical force. De-escalation techniques should be used when possible, instructors explained, but should never be prioritized over officer safety. Doing so, they warned, would result in catastrophe for the cadets and other officers. At Rollingwood, the instructors issued this warning in many ways throughout the De-escalation class, including by showing a clip from the 1966 film *The Good, the Bad, and the Ugly*. In the clip, a bounty hunter corners the character Tuco as he takes a bath. The bounty hunter rants about his long, tired search for Tuco and expresses glee that Tuco is exactly in the position that he hoped he would be: trapped and vulnerable. Tuco interrupts the bounty hunter's speech by shooting him multiple times from the bathtub, delivering his line: "When you need to shoot, shoot. Don't talk." As the clip ended, the academy classroom erupted into laughter.

This message was even more explicitly delivered later in Rollingwood's De-escalation class, when Brett reminded the class, "We're not telling you that you can't go hands-on. If the opportunity allows and officer safety allows for it, try to talk to people." To illustrate his point, Brett showed the video of Deputy Kyle Dinkheller's murder. Dinkheller issued dozens of verbal commands, to no avail, and ended up paying the ultimate price. Again, the class listened to Dinkheller's strained, shallow last breaths as he bled out at the side of his patrol car. Brett concluded the video by saying, "I hate going to funerals. Don't make me go to your funeral because you were using your words when you shouldn't be." De-escalation was a useful tool at their disposal, cadets learned, but it should be used cautiously.

That videos of officers being beaten and killed were repeatedly shown during de-escalation training and that instructors continually issued warnings about the dangers of de-escalating speaks volumes about the institutional approach toward violence in policing. Equally telling was the absence of any kind of de-escalation evaluation exercise. As I have described here, cadets were repeatedly tested on their competence in using physical force, from verbal commands to firearms. There was, at the time of this research, no exercise at the academy that specifically evaluated cadets' ability to de-escalate. Admittedly, the inherent vagueness of the concept and the fact that instructors felt that de-escalating did not encompass a new or novel set of skills made it difficult to test de-escalation. The de-escalation training that cadets did receive consisted of classroom work and a written exam. Their instructors framed de-escalation as useful insofar as it made the work of policing easier and safer. They did not, however, discuss de-escalation as a way that they could do their jobs more ethically, morally, or peacefully. Rather, cadets learned that they should be polite in the way they approached an interaction because it would enable them to solicit information more easily and decrease the likelihood of their being attacked. Being polite, however, did not preclude maintaining a warrior mentality. Cadets learned that they must stay vigilant, on guard, and ready for violence at a moment's notice.

* * *

When video footage of the police surfaces on the internet, they are often criticized for the ways that they talk to and interact with civilians. Those who are critical of the videos usually comment that the officer's voice and commands were overly aggressive, that they touched the civilian's body in a forceful and/or violating way, or that they needlessly escalated the level of violence. Especially in cases where a police officer shoots someone who is unarmed, public outcry centers around the officer's mistaken assumption that this person—who is often a man of color—had a weapon.

The cadets at these academies were taught to talk to and interact with civilians in exactly the ways that are shown in this kind of video footage. Instructors urged cadets to use a loud, deep voice to issue commands, to get physical at the first sign of noncompliance, to forcefully position other people's bodies to communicate dominance, to fight in ways that hurt other people, and to shoot as soon as they perceived a potentially lethal threat. Through repetition and disciplining, the cadets learned to embody their new role by mastering violence and domination. The police officers shown in most of these publicized videos (there are, of course, cases that even officers categorize as inexcusable), then, are simply acting like police officers.

Cadets were taught that they would have to make life-or-death decisions and that in those situations, they should choose their own lives, even if it means that someone else would die. Of course, instructors did not encourage cadets to shoot unarmed civilians, but they did train the cadets to assume that everyone is armed and to shoot as soon as they felt that their life might be threatened. Given this training, it is not hard to understand why police officers repeatedly end up shooting unarmed civilians who run away, turn around suddenly, or reach into their pockets to grab a phone or wallet. Quite simply, they were trained to react in this way.

Those who are pushing for police reform often suggest that adding more women officers and implementing de-escalation training will help reduce the use of violence in policing. On the basis of what I saw at these academies, I have no reason to believe this to be true.

Although women cadets certainly experienced gendered dilemmas in the academy around using violence, they could and did excel in these spaces. Women faced added barriers to performing well at the academy, but they, just like their male classmates, were taught to use violence to control and harm others.

The de-escalation training incorporated into the academy at the time of this research was limited to just eight hours. Officers did not believe that the concept was new or different, and instructors urged cadets to use extreme caution when attempting to use de-escalation techniques. I was not ever able to gather a clear understanding of what specific set of skills or techniques constituted de-escalation. Even if there had been, though, it seemed that de-escalation techniques in no way challenged existing ways of doing police work. Instructors presented de-escalation as a way to approach civilians politely but warned cadets to maintain their warrior mentality and always be prepared and willing to use violence.

How cadets were taught to use violence assumed a troubling control over people's bodies. They were taught not just to defend themselves but how to control, incapacitate, and harm other people in the name of the greater good. At the academy, officers often told cadets that in a high-stress situation, they would not "rise to the occasion" but, rather, "fall back to their training." Cadets' physical bodies were conditioned, through repeated drills and institutional disciplining, to react in specific ways. The outcome of this kind of training is clear: the police are trained to use violence, and civilians are dying as a result.

6 PUSHED OUT OF POLICING

On my last day of fieldwork for this project, on a cold and windy day in February, I attended Terryville's academy graduation. I had spent hundreds of hours with these cadets: we ran miles together in sweltering heat, I helped them study for exams, we fought each other during tactical training, we ate lunch together, and we sat next to each other in the classroom for dozens of hours. Graduation day started at the academy facility, where the class had a potluck breakfast while they got ready for the ceremony. I got to the academy just before 8:00 a.m. and placed the fruit bowl I bought on my drive over on an already-full table of donuts, pastries, bagels, and orange juice. When I entered the classroom, I saw the cadets, for the first time, wearing their full officer uniforms. Their shiny name tags were clasped neatly on their chests, their long sleeves were firmly pressed, and their duty belts were now complete. The only thing missing were their badges. They were now nearly indistinguishable from their instructors, who wore the same formal uniform for the ceremony.

Around 11:30 a.m., we headed out to our cars and drove the short distance to the convention center downtown, where the graduation ceremony would take place. The convention center auditorium had a large stage on the far end of the room with over two thousand seats facing it. For about an hour, the instructors ran the cadets through a rehearsal of the ceremony while I sat with Haley a few rows back from the stage. Although this was her academy class, Haley broke her leg during defensive tactics and had to make up several blocks of missed training before she could graduate. Despite the setback, Haley was in good spirits, telling me that her recovery was going well; she was out of the boot now, which was good, but her bone was still disconnected, she said. After several run-throughs of the ceremony, the instructors directed the cadets into a room nearby, where they would wait until their formal entrance into the auditorium.

When the auditorium doors finally opened to guests, the cadets' friends and family members flooded in. I glanced around the room and recognized what were by then very familiar facial features on the cadets' parents, grandparents, and children. Once everyone was seated and it was time for the ceremony to begin, the academy captain, Terry, greeted the crowd, thanked everyone for being there, and formally invited the cadet class to enter the auditorium. Manny held the class guidon—a flag customized for the class—at the front of the formation, leading his classmates in the procession as they marched in unison through the doors, down the aisle, and onto the stage. The cadets filed into the two rows of seats arranged on the stage and stood at attention, just as they had practiced. Kevin, their instructor, shouted, "POST!" prompting Manny to carefully lower the guidon into a stand at the front of the stage. "SEATS!" Kevin yelled, and the cadets all sat down. A Terryville officer then sang the national anthem, and the captain gave out awards to the top cadet in physical fitness, shooting, academics, and character.

Finally, the cadets received their badges. The captain stood at the podium and read each cadet's name, in alphabetical order. One of the training officers then brought the badge and a certificate for each cadet to the chief, who stood on an X in the middle of the stage. Another X was taped next to him, marking where the cadet should stand to get pinned. Each cadet walked proudly to the middle of the stage, shook the chief's hand, got pinned with their badge, and walked across the rest of the stage to shake hands with various members of the command staff and city council. Once everyone was pinned, the chief gave a short speech. He reminded the audience that this was a celebration and a major accomplishment for these new officers. He explained that this class was coming into policing at a "different time and context." He paused dramatically, scanned the crowd, and added, "a different world." These new officers needed to be "problem solvers" and "public servants," he said. Echoing the sentiment that I had heard repeatedly over the past year, the chief declared that in today's dangerous and unpredictable world, police officers must be "warriors and guardians," that they needed to be "the kindest" people but also ready for "a battlefield." He went on to say that it was not easy to get hired or to make it through the academy, so the group of people in this cadet class was really special.

Several cadets who had started the Terryville academy with this class were not standing on the stage. As the chief reminded the audience, not everyone could cut it, and it took a special type of person—someone who was kind but also ready for battle, he said—to make it through the hiring process and the required training. Terryville was not the only department that lost cadets along the way, and indeed, every academy class that I observed lost several, if not dozens of, cadets before graduation. This level of attrition reflects national trends as reported by the US Department of Justice, which collects data every four to seven years about law enforcement training academies across the United States. Its 2018 report indicated that 14 percent of cadets who started a local or state academy in that year did not complete their training. This amounted to over eight thousand people who either left or were removed from an academy that year.[1] So, who stays and who leaves? And, perhaps more importantly, for what reasons do cadets wash out?

Just as with the hiring process, the academy included formal requirements for continued employment as well as informal evaluations—by both instructors and the cadets themselves—of occupational fit. To make it to graduation, cadets needed to meet both sets of standards: they needed to pass their tests and show competence in basic policing skills, but they also needed to successfully demonstrate their socialization into state violence, proving that that they could look, think, and act like police officers. The cadets who either could not or did not want to meet either of these requirements were pushed out.

Official Qualifications

On the first day of Hudson's academy, each of the instructors introduced themselves to the new cadet class. Jon, the corporal at the academy, was the second instructor in this lineup of introductions. Jon was Latino, in his forties, slender, and around five foot ten. Anytime I met with him, he spoke about his job with enthusiasm and passion, eagerly sharing stories from his time on patrol. He also bordered on oversharing at times, for example, disclosing both to me individually and to the class of cadets that his wife had recently left him and that he could not "seem to let it go." Jon used most of his time in front of the class that first morning delivering the warning that 17 percent of them would not graduate, insisting that they take the training seriously and put in the work. Throughout the next few days, Jon and his fellow instructors brought up this percentage repeatedly, reminding the cadets that if they did not study hard enough or train seriously enough, they would not make it through the academy.

At the most basic level, in order to graduate, cadets needed to show up, follow the rules, avoid injuries that would prevent them from doing basic job tasks, and pass their exams. If they did these things, they remained employed. If they did not, they risked getting fired. However, cadets were very rarely officially fired. Most of the time, cadets either voluntarily resigned or were brought into the academy offices and highly encouraged to resign by the training staff. In the latter situation, cadets were given the option to voluntarily resign—which would maintain their eligibility to apply to other departments—or be terminated. Given these options, of course, most cadets chose to resign.

One of the most common reasons that cadets were formally fired was failing a maximum number of written exams.[2] The cadets took a written exam almost every week for most of the academy. Cadets needed to learn the penal code, the code of criminal procedure, and use of force policies, among many other topics, and then demonstrate a mastery of the material just a few days later. Each department had a set of policies that dictated the testing process; at one academy, for example, cadets were allowed to retake an exam, but their new score would not contribute to their overall academy grade point average. When I asked instructors what some of the most common reasons were for cadets to leave the academy, almost all of them mentioned test failures. Just a few months into the Rollingwood academy, Chris, the lieutenant in charge of hiring, told me that Rollingwood had already lost about 15 percent of the current class. When I asked why, he explained that a few decided it "wasn't for them or had family reasons," and the rest were test failures. Referencing test failures, Chris added, "Yeah, I think that's probably the biggest thing."

Similarly, cadets were sometimes fired for failing their physical fitness tests. When this did happen, it tended to be concentrated toward the beginning of the academy, before the cadets had built up their strength and endurance. Several cadets typically resigned within a few days of the first workout, which usually took place in the first week or two and lasted between two and four hours. This first workout happened on the third day of Hudson's academy. During the workout, as I detailed in chapter 5, several cadets vomited, and one needed to receive oxygen. The following day, we learned that one cadet in the class had decided not to come back. I was told by several Rollingwood cadets and instructors that Rollingwood's version of this initial workout always resulted in one or more cadets needing to receive oxygen or other medical treatment. Every now and then, a cadet was taken to the hospital for treatment, though instructors assured me that this was rare.

Those who struggled with the physical fitness training were usually helped along by their instructors to ensure that they would pass their physical fitness tests. Instructors spent extra time with these cadets after class, created specialized fitness plans for them, and maintained systems of accountability to check in on them. PT (physical training) exams were considered a test not just of physical ability but also of mental fortitude. When cadets demonstrated that they wanted to improve, instructors helped support them. Paul, one of the Rollingwood instructors, explained this sentiment: "If they're just physically weak but they're emotionally and mentally strong, we're able to take someone and build 'em up, give 'em the tools. We start really slow PT-wise. Then at the end, PT is considerably more challenging, but they're able to handle it. We give 'em the tools." Despite this extra help, the cadets who repeatedly failed the PT tests were eventually terminated.

There were, of course, other miscellaneous reasons why someone might leave the academy because they failed to meet the official requirements. Some cadets had personal or family issues arise that made the academy schedule untenable for them. A few cadets could not pass their driving or firearms exams. In every class that I saw, a few cadets sustained injuries that made it impossible for them to complete the required physical training. At Terryville, for example, two cadets broke their legs during two separate afternoons of defensive tactics training. When cadets were injured, they were usually either "recycled"— meaning given the option to start the next academy—or offered a civilian position at the department. Sometimes, though, when the injury healed quickly enough, they were able to make up the missed training and walk with their class at graduation. Although uncommon, instructors told me that every now and then, a cadet would get arrested, leading to their swift removal from the academy. Disciplinary issues—like talking back to instructors, lying, or cheating on exams— were also rare but, when egregious enough, would result in removal from the academy.

To remain at the academy, cadets needed to fulfill the basic requirements. They needed to learn the law, their department's policies and procedures, and how to use the equipment—like patrol cars, computer systems, and guns—that their job required. When cadets could not pass their exams, follow the rules, or physically complete the training, they were removed from the academy.

Institutional Fit

On the first day of DT (Defensive Tactics) Week at Rollingwood, the cadets spent the day learning how to work with a partner to take someone to the ground. The instructors called this a "2 vs. 1 takedown," and after lunch, they selected pairs of cadets to practice the technique in front of the class. Will and Stacey were the second pair of cadets chosen for this exercise. Will, an Asian cadet in his twenties, was struggling to make it through the training; his instructors relentlessly harassed, criticized, and humiliated him for the entire length of the academy. Stacey, a Latina woman in her twenties, consistently performed well academically and in tactics. The instructors picked James, a top cadet who previously served in the military, to play the role of the "suspect" in this scenario. James's job was to avert Will and Stacey's efforts to overpower and handcuff him.

As soon as Will and Stacey approached James, he took off running, forcefully swinging his arms around to avoid being detained. Will and Stacey chased after him and tried, but failed, to take him to the ground. When they eventually pinned James down, Stacey yelled, "Head strike!" several times while she imitated hitting him in the head. Stacey tried to secure James's arms and torso while Will grabbed onto his legs. As Will tried to pin James's flailing legs, James began choking Stacey. Stacey called out to Will for help, but not hearing her, he continued trying to secure James's legs. She shouted again, with strained breathing now, "He's choking me!" and finally, Will looked up and intervened by striking James.

Each group of cadets that demonstrated a 2 vs. 1 takedown debriefed with the instructors afterward in front of the class. After Will and Stacey's turn, the instructors spent several minutes berating Will. "Will, you spent half the time in James's nut sack while Stacey fought," Josh bemoaned. "What do you do when you're on the bottom?" Josh asked rhetorically, immediately answering his own question: "You get on top!" "Did you know what James was doing?" Josh continued. "You had no situational awareness, no communication." Another instructor chimed in, "Will, you were worthless in that situation." Another added, "You did all of the technique wrong." As Will's instructors lobbed critique after critique, he just stood there, taking the public criticism without a twinge of expression on his face. Will was used to this by now, having been the focus of intense scrutiny and chastisement for months.

Later that day, Neil, one of the firearms instructors at Rollingwood, leaned over toward me and told me, "Will needs to leave," adding, "He sucks." Neil explained that the academy was not for everyone, and if someone quit because it just was not for them, he would shake their hand and take them out for a beer. If, however, someone stuck it out, even though they "suck," and then began patrol work and got someone else hurt, that person would be "dead" to him. Neil expressed a sentiment that I heard across academies: some people were just not cut out for this job.

More than just fulfilling the formal requirements of police work, to make it to graduation the cadets also needed to prove to their instructors that they were, in fact, cut out for this job. Getting through the academy required more than just knowing criminal law or being able to pass a physical fitness test. It also required that cadets were able to tolerate the academy environment, which involved high levels of stress, pain, discomfort, and humiliation, and that they were willing and able to use violence. These were the intangible elements that, according to the instructors, made a cadet a good fit for police work. Much of what was considered a good fit hinged on normative expectations of whiteness and masculinity, making "fit" an elusive task for those who did not occupy these social positions. Will, for example, was a slender Asian man, which meant that he had to navigate conceptions of race that associated Asian men with femininity. Thus, being a man, in and of itself, did not necessarily guarantee acceptance into the institution. Rather, those cadets who convincingly embodied the warrior by looking, sounding, and acting like police officers, regardless—or at times, in spite—of their gender and race were considered a good fit, granting them access to the job.

Whatever It Takes

On the second day of Hudson's academy, I arrived around 7:30 a.m., parked my car in the dirt lot near the main building, and headed to the locker room to quickly change out into my PT clothes—a plain white shirt and black athletic shorts—before morning formation. Hudson was a large police department, so there were multiple academy classes running simultaneously. I was participating with the "baby class," having just started the day prior, so we set up our formation all the way on the left side of the parking lot. Julian, the class leader, reviewed the drill commands we had learned the day before, guiding us through the body positions and movements for "attention," "parade rest," and "face right," among others. As the four-person detail from another cadet class raised the US flag, our class was instructed to turn to the left and salute. We had not yet learned how to correctly salute, so I tried my best to mimic Karol, the cadet to my left, since I knew she had military experience.

After detail, Charlie, the academy sergeant, moved from one class formation to the next, shouting as he asked if everyone was present. Each class leader responded loudly that the class was either all present or all present and accounted for. Our formation, however, was not complete; we were missing one person. We continued to stand at attention while the other classes completed push-ups for an assortment of missteps from the previous day. When given permission by the instructors, we then marched into the main building, one class at a time.

When we got to the classroom, we learned that our formation was incomplete because one of the cadets in the class had quit the night before, after just one day of the academy. Henry, one of the Hudson instructors, assured the class that the cadet quitting was "no loss to us" since he "didn't want to do it." "You know how I responded to that text? Okay, whatever," he went on, "Fuck him. We don't need him." Derek, the Hudson PT instructor, told the class it was better that the cadet dropped out and figured out this was not for him earlier rather than later, adding that this job was not for everyone. This cadet, according to his instructors, simply did not want it badly enough.

According to the instructors, making it through the academy required a certain mentality. Low-performing cadets, they explained, did not have the willpower, mental tenacity, or passion for police work that they needed to carry them through the academy and out onto the streets. Paul, a Rollingwood instructor, told me that both physical and mental preparation were needed to survive the academy, explaining, "If they show up, they're mentally unprepared and physically unprepared, they're more likely gonna have a really hard time, if they make it. Or they just won't make it." Instructors expected cadets to show up ready, both physically and mentally, to do whatever it took to walk across the stage at graduation.

Paul described to me two examples of cadets from prior classes who had lacked mental preparation and, as a result, left the academy. The first, he explained, was not ready or able to handle the mental stress involved in training. Paul recounted this cadet's exit interview, when she explained to him that she had "heard one the instructors yelling and cussing at another cadet" and said, "That's just wrong. And I don't wanna be part of that." She chose to leave the academy, which Paul considered a success: "She reacted negatively to someone cussing and getting in someone's face and yelling at 'em, which is fine because it worked. . . . She wasn't able to do that; therefore, the training worked."

The second cadet whom Paul described decided to leave on the second day of the academy. Paul recounted his exchange with this cadet when he decided to quit:

> Out of this most recent class, it was the second day. He came in in the morning like, "Day one was enough." He came in, and he's like, "Well, I don't think that I was doing very good, and I wasn't prepared." I was like, "But we explained it in the beginning that this is what's coming.

Right?" And he was like, "Yep. You did." I was like, "You were told that it's gonna be physical from the beginning." And he was like, "Yep." "And we gave you the cadet manual, and we said there's no tricks. Everything is in here. You follow this, then you're good." He's like, "Yep." Then I said, "Was yesterday like at a ten?" He was like, "Yes. I thought it would be more of a seven or an eight." I was like, "Oh, so you probably prepared for like a five or a six?" And he was like, "Yes." So, there's not having the emotional or mental part that says, "You know what, it sucks, but that's what I wanna do, so I'm gonna pay the price to get there."

Getting through the training, according to Paul, required that cadets push through the parts of the academy that "sucked" to get to the other side. If someone wanted it bad enough, instructors reasoned, they would willingly endure the pain, discomfort, and stress of the academy. This particular cadet, Paul explained, did not come prepared and, perhaps more importantly, was not willing to "pay the price" to be an officer.

Bill, who oversaw tactics training at Rollingwood, similarly explained that cadets needed to be willing to do whatever it took. He described feeling frustrated by cadets who did not give it their all and added,

> I can't take it personal. I've learned that. I have to realize that we're not all cut out for this job. There's a reason God built us the way we are, . . . [but] it's frustrating because I know, like me personally, I want it so bad that I would work hard enough to where if it killed me, that's fine. That's how bad I want something. But there's other people—you don't see that from them, and it's frustrating, because it's a waste. It's a waste of talent and ability. The department's not getting what it needs, the city's not getting what it needs. . . . I just have to come to that realization: maybe they're just not cut out for this job.

The academy training revealed who was willing to do whatever it takes and who was not. The cadets who were unwilling or unable to meet this level of intensity in their training, according to Bill and other instructors, were not cut out for the job.

The cadets who were most successful at the academy subscribed to this do-or-die approach. James, a white cadet in his twenties, told me that he respected people when they put their all into something, even if it did not come naturally to them. He criticized his classmate Will for what he felt was a lack of commitment to the training. Commitment was often displayed at the academy physically, either through workouts or fighting, in which pushing through the pain was highly valued. This tolerance of pain marked cadets as physically strong, invoking conceptions of masculinity that prize pain and suffering, a relationship that is visible in other masculinized occupations and activities, like martial arts and athletics.[3] James invoked this sentiment when he compared his own approach to Will's:

> During the workouts, I wanted to almost die. I wanted to throw every single thing that I had out there on the table because, I don't know. I told you. I don't like losing. I wanted to be the best or whatever. In Will, I never felt like he would match my level of intensity or match my level of grind or grit. And, like, he would be done with these runs, and he would just not be out of breath. He would just be trotting around the track. . . . I don't care how good you are. If you're willing to lay everything out on the table, you're cool in my book. Do you know what I mean? If you are willing to die in the ring fighting—you can be the shittiest fighter. You can get your ass kicked every single day of the week, but if you're willing to go into that ring and face everything head-on, cool. I don't think Will was one of those guys. It doesn't mean he's any less of a man. It doesn't mean he's any less as a person. . . . Some people can be a cop. Some people can't.

James, in a similar way to his instructors, expressed a deep commitment to demonstrating his desire to be a police officer. During the workouts, James explained, he pushed himself to the brink of physical failure. Will, on the other hand, did complete the workouts, but not

with the same level of "intensity," "grind," or "grit." Will was not willing to put it all on the line to reach his goal, James explained, which
indicated that he was not cut out for this job. James also made connections between these kinds of physical displays of commitment and
fighting, explicitly associating this approach to his job with violence.
James made it to graduation and out onto patrol; Will did not.

The academy was a tough environment to endure, especially for cadets who had no former policing or military experience. Instructors
yelled at cadets—sometimes within inches of their face—mocked and
berated them, and embarrassed them in front of their classmates. Cadets were required to follow a long list of rules, knowing that their
instructors quietly kept track of any infractions. A boot not adequately
shined, a missing item from a duty belt, or not greeting an officer in
the hallway with enough enthusiasm or professionalism could all lead
to the entire class being punished. At times, it felt like instructors just
made things up so that they could punish the class. Cadets needed to
keep up with the academic curriculum of the academy while physically
exhausted from twelve- to fourteen-hour days that usually included
hours of tactics or physical fitness training. It did, in fact, take a high
level of mental and physical fortitude to make it through the academy. There were moments when I, too, questioned if I wanted to keep
doing this research, and I was not subjected to nearly the same level of
scrutiny as the cadets.

All of this begs the question: Why? Why was the academy designed
to encourage attrition? Why did cadets need to be willing—as Bill
said—to be "killed" by the path to police work to make it through the
academy? Instructors justified this approach by explaining that cadets
needed to be able to handle the stressors they would encounter on the
streets. Paul, for example, clarified why the instructors yelled at the
cadets: "When you go to the street [work patrol] and someone comes
up to you and they're yelling and cussing at you or there's a large group
of people and you might be in fear for your safety, you have to be able
to work through that stress." However, this reasoning does not explain
why cadets needed to endure eight months of stress, anxiety, humili-

ation, degradation, and exhaustion to be a police officer. This test of wanting it bad enough means that every year, otherwise-qualified cadets who are unwilling to endure the abuse of the academy quit.

The academy's requirement that cadets do whatever it takes and that they display this commitment by enduring pain is characteristic of many masculine institutions. Fraternities, all-boys schools, sports teams, and the military all engage in hazing techniques and rituals that require new members to demonstrate their commitment to the organization by participating in painful, degrading, and sometimes life-threatening activities.[4] In 2021, Stone Foltz, a twenty-year-old sophomore at Bowling Green State University, died following the forced consumption of alcohol at an initiation ritual at the Pi Kappa Alpha fraternity.[5] In 2018, a video surfaced online that showed students at St. Michael's College School, an all-boys school in Toronto, pinning down a classmate in the locker room and sexually assaulting him with a broom stick.[6] In 2016, five Wheaton College football players abducted a new teammate, put a pillowcase over his head, bound him with duct tape, and abandoned him in a baseball field as part of an initiation ritual.[7] In 2011, a Marine deployed in Afghanistan was punched, kicked, and forced to exercise to exhaustion by a fellow Marine as punishment for falling asleep while on guard.[8] In all of these highly masculine organizations, perseverance, endurance, grit, and suffering are prized characteristics that must be demonstrated physically. Scholars who study hazing in many different contexts theorize that this part of the initiation process can serve multiple purposes: it generates and enhances group solidarity, reinforces group hierarchy, ensures the selection of only committed new group members, and communicates group-relevant attitudes to new members.[9]

Police academies across the country—in Goodyear, Pennsylvania; Austin, Texas; Atlanta, Georgia; Baltimore, Maryland; Springfield, Massachusetts; and Baton Rouge, Louisiana, to name a few—have been accused of hazing, harassment, and abuse of cadets.[10] Cadets at the academies involved in these news reports and lawsuits describe being subjected to racist, sexist, and homophobic harassment, pushed to the point of physical illness or injury, and, in some cases, put in situations that resulted in permanent physical impairments, including brain damage. In the Goodyear case, officers accused members of the SWAT team of handcuffing them, putting a bag over their head, and forcing them to run while spraying water in their face as part of their initiation ritual, called "Hell Day."[11] At Austin's 2018 police academy, five cadets were sent to the hospital following their first workout; one of them then spent the next thirty days in the hospital recovering.[12] This kind of environment, and the requirement that cadets be willing to do whatever it takes, does not appear to be isolated to the academies included in this study but, rather, describes a broader trend in police socialization.

Being Bad at Violence

The Rollingwood academy included several weeks that were dedicated exclusively to defensive tactics training. During the first of these weeks—called DT Week—the cadets learned how to strike and disarm another person and take someone to the ground, both by themselves and with another officer. On the first day of this week, the cadets spent the morning practicing 2 vs. 1 takedowns, which involved a range of techniques they could use with a partner to get someone onto the ground and into handcuffs. The instructors emphasized that one of the officers should "go high," meaning grab the person's chest and arms, while the other officer "goes low," shoving their shoulders into the person's thigh and wrapping their arms around their hips.

When we came back from lunch, the instructors selected three cadets at a time to demonstrate the skills they had learned that morning. Two cadets played the role of officers, and the third played the role of the "suspect." The last group to demonstrate included Lucas, Steven, and Adam. Steven, playing the role of the "suspect," immediately took off running, trying to evade Lucas and Adam's attempts to get him onto the ground. At one point in the scenario, Adam shouted "KNIFE!" receded from the fight, and drew his (fake) pistol. Looking flustered, Adam aimed his pistol toward the "suspect" and his partner, who were still engaged in a fight on the ground. He then reholstered his gun and reengaged in the fight, eventually getting Steven into handcuffs.

Afterward, the instructors debriefed the scenario in front of the class, critiquing the cadets' tactics throughout the fight. They asked Adam where he saw a knife, adding that he could not see Steven's hands, so it would not have been possible to see a knife. One of the instructors concluded that the "takedown was good" but everything else "went to shit." "You did the opposite of what you should do," the instructor went on, pausing and then adding, "I don't know what to say." Neil, one of Rollingwood's firearms instructors, leaned over to me and groaned about Adam, telling me that it was tough because they could not fire Adam yet since he was technically passing his tests. But, he added, Adam should absolutely be fired. Turning then to the class, Neil shouted, "You better pray that you show up with backup worth a shit," and warned them, "Do yourself a favor and don't be that fucking person," referencing Adam's performance.

Throughout the academy, the instructors fixated on a handful of cadets who struggled with the defensive tactics training. At Rollingwood, Adam was one of these cadets, and he was eventually pushed out of the academy. When cadets showed any sign that they may be either unwilling or unable to use violence, instructors zeroed in on them, adding a higher level of pressure and heightened visibility to their performances of violence. Sometimes cadets decided that they did not want to use violence and, as a result, opted to leave the academy. For others, like Adam, the institution removed them.

Adam was white, blond, about six feet tall, and thin. He had a deep voice and southern drawl and spoke slowly, his mouth hanging open for a moment after he finished each sentence. Despite being a tall, white man, Adam had trouble embodying the masculine ideals of this institution. He was not particularly muscular, and his instructors picked at the parts of Adam that they felt did not fit within the institution, often pointing to characteristics or behaviors that did not align with their expected performances of masculinity. They mocked his lanky figure, his use of an expansive vocabulary, and his slow, methodical manner of speech. Rob, one of the DT instructors, repeatedly made fun of Adam for using what he felt were large words, like "accost" and "agaze," in his reports. "You're not fucking William Faulkner," Rob complained to me about Adam. "You [should] write like the [news] paper reads so that people can understand you." More than anything else, though, the Rollingwood instructors ridiculed Adam for being physically weak and bad at fighting.

Shortly before Adam was scheduled to graduate, the academy staff pulled him into the administrative office and gave him two options: be fired or resign. Adam wanted to remain eligible for other police departments in the state, so he agreed to resign. A few months later, I interviewed him at a Starbucks in Rollingwood. On the day of our interview, he wore work boots and a collared plaid shirt, and giving away his southern roots, usually finished each sentence during our conversation with "ma'am."

About fifteen minutes into the interview, Adam told me that he felt like he chose the "wrong" department for his "first academy." When I asked what he meant, he clarified:

> So obviously I've got no military experience. I didn't go into this with a fighter's mind-set. And I don't know how to keep my head down. So, my tendency to use large words to talk about small things I think drew a target on my back. And I just couldn't punch hard enough to make them shut up about it. So, the general environment here is more focused on your ability to punch the problem. And I didn't expect it because I hadn't talked to anyone, so I didn't go in with that same mind-set. I went in with the image of the police officer that I had from my experience. Like I said, I don't have occasion to deal with the "warrior" cop.

As he mentioned, Adam was indeed put under a microscope by his instructors. During one day of scenario training, for example, an evaluator entered the conference room to report that Adam had failed a scenario. The instructor tracking the cadets' performances on an Excel sheet exclaimed, "Oh yay!" and tapped his fingertips together, giddy with excitement. Later that day, when Adam was about to begin a scenario that involved a foot pursuit, this same instructor announced, "Does anyone wanna see Adam chase someone? Just sayin'. It's fair game." A few instructors jumped at the opportunity, asking where on the academy campus the scenario was happening.

During Adam's tactical training week, instructors constantly berated him, both to his face and in back offices, for what they described as his inability to fight. On the last day of the first tactics week, the instructors paired up the cadets and required them to fight one another in a mud pit. This ritual came up when I asked Adam about his experience during tactical training:

> I had a hell of a lot of fun with both of them. But then, you come around to your final implementation for each one, and then the last day of week one was fighting in the mud pit. And, you know, you do it until you're done. And my opponent was James, especially chosen for me. And he was told that he was to go 100 percent and, if he didn't, that we would be there all day. So he did, which I thank him for because I would rather have gone through it all at once than spend all day. But his 100 percent and my 100 percent are worlds apart. He was in training to do Navy Seals, and that's not me. So, sparing every detail, at the end of it, he apologized to me because we were at it for a while, and I had spaghetti arms by the time we were done.

The instructors frequently set up Adam to fail, particularly when it came to fighting. Other cadets, including James, echoed this observation, explaining that "the instructors would pit the class against those guys [referencing Adam and another cadet, Will] as some of the lower performers." In the example that Adam recounted during our interview, the instructors paired him up with James, one of the top cadets in his class, who weighed around seventy pounds more than Adam did, to fight. Another time, the instructors told me that they intentionally scheduled a scenario that involved an ambush so that Adam would go through it at night, when there was less visibility, to make it more challenging for him.

The instructors frequently talked to me, and to each other, about wanting to fire Adam. They felt that Adam was weak, scared, and incompetent, particularly when it came to using force. The DT instructors often expressed frustration and contempt about Adam's motivations for pursuing police work. Instructors told me multiple times that in his interview for the department, Adam apparently informed the hiring officers that he had never been courageous and hoped that the academy would make him braver. During a conversation about Adam's motivations with a group of instructors, Rob exclaimed, "This isn't the place to figure that out!" Another instructor added, "That's kind of just something you need to be born with. We can't teach you that." Throughout the first week of intensive tactics training, Josh regularly yelled at Adam for what he described as "whimpering" during a fight or for showing any physical sign of pain or discomfort during workouts.

Adam tried to adapt to his instructors' feedback and use force the way that the academy required. He responded to the constant complaints of his being weak by using too much force. When he was then reprimanded for using too much force, he would scale it back again, to then be told he was not using enough force. Bill, who supervised the defensive tactics instructors, described this pendulum swing, as Adam attempted to apply his instructors' feedback, without success:

> He [Adam] was repeatedly counseled, so we would monitor and make sure or put him back in those same situations [scenarios or tactics drills]. So, we've talked to him about it, remediate it through more reps, and apply that same pressure or that pressure from a different angle maybe, and we were coming up with the same result, to the point where he then wasn't using his firearm—he would just go ahead and use another force option, say, the baton, inappropriately. And we'd ask him why. And he's like, "Well, I've already been talked to about pulling

my gun too much, so I used my baton." He's not getting it. You're not applying what you're learning in the classroom and in the gym simultaneously, so he wasn't able to understand when and why he can do certain things. And I felt it was a huge liability, and unfortunately, we had to get rid of him.

Adam could not quite get it right. His instructors, from the start, did not want him to graduate. Although he made it within a few days of graduation, ultimately, he was pushed out of the department. According to Adam, and his instructors, he did fine academically and was able to pass his physical fitness tests, but he was unable to fight or make quick decisions. He resigned, left the academy, and, despite his experience, told me he still intended to apply to other departments in the future.

Being Unwilling to Use Violence

I interviewed Paul in the large conference room at the Rollingwood academy about six months into my year of fieldwork. We sat on the same side of the table, next to each other, for almost two hours talking about his motivations for pursuing law enforcement, his experience training cadets, and his opinions about the current political climate. I asked Paul what made someone stand out as either a high-performing or low-performing cadet, and in his response, he discussed both physical and mental strengths and weaknesses. Continuing with his line of thought, I asked Paul if there were certain points in the academy when what he referenced as mental weaknesses revealed themselves. Paul replied that yes, there were, but that what was considered stressful depended on the cadet. One cadet, for example, quit after hearing the audio recording of an incident that included a lot of screaming, explaining to his instructors that hearing that level of distress triggered his PTSD symptoms from prior deployments to Afghanistan. Other cadets, Paul explained, "quit in role-plays based upon the amount of stress": "They realized that 'I just can't function like this. It's just too much.'"

I told Paul that during my fieldwork, I often heard instructors express concerns about cadets coming into the academy without any experience with fighting. "Does that concern you? Do you worry about cadets who are coming in like that?" I asked. "No," he replied while laughing, "'cause when they go to their first defensive tactics week, they're gonna get punched." He went on to explain:

> But at the same time, it's by an officer. You're wearing gloves, and it's all set not to knock you out or take you out or inflict pain. It is to get you exposed to it. And at the same time, if it's never happened, some people realize, "Whoa! That is not for me." Part of it, from what I've seen, is not so much having pain inflicted on me but having to do that to somebody else, which I never really thought about. Then we had a couple of cadets that quit. That was what they said is that "I don't wanna hurt anybody." I'm like, well, I get that. Like, I don't wanna hurt people either, but they weren't able to make the distinction that I'm gonna have to hurt them to control it, so that I can help them or help somebody that they were hurting. They were just like, "Yeah. I just can't do it." I'm like, "I can take a beating [laughs], I guess, but I can't inflict pain."

According to Paul, these cadets chose to leave the academy because they were unwilling to inflict pain. In his response, Paul conceptualized the violence that police enact as necessary to help others and explained that although he did not want to hurt people, he needed to. These cadets, he said, were not able to make this distinction and were unwilling to physically hurt other people in the course of their duties.

This same process played out for Elisa, who quit just four months into Rollingwood's academy. Elisa was white, blond, around five feet tall, and athletic. She had a black belt in karate and participated in competitive cheerleading and CrossFit. I initially found out about Elisa's experience at the academy from her classmates, who spoke highly of her and expressed disappointment that she had decided to quit. Jacob, the class president at Rollingwood, told me, "There was a very capable girl in my academy class who I'm still good friends with.

Her name's Elisa. . . . She could move more weight than a lot of the guys, but she was also about five foot two. . . . She ended up resigning." Patrick, another classmate, told me, "After the first tactics week, she [Elisa] was like, 'I just don't think being aggressive and putting hands on people is for me.' She was back and forth for a while, and then she finally just said, 'I'm done.'" When I interviewed Elisa a few months after she quit the academy, she explained that she began to have doubts after the first week of tactical training. As she described it, she froze during a use-of-force scenario at the academy and "couldn't make the move" to go hands-on. She explained what happened during the scenario:

> I was with my partner. He was a male, also not very big. And we were at a bar [in the scenario], and the bar owner had asked this guy to leave. . . . Of course, he was the biggest dude in the room. . . . So, we walk in, they start harassing us, and eventually they start throwing drinks at us, like cups, which is immediately like, we could have just cuffed them then because they were throwing stuff at us. . . . And I just—I couldn't make the move. And eventually, my partner tried Tasing him. I tried batoning him—it's like all imaginary—but my partner pulled his gun, like, in a bar. It just downward spiraled, but in the whole thing, I didn't do anything. And even when he [her partner] pulled his gun, I was like, "Holy shit, why'd you pull your gun? Why'd you pull your gun?" But I hadn't done anything, so he was just like, "I'm gonna pull my gun." . . . And it took me forever to go in and handcuff him. It was just that I couldn't make the move. . . . I had so many opportunities to go hands-on, and I couldn't do it. And it was stifling fear of like, "I know this is fake. Why am I not doing anything? What is wrong with me? Why can't I do it?"

Despite having a background in karate, Elisa explained that when the tactics training began at the academy, she could not will herself to initiate a physical contact. When I asked her what specifically she feared, she responded, "It was just like a fear of making the wrong move, for one. You're being watched by the whole instructor board, especially me, because everyone wanted to know: Is she gonna fuck up? And, like, the fear of getting it wrong was probably the biggest thing for me, and I think that just added to the flame of, like, stifling me." Elisa pointed directly to the heightened visibility of her performance and a fear of making the wrong decision in front of her instructors. This fear, she explained, initiated a spiral in her mental health, which ultimately led her to quit. During her defensive tactics and scenario-based training, Elisa explained,

> I would go home and simmer on scenarios that would just fill my head. . . . Like, the week of DT, . . . I would go home and be like, "Okay how am I gonna use this? Where would I be stuck in that position?" And you create these things, and it's like a rabbit hole, and I would keep myself up, like, "Okay how would this happen? What would happen to me? What would I do?" It was kind of a train wreck for me. I just couldn't turn it off. . . . I was literally making myself sick. Like, it was eating me alive.

After a few weeks of feeling tormented, trying to decide if she should continue the academy or leave, Elisa quit.

Elisa described feeling a fear of being overpowered by someone bigger than she is, but ultimately, she said she quit the academy because she felt unable to initiate a physical interaction. After some back and forth on this, I tried to clarify with Elisa:

> SAMANTHA: So, some cadets I think had trouble towards the end of it [the academy] with how to apply the law or making an on-the-spot decision and stuff like that. So it sounds like—I'm just trying to make sure I get it—it sounds like for you, it was this physical conflict that you weren't sure about. Is that what it was about?
>
> ELISA: Yeah, mostly the physical, like, being able (1) to go hands-on first, like to make the first contact, and then (2) make the right decision when I go hands-on. Like, I think—I never did this—but like overreacting, kinda like my partner pulling a gun, and knowing,

like, there's serious consequences if I do that. And that would send my brain into overdrive. So, just thinking about like, "Okay, you gotta apply policy, and you have to apply the law," and knowing all these things, and be able to react. It was overwhelming for me. But the biggest thing being the physical barrier of not being able to step into that first contact, going hands-on.

Elisa was unwilling, and as a result unable, to initiate physical control over another person. Her experience differs from Adam's, though, in that her instructors asked her to stay, and despite this, she decided to leave. In contrast to Adam, her instructors believed that she had the ability to engage in violence and that through more practice, she would improve. Elisa was considered a good fit for policing by her instructors, if she could get over her fears and engage with others physically. Despite being a woman, Elisa was better able to fulfill the masculine expectations of the institution; she had experience fighting, and she competed in weightlifting, for example. However, ultimately Elisa could not get through the tactics training.

Everyone Elisa spoke to about the situation, she said, "tried to get me to stay, begged me to stay." She recounted, "I had all the other boxes checked. I was fit, I was good in the academics, I wasn't socially awkward. . . . I could speak Spanish. Everything else was good for me." When she initially approached her instructors expressing her doubts about continuing with training, she explained, "They all wanted me to stay. They were like, 'I would call you as backup any day of the week. There are other cadets here who shouldn't be here. You're not one of them, and just keep training.'" Elisa said she "tried to do that" but told me, "I didn't feel like it was something that could be trained out. Like, I didn't feel physically inadequate. It was like a combination of my size, like, going into all these things, and mentally feeling like I can't do it." Despite having years of experience competing in sports and practicing martial arts and being encouraged to stay by her instructors and class-mates, Elisa did not feel like she could train her way to go "hands-on." This decision was tough to make, Elisa told me: "I was super proud to be in the academy, and to walk away was really hard." She did not regret her decision, though, and expressed relief that, at the time of our interview, she was not out on the streets working patrol with her prior classmates.

* * *

The academy is designed to be stressful, rigorous, and unrelenting. Not just anyone can be a police officer, and indeed, most people would probably agree that not just anyone should be a police officer. The academy acts as a filter, letting through those who are deemed qualified and eliminating those who are considered unfit for the job. Some cadets excelled in the academy environment, passing all their exams, leading the class in physical fitness training, and mastering defensive tactics techniques. The top cadets usually came into the academy with prior military or policing experience and, as a result, fit seamlessly into this highly masculine, regimented institution. The cadets at the bottom of the class garnered considerable attention, scrutiny, and ridicule from their instructors. These cadets sometimes performed fine academically, followed the rules, and avoided injuries. They did not, however, embody the ethos of policing. They were not, according to their instructors, willing to do whatever it took to become a police officer, and they did not use violence either enthusiastically or competently or both.

The academy instructors I met justified the intensity of the academy by pointing to the ways that this training ostensibly prepared cadets for what they would face out on patrol. The cadets needed to prove that they could follow rules so that the department could trust them to abide by policies when they had more discretion and were under less direct supervision. The instructors induced stress—including yelling, flashing lights, loud music, and intimidation—throughout the training so that cadets learned to stay focused while immersed in chaos, which would inevitably happen on the streets. Cadets needed to be willing and able to use violence so that they could subdue and control people under arrest and protect themselves, their partners, and the public.

The instructors put the cadets through physical discomfort and pain because it revealed who would be willing to do whatever it takes to make it out of an interaction alive. Officers, they explained, needed to have a warrior mentality, which included pushing through pain and exhaustion to survive. The academy, these instructors insisted, was this way because police work demanded it.

Through the relentless antagonism of cadets, though, the academy training modeled a certain kind of accepted interactional dynamic in police work. The environment, and particularly the requirement that cadets be willing to quietly take the abuse, taught cadets that aggression results in compliance. It was not just about being able to handle the stress of someone shouting in a cadet's face once they were out on patrol; it was also about introducing cadets to a world where yelling at, degrading, humiliating, and physically punishing others were regarded as acceptable, and indeed essential, behavior. Cadets who were able to weather the academy were those who learned these lessons best. The cadets who could not, or would not, were pushed out.

7 THE FUTURE OF POLICING

The Rollingwood academy concluded with a two-week block of scenario-based training. The academy staff set up scenarios all over the training facility to test the cadets' ability to apply their skills in real time in a range of situations. For most of these two weeks, I rode around on a golf cart with one or two officers, making periodic stops at each of the scenarios. I also spent time in the "war room," where officers tracked the progression of each scenario. On the eighth day, while I sat in the war room, a young, stylish, white man walked in with a bunch of camera equipment. He had dark-brown, curly hair and wore round, turtle-shell glasses, khaki shorts, and a floral-print, dark button-up shirt. I would not have needed to spend a year at police academies to immediately recognize that he was probably not an officer. He walked in the room with Steve, one of the sergeants at the academy, and I gathered from their conversation with the other instructors in the room that he was there to film the scenario training as part of a marketing video for the department.

The videographer explained that the chief of police was "looking for more of a guardian than a warrior vibe" for the video. Steve asked Keith and Paul which scenarios were currently running and, of those, which ones might be good options for the videographer to film. The intensity of the scenarios had increased over the course of the two weeks, so now, on day eight of ten, almost all the scenarios involved deadly force. Keith and Paul described the scenarios currently running, and the videographer replied, "Yeah, I don't think that's what they're [the command staff] wanting." Steve explained that the chief and commanders were looking for more of a "community policing vibe." Keith turned from looking at the whiteboard, where the scenarios were listed, back toward the table and in a prickly tone retorted, "Yeah, well, nothing we're doing today is going to be what you're looking for." Steve and Paul decided to set up a scenario that was not actually running that day specifically for the videographer to film. Facing each other, they each suggested different scenarios: Maybe a park disturbance? Maybe a littering call? Something civil related, they agreed. In the meantime, the cadets were actually running through scenarios in which they were ambushed by a man with an AK-47 and, later on, required to go through a series of back-to-back lethal use-of-force scenarios.

The videographer left the room with Steve and Paul. Brett, another instructor, lamented to Keith, "You know what? People don't want violent cops until violence is brought to them. Then they want violent cops. But if we have to pretend we aren't violent to make people happy, then so be it. And we will *still* be there to protect them when they need us." This interaction has stuck with me for years after I finished this fieldwork. To me, it exemplified larger, integral debates about violence in policing, including what it means, how it looks, when it should be used, and how the public interprets it. Should police officers be guardians or warriors? Is there a meaningful distinction between the two? What does the public want from the police? And how should new officers be trained to use violence? These are all questions these officers negotiated, in real time, in the room that day.

Brett's comment in the war room illustrated the primary argument that I make in this book: that violence is an essential, constitutive, and structural requirement of police work. During my time in the field, violence pervaded every inch of these spaces: it was in posters on the wall, on the clothing officers wore off duty, in the conversations I heard, on the websites officers talked about, and in the videos shown at the academy. This violent ethos shaped the selection and training of cadets, structuring their socialization into state violence.

Hiring and Training for War

When I have told people about my research on the way police officers are trained, I usually get a couple of common reactions. First, I get the question, "Isn't having 'bad' police officers really about a bad selection process?" In other words, isn't there just a need for more or better or different screening to determine who gets into the police academy? This question suggests that police violence happens because police departments are hiring already-violent and/or already-racist people. If we could just weed out these people, the logic follows, then we could rid our society of excessive and racist police violence. The United States is heavily invested in individualistic understandings of both successes and failures. Billionaires are thought to have achieved their level of wealth by pulling themselves up by their bootstraps, and people in prison are thought to have landed in their position because of poor decision-making and selfishness. It is not surprising, then, that in this country, an attractive answer to the question of why patterns in police violence persist is that there are racist, sexist, and violence-prone people who then become officers.

The proposed solution to the issue of selection is usually the implementation of more stringent hiring requirements and more rigorous hiring procedures. While, of course, there are police officers who engage in acts of egregious violence and who are racist, sexist, and homophobic—just like in every institution—I would argue that the answer to the problem of violence in policing is not simply detecting and removing individual applicants or officers. That is, a better screening process will not fix this.

There is also a push from other policing reformers to hire more women as a solution to the issue of selection. Proponents of these efforts argue that women are better at communicating and less inclined toward violence than men are, making them the key to "fixing" policing. This initiative has rapidly gained popularity with policy makers, the public, and the police themselves. At the time of this writing, 187 US law enforcement agencies have signed a pledge with the 30×30 Initiative, a nationwide coalition whose goal, according to its website, is to "increase the representation of women in police recruit classes to 30% by 2030."[1] Seemingly every week, articles, news stories, and podcasts pop up making the pitch that women officers are the cure for policing. For example, National Public Radio (NPR) posted an article titled "Increasing Women Police Recruits to 30% Could Help Change Departments' Culture"; the *Washington Post* also published an article titled "This Police Chief Is Hiring Female Officers to Fix 'Toxic' Policing"; and CNN posted an article titled "Want to Reform the Police? Hire More Women."[2]

These proposed solutions, however, rely on individualized understandings of why excessive and/or racist police violence continues to happen. Within this frame, individual officers are to blame for these systemic patterns, and changes in the demographic composition of police forces are offered as solutions without any meaningful changes suggested to the practices or institutional culture of policing. Simply placing women, for example, into academy classes without changing the ethos of masculinity and violence that permeates the organization will only perpetuate the same problems but with different bodies. The hiring and training processes at these departments ensure that those who make it out onto the streets, regardless of their gender and race, are equipped and willing to engage in violence.

The second reaction I get to this research holds civilians—especially Black and Latino communities, which are disproportionately subjected to police violence—responsible for police violence. This reaction is illustrative of larger public conversations in which it is suggested that building trust between the public and the police will reduce rates of police violence. If members of the public trusted the police, this logic goes, then they would be more compliant and deferential in their interactions with the police, and the police would not feel the need to use force.

Often, the proposed solution to the issue of "trust," particularly between Black and Latino communities and the police, is to hire more Black and Latino officers. These officers are expected to act as bridges between the racial-minority communities of which they are a part and their departments.[3] These kinds of demographic diversity initiatives conceptualize race and ethnicity as static identities and are, themselves, a form of "racecraft," which describes discursive maneuvers that blame effects of racism on seemingly neutral conceptions of race or racial difference.[4] This way of framing the issue places responsibility on civilians rather than the police by focusing on distrust, not police abuse and/or misconduct, which severely limits the capacity of these initiatives to change policing.

The third most common reaction I get when discussing my research focuses on the danger that officers face on duty. People who have this reaction point to the sacrifices that police officers make in doing their jobs and ask some version of the question, "What are police officers supposed to do when faced with lethal threats?" This question presents a very real dilemma for those who are engaged in police reform. It is true that officers across the country respond to tragic and dangerous calls for service. Every year, some of these officers are killed while carrying out the duties of their jobs. Given this reality, it makes sense that officers are fearful and that academy instructors encourage cadets to be cautious and mindful about their safety.

However, the way that academy instructors interpret and communicate what constitutes caution and safety supports a worldview that pits the police against the public. These departments framed their relationship with the public as a war, which heightens, rather than diminishes, the perceived necessity of violence. The cadets at these academies entered a world where bad guys were around every corner, only other officers could be trusted, and evil people hunting down and killing police officers were increasingly gaining momentum. Instructors insisted that cadets learn how to identify their enemy, to interpret the presence of a threat through embodied markers, and to do whatever it takes to survive. Even in situations in which verbal de-escalation skills were taught, instructors emphasized the necessity of violence for officers to make it home each night. Holding onto this worldview every day would indeed be a scary way to live. Without diminishing the fact that officers are hurt and killed on the job, it is important to highlight that the job has not, in fact, gotten less safe over time and that this way of seeing the world is dangerous for the public.[5]

The final reaction I often hear when I describe my research is an expression of disgust toward the police, usually coupled with absolute dismay as to how I could stand being around police officers for a year. As I think is clear in this book, I have major critiques of the police, and I was, indeed, deeply troubled by much of what I saw during my year at police academies. I do not, however, find it useful or gratifying to dehumanize or villainize the human beings who work as police officers. I approach all my research with a genuine sense of curiosity and compassion, and I do not think it would be possible or ethical for me to have done this project if I went into it with a disdain for the people I intended to study. The arguments I make in this book focus on the ways the policing organization sustains itself, regardless of whether individual "good" or "bad" people occupy the positions within it. There is indeed enough space to hold the police accountable while still recognizing the humanity of all people.

Pathways Forward

In most sociological work, this is the section of the book where authors make concrete policy suggestions on how to address the issues raised in the preceding chapters. Readers of this book might hope to find here a list of possible reform efforts to improve how cadets are trained at the police academy and, by extension, to change the state of US policing. Unfortunately, however, I am increasingly pessimistic about the potential for reform efforts to change policing. If history tells us anything, it is that the police institution is highly resistant to reform efforts and instead shape-shifts in ways that further entrench its role of enforcing social hierarchy.

We are stuck in what feels like a never-ending cycle of crises in policing, in which instances of police brutality and corruption result in public outrage and calls for action. For almost a century now, US presidents have assembled commissions to investigate the state of the criminal legal system, each time outlining eerily similar causes for concern and recommendations for reform. In a 1931 series of reports, President Herbert Hoover's National Commission on Law Observance and Enforcement, commonly known as the Wickersham Commission, detailed instances of police brutality and corruption in cities across the United States. In its recommendations, the commission described the existing police training as a "weakness" and advised that police work required more expansive training.[6] Almost forty years later, in 1967, President Lyndon Johnson's Commission on Law Enforcement and Administration of Justice published its report, *The Challenge of Crime in a Free Society*, including a full chapter about the police. In it, the commission recommended implementing higher educational requirements and better training for new officers, improving relations between the police and the communities they serve, and hiring more officers of color.[7] Again, almost fifty years later, in 2015, President Barack Obama's Task Force on 21st Century Policing advised that police departments embrace a "guardian" approach to their work, engage in community-oriented policing practices, improve training, and implement demographic diversity initiatives in hiring.[8] Although these suggestions for police reform might feel novel or contemporary in current conversations about the police, they are not.

Sociologist and policing scholar Alex Vitale explains that these reform efforts have not changed policing because they do not alter the police role or function in any way. Vitale explains that the police have always been tasked with enforcing social hierarchy, which has historically involved "the suppression of workers and the tight surveillance and micromanagement of black and brown lives."[9] Vitale urges us not to rely on procedural reforms for policing and instead reconceptualize the role of the police. Highlighting the shortcomings of procedural reforms without substantive change to the institution's function, Vitale poignantly observes that "a kinder, gentler, and more diverse war on the poor is still a war on the poor."[10]

Abolitionist scholars and activists have been wrestling with the question of how to address police reform for a long time and, through their work, offer a way of reimagining our current system of addressing harm. Although there is heterogeneity among abolitionist frameworks and perspectives, abolition generally describes the ongoing project of dismantling systems of state violence, which have included slavery, prisons, and the police. Contemporary movements to abolish the criminal legal system are one part of a larger project of dismantling racial hierarchy and capitalism more broadly. Abolitionists draw connections between different systems of harm, for example, highlighting the integral role that racial hierarchy and domination has played in building and sustaining capitalist economies in the United States. The police have historically helped enforce racial hierarchy and protect capital and, thus, are a key institution in sustaining these systems.

The idea of abolishing the police can elicit strong reactions, including expressions of hostility and fear. Those who advocate for a world without police, and the current criminal legal system more generally, are often painted as naïve and utopian. Pushing past these kneejerk reactions of dismissal, though, provides an opportunity to engage with abolition as a real pathway forward.

Following the police killing of George Floyd in Minneapolis in 2020, the idea of "defunding" the police cemented itself in the public lexicon as demands for defunding police departments gained significant momentum. There was an immediate backlash against these organizing efforts, which was, predictably, steeped with gendered and racialized rhetoric that stoked white fears about crime, danger, and violence. A television ad released at the time by then-President Donald Trump's reelection campaign, for example, drew on these narratives. The ad shows an older white woman at home alone watching a fictional news report about Seattle's police department losing up to 50 percent of its budget in response to demands for defunding, including removing 911 dispatchers. As this woman watches the news report, the viewer of the ad sees the silhouette of a man outside her door trying to break in. She calls 911, but after several rings, an automated voice picks up and says, "Hello, you've reached 911. I'm sorry that there is no one here to answer your emergency call. But leave a message, and we'll get back to you as soon as we can." The ad concludes with the man entering the woman's home and forcibly grabbing her as the phone drops to the floor.

This caricaturing of efforts to abolish the police dramatically mischaracterizes abolitionist visions of the future. Abolitionists do not deny that there is, and will continue to be, violence and harm in the world. Abolishing our current systems of enforcement and punishment cannot eliminate harm, but it can offer an opportunity to build new and better societal responses to harm. As lawyer and activist Derecka Purnell explains, "rather than thinking of abolition as just getting rid of police, I think about it as an invitation to create and support lots of different answers to the problem of harm in society and, most exciting, as an opportunity to reduce and eliminate harm in the first place."[11]

Importantly, abolition prescribes both a dismantling and a building of systems. Prominent abolitionists like Angela Davis, Ruth Gilmore, and Mariame Kaba emphasize this point in their work, explaining that simply eliminating the police without creating new systems of support would not be effective or advisable. Davis conceptualizes abolition not just as a "negative process of tearing down" but also as "building up, about creating new institutions."[12] Dozens of activist organizations and networks, like INCITE, Critical Resistance, Black Visions Collective, and the Black Youth Project, to name just a few, are already engaged in this work, building processes and systems to address harm that do not rely on state-sanctioned surveillance, punishment, and violence. These organizations focus on building up their communities by improving access to employment, supporting workers' rights and unionization efforts, and increasing levels of civic engagement.

Those who are in opposition to abolitionist efforts often express fear that without the police, crime and violence would proliferate and intensify. This imagining of violent chaos, reminiscent of a scene out of the movie *The Purge*, necessarily depends on a conceptualization of the police—and our current criminal legal system more generally—as an effective system of deterrence and security. Within this frame, the police are thought of as a historical inevitability, as the only and best way we have ever dealt with those who harm others. Although abolitionists do not necessarily have all the answers on how to build a future of community safety and support without the state, they are right to point out that our current system is not effective at taking on these tasks either. As the political scientist Charmaine Chua explains, "As defund and abolish campaigns proliferate across the globe, skeptics have (perhaps rightly) suggested that abolitionists do not have all the answers to problems of ongoing harm. This may be so. Neither, however, does liberal racial capitalism."[13]

Abolition is not a finite, specified destination but rather a continual, evolving process. Chua describes abolition "not as an event but a horizon, requiring radical participation in a fight for meaningful freedom."[14] Abolition requires a continual effort of working toward and pushing further. In this way, abolition does not provide a checklist of tasks but rather describes an approach, perspective, and vision for the future.

I understand that a world without police may sound like a whimsical idea at best, and a terrifying prospect at worst, for some people. After spending a year at police training academies, I do not see any other way forward. I join other abolitionists in their critiques of reformist approaches, seeing firsthand that even with demographic diversity initiatives, de-escalation training, and racial-bias training, violence remained the guiding principle of these academies. Another world is possible, and abolitionist frameworks give us the tools to keep trying to get there.

* * *

While abolition remains a goal, it is also vitally important that other kinds of harm are also addressed, including gun-related injuries and deaths. The police do not operate in a vacuum but, rather, within a broader landscape of violence. The United States has the highest gun-ownership rate in the world, with an average of eighty-eight guns per one hundred people, as well as much higher rates of gun-related deaths than in peer countries, like Canada, Australia, and the United Kingdom.[15] As I show in this book, the cadets at these academies were taught that they would be in grave danger while on the job. Cadets were repeatedly shown graphic videos of police officers getting killed. Instructors issued warnings about bad guys who had weapons and were not afraid to use them against—and indeed, sometimes specifically targeting—police officers. In the academies' tactics and scenario-based training, instructors punished cadets for missing weapons during a search, reminding them that it was not just their life on the line but also their partner's. This responsibility, to protect themselves and their partner and to go home to their family at the end of the night, became all-encompassing. One tiny, momentary slip in this intensity—of watching someone's hands, of conducting a completely comprehensive frisk or search, of approaching a vehicle tactically—the cadets were taught, would lead to their and their partner's violent murder. It makes sense, given this kind of training, that officers often feel paranoid and reactionary and are quick to assume the worst.

The number-one fear that officers expressed, both in conversations and during training, was dealing with someone who had a gun. The cadets were trained to deal with other kinds of weapons, like knives or razor blades, as well, but by far, guns were considered the most serious threat. During scenario-based training, when a cadet found a gun on an officer/actor, they were taught to shout "GUN!" at the top of their lungs, so that their partner would hear it, and immediately handcuff the person, take the gun, clear the gun of any ammo, and search for any other weapons or drugs. As soon as a cadet shouted "GUN!" their anxiety became palpable and contagious as their movements quickened, their eyes widened, and their voice elevated and strained. They were, understandably, afraid.

The assumption that anyone could be armed at any time has real consequences. At the academy, I watched almost every single cadet make the decision to shoot (with a fake pistol) their unarmed partner, who pulled a miscellaneous item out of their pocket quickly, because they thought the item was a weapon. Instructors told me about their time in the academy, when they ran through a scenario in which, after going through several lethal-force situations, they had to conduct a routine traffic stop. They explained that the person sitting in the driver's seat threw her arm out the window with her driver's license in hand. Every officer who told me about this scenario said that they thought she was pulling out a gun, so they shot her.

This relationship between civilian gun ownership and police violence appears in national trends. In a recent study, the authors analyzed fatal police shootings between 2015 and 2017, which included 2,934 civilian deaths, to determine whether rates of gun ownership affected the prevalence of fatal police shootings in individual US states. On the basis of this analysis, the authors found that even after controlling for state characteristics, including violent crime rate, racial composition, poverty rate, and urbanization, the police fatally shoot people at higher rates in US states with higher firearm prevalence. In the ten states with the highest firearm prevalence, including Alabama, Georgia, and Idaho, the incident rate for fatal police shootings was 3.6 times higher than in the five states with the lowest firearm prevalence, which included Connecticut, Massachusetts, and New York.[16] In another study, the authors found that between 2015 and 2016, the police killed fewer civilians in states with more stringent gun laws.[17]

The academy training relied on this fear and taught cadets that it was better to assume the worst—that someone was armed—and overreact than to assume they were not armed and be killed. This dynamic could be different, I think, if the US public was not as armed. One way to work on reducing police violence—and violence more generally in the United States—is to dramatically lower rates of civilian gun owner-ship in this country.

* * *

When I spoke with officers in the field, they would often ask me, in a disheartened, genuine tone, to tell their story "right." Standing in the parking lot outside Terryville's academy one afternoon, one officer pleaded with me, "Do us right," adding, "A lot of people don't do us right, so do us right. Do us some justice. We're people. We bleed red just like everyone else." Many, though certainly not all, of the officers I met told me that they felt misunderstood by the public, misrepre-sented by the media, and generally resentful, anxious, and guarded about their jobs.

Just as with other highly contentious topics, like gun rights or abor-tion access, conversations about the police tend to devolve into a two-sided debate, in which one can either be pro- or anti-police. Indeed, while conducting this fieldwork, I was often asked by police officers themselves if I was "pro- or anti-cop," giving me just two, overly sim-plified options to describe my orientation toward our system of law enforcement in the United States. This binary framing is perhaps use-ful in rallying public support for political candidates or policy initia-tives, but it does not accurately describe the wide range of positions and feelings to be had about the police. Recognizing the complexity of this issue does not mean that we must resign ourselves to contin-ued police abuse or absolve police organizations of the harm for which they are responsible.

My goal for this book has never been to suggest that all police of-ficers are evil or maladjusted people who go into police work so that they can commit acts of violence. I do not believe that, and I do not think that the data I have presented in this book would support that claim. I am, however, arguing that this institution's hiring and training practices position police officers to continue engaging in racist vio-lence. I am not in a position to doubt that most police officers want to help people, that their jobs are difficult, and that they face dangers as part of their jobs. While I acknowledge the challenges of these officers' experiences, I maintain that it is vital to keep a critical eye on the institution that is responsible for training them and the ways that this organization's hiring and training practices shape these persistent patterns of violence. This, I think, is the only way forward.

Acknowledgments

Writing this book was incredibly intellectually and emotionally challenging, but it was made much easier by my wonderfully supportive, compassionate, and spirited community of family, friends, and colleagues. I began this research while in graduate school in the Department of Sociology at the University of Texas at Austin, and I remain ever indebted to the mentorship and friendship I received there. Thank you to Harel Shapira, Sarah Brayne, and Jennifer Glass for your unwavering support of me and my research. I am especially grateful for and indebted to Christine L. Williams, whose mentorship and intellectual guidance have shaped me and my approach to research in innumerable ways.

This book benefited greatly from the thoughtful and engaged feedback from many of my brilliant colleagues and friends. I want to thank Michael Sierra-Arévalo for his constant encouragement and for his invaluable and honest notes on several of the chapters that make up this book. Thank you also to Forrest Stuart, Jennifer Carlson, Becky Pettit, Carmen Gutierrez, Thatcher Combs, Brandon Robinson, Shannon Malone-Gonzalez, Katie Rogers, Rachel Donnelly-Mason, and Rachel Ellis for your intellectual engagement with this work—you have all made me a better scholar. Thank you also to my colleagues in the

Department of Criminology and Criminal Justice at the University of Missouri, St. Louis, where I finished writing this book. Thank you especially to Kelsey Cundiff, Marisa Omori, Katie Quinn, Devin Banks, and Elaina Johns-Wolfe for your friendship and for helping me maintain the endurance I needed to complete this book.

I am forever grateful to my family. To Elaine Jones, my wonderful mother, thank you for introducing me to feminist perspectives, for supporting me even when it came with personal costs, and for finding and pursuing opportunities for me to discover my interests. To Paul Simon, my father, thank you for teaching me to work hard and persist, for encouraging me to form evidence-based opinions, and for supporting and trusting every professional decision I have made. To Emily Simon, my sister, thank you for endlessly, persistently, and enthusiastically supporting me in every part of my life but especially in my professional pursuits. You have always kept me grounded, reminded me that I could, in fact, do things that at times felt impossible, and given me too many laughs to count. To Nick Baranowski, my brother, thank you for always showing an interest in my work and for your enthusiasm and humor. To Dan Baranowski, my brother, thank you for opening the door to education for me. Without you, I am not sure I would have ever found sociology.

Thank you also to my incredible friends, who have filled my life with laughter and love. Thank you to Alanna Powers, Marsi Taylor, Elise Gan, Miriam Tischler, Jinny Kim-Baker, Lissette Martinez, Nicole Cappabianca, Joe Forzano, Victor Garcia, Cerita Kelly, James Kim, Laura Francis, Carolyn Chen, and Alex Cole.

Finally, I would like to thank the police cadets and officers who allowed me to witness and experience their lives. In this book, I am often critical of policing and of the ideologies and practices that I observed at these departments. However, I also feel a great sense of gratitude to the officers and cadets with whom I spent hundreds of hours for answering any question I asked, inviting me to departmental events, welcoming me into their space, and cheering me on when I struggled. Thank you for giving me your time, for offering your candid opinions, and for teaching me about your world.

Methodological Appendix

In the summer of 2016, I started working with Dr. Harel Shapira on an ethnographic project about gun ownership. At the time, Harel was studying the rise of civilian gun carry in the United States, and, that spring, he asked if I would be interested in conducting field-work and interviews for the project. I had almost no experience with studying—or just generally using—guns or violence; but I knew I was interested in gender, masculinity, and inequality, so I enthusiasti-cally started working on the project with him. As part of this project, I attended civilian firearms-training classes, license-to-carry classes, events organized by a women's gun club, shooting competitions, and gun shows. I learned how to shoot pistols, rifles, and shotguns, com-pleted the (at the time) mandatory training to receive my license to carry, and spent time with gun owners from a range of backgrounds. The people I met during this project introduced me to an entirely new way of seeing the world, one that was steeped with fear, danger, pride, and violence. According to their worldview, life was becoming increasingly dangerous, unpredictable, and volatile, and the only way to protect myself from these threats was by carrying and using a gun.

As I continued to meet and interview the instructors of these civil-ian firearms classes, I found that most of them were current or former police officers. I was conducting these interviews about a year and a half after a Ferguson police officer fatally shot Michael Brown. The police killing of Michael Brown and the subsequent uprisings in Ferguson, Missouri, sometimes came up in conversations with firearms instructors, usually as a data point to support their beliefs about danger, crime, and the police. At this point, Black Lives Matter (BLM) had gained significant momentum as a movement and had solidified itself as a part of the public lexicon. Countermovements to BLM popped up around the United States, most notably Blue Lives Matter, whose stated goal was to defend officers against a "war on cops."

Following the uprisings in Ferguson, public conversations predictably started to focus on ways to reform the police. These suggestions included a push for de-escalation training, antibias training, and demographic diversity initiatives in hiring. As I continued to interview firearms instructors, many of whom were police officers, I started to wonder how the civilian firearms training I had watched and participated in either differed from or resembled the training that officers received at the academy. How were new officers being trained to use force? What did de-escalation training even look like? And how, if at all, would the demographic composition of a police force shape these processes? The answers to these questions, I thought, could potentially help explain why Michael Brown and so many others before and after him were killed by the police. I did not know what I would find at the police academy, but I had a sense that whatever happened there was an important part of understanding this repeated and tragic loss of life.

My original plan was to go through Rollingwood's academy, every day, from start to finish. A friend had recently graduated from this academy, and once I told her about the project, she offered to put me in touch with Diego, the sergeant who oversaw the academy training. I first emailed Diego in December 2017 to ask if he would be willing to talk with me about my research project on police academies. I knew that Rollingwood's next academy was set to start in March, so I hoped I would be able to get permission from Rollingwood in time to get the logistics ironed out. Much to my relief, Diego emailed me back, but he told me the meeting would have to wait until the new year, when his schedule opened up. I followed up with Diego in early January, and we set up a time to meet in his office at the Rollingwood academy.

The morning of the meeting, I got to the academy building early and sat in my car for ten to fifteen minutes trying to calm my nerves. A lot was riding on this meeting, but I was hopeful that it would go well and that Diego would let me participate in the upcoming academy. The doors to the main building were locked, so I called Diego to let me in. We walked to his office and sat down, and I asked if I could audio record the conversation. He waved his hand in confirmation and said that would be fine.

I had decided to treat the meeting like an interview, so I asked Diego questions about his motivations for pursuing a career in law enforcement, his experiences going through Rollingwood's academy, how he ended up working in training, and how the academy was structured, among other topics. At the end of the interview, I thanked him for his time and nervously pitched my idea of participating in the upcoming academy, explaining that I was interested in gaining a hands-on understanding of the training. Diego quickly said that would not be possible, pointing to the city's legal department being unlikely to approve my proposed fieldwork. I tried my best to negotiate at least some access, asking if there was some combination of observing and participating that might be approved. "It would be very little, just to be honest," Diego responded. "It's just not something—it's not open to the public like that."

Diego suggested other avenues that I was not interested in pursuing, like going through the department's citizen academy (an educational program designed for civilians to learn more about the police department), watching YouTube videos about police academies, going on ride-alongs, or applying to get hired as an officer by Rollingwood. I had considered the last option—getting hired—but knew it could take up to a year to go through the process. Diego eventually offered that I could maybe watch the cadets go through one or two scenarios but warned that he would first need to "send it up" to his command staff to get approval. During our meeting, he also suggested that I get in touch with Rollingwood's recruiting office, which he said would be better suited to answer some of the questions I had about cadet selection. I left the meeting with Diego feeling defeated and panicked, not knowing when, or if, I would be able to start fieldwork at Rollingwood.

Despite this initial setback, I was determined to get the project off the ground. While I waited the few weeks until I could follow up with Diego, I reached out to the Rollingwood recruiting office via a contact form on its website. Chris, the lieutenant in the office, promptly emailed back and said he would be happy to meet with me. When I arrived at the recruiting building for our meeting, I signed in at the front desk, showed the receptionist my driver's license, and sat down in a small waiting area. After a few minutes, a tall white man with thin, wispy hair and glasses appeared and said, "Sam? I'm Lieutenant Brennan," while he extended his arm to shake my hand. For the next hour, I asked Chris questions about hiring at Rollingwood, including the career fairs that the recruiting office attended, the testing process, and the strategies the hiring officers used to recruit women and racial-minority candidates. Chris was much more receptive to my project than Diego had been and granted me access to anything I wanted to observe at the recruiting and hiring office. Though I did not originally plan on observing the recruiting and hiring process, doing so turned out to be a key part of this study.

Even with access to the hiring office, I still wanted at least to observe Rollingwood's academy training. Per my prior conversation with Diego, I followed up with him in March, once the newest academy had started, about watching the cadets go through scenario-based training. Diego emailed me back to let me know that he had moved on to a different role within the department, and he suggested that I get in touch with Steve, his replacement at the academy. I met with Steve, and after jumping through some bureaucratic hoops with Rollingwood's public information office, which required the approval of an assistant chief, in April 2018, I was finally granted access to Rollingwood's academy.

Selecting Field Sites

While I waited for approval from Rollingwood, I also reached out to contacts I had at other police departments. I knew some of these officers through fieldwork I had done at civilian firearms-training classes, and others I met through friends or colleagues. By then, I decided I wanted to expand my fieldwork to include multiple departments, rather than focus on just one. Studying multiple departments would introduce important forms of variation, for example, departmental structure, city context, and demographic composition. I thought that this variation might reveal ways that police training differed, offering a chance to see potentially better or worse ways to train new officers. I ended up conducting fieldwork at four departments: Rollingwood, Terryville, Hudson, and Clarkston. Assigning pseudonyms to the departments and participants was key to my gaining access to observe their academy training, although it does in many ways limit the amount and type of information I can use to describe them in this book.

Once I had one department on board with the project, it was significantly easier to gain access to additional departments, though I still experienced several starts and stops throughout my year in the field. After just a few weeks of fully participating in Hudson's academy, for example, the academy sergeant pulled me into his office to let me know that the academy's commander had changed his mind and would no longer allow me to conduct fieldwork there. I tried to negotiate continued access in some way in a meeting with the command staff a few weeks later but was ultimately not allowed to continue my observation there. I was, however, able to stay in touch with several of the cadets in the class. Even with these occasional hurdles and barriers, I was able to spend about six hundred hours participating in and observing the hiring and training process, the majority of which was spent at Rollingwood and Terryville.

These four departments varied in size; they served cities that differed in their demographic compositions and political leanings; their training academies varied slightly in length; and the demographic makeup of their police forces varied. Even with these differences, the departments shared several similarities: they were all located in the same southern state; they were all located in mid- to large-size cities; the hiring processes at all the departments were similar; they recruited at many of the same events; they all taught the same six hundred hours of state-mandated instruction to cadets; they all had instructors who specialized in classroom curriculum, defensive tactics, or firearms; and they all added a substantial amount of training to their academies that was not mandated by the state, primarily focusing on department-specific policies, physical training, tactics, and scenario-based training. Table A.1 includes the basic characteristics of each of these four departments.

Table A.1. Description of Field Site

	Rollingwood	Terryville	Hudson	Clarkston
Size of police force	1,500	400	3,000	5,000
Size of city population	800,000	300,000	1 million	2 million
% women	10	10–20	18	15
% Black	9	3	25	23
% Hispanic	21	48	18	44
% Asian	2	0	2	6
% white	70	49	54	45
Length of academy training	8 months	8 months	8.5 months	6 months
Size of academy class	50–120	20–30	50–60	60–70
Number of academy classes per year	1–2	1	3–4	3–5

Source: Michael Maciag, "Police Department Race and Ethnicity Demographic Data," Governing, August 27, 2015, www.governing.com; departmental websites; and data collected from this research.

"Do I Need My Lawyer Present?": Building Rapport

My first day at Rollingwood's academy was, in some ways, the absolute worst-case scenario for establishing rapport with police officers. I arrived at the academy campus around 6:45 a.m. and met Steve, the sergeant who oversaw the academy, at the front door to let me into the otherwise-locked main building. At this point, Steve and I had emailed back and forth several times and met once in person to discuss my project. The cadets were now about two months into their academy training, and this week, they were working through several different use-of-force scenarios to practice applying their classroom instruction. As soon as Steve opened the front door, he let me know that there would also be a reporter coming to the academy that day. He intended to put me and her together since he figured we were interested in seeing the same kind of stuff. I immediately felt irritated by this news, knowing full well that police officers are generally quite wary of the media. The last thing I wanted, on my very first day meeting the Rollingwood academy instructors and cadets, was for them to think I was a reporter.

Steve also informed me that Michael, the lieutenant at the academy, would be accompanying both me and the reporter for the day so that he could answer any questions we had about the training. After about fifteen minutes of waiting on a couch in the front entryway, Michael emerged from the back offices and introduced himself to both me and the reporter. Michael asked how long I would be there today, and, confused, I responded, "I thought the whole day, but I'm not sure." He laughed and said he hoped not since he had things to do that afternoon. It became clear, between that comment and conversations I had with Michael a few hours later, that the plan at that time was to have an instructor essentially chaperone me whenever I was at the academy. This was certainly not what I had imagined, but luckily, this arrangement quickly dissolved as I spent more time at Rollingwood.

Even after some of the instructors became friendly and welcoming, the defensive tactics (DT) instructors remained guarded and aloof. Each of the academies I studied—which were all at relatively large departments—had several instructors who specialized in teaching defensive tactics, and at every academy I visited, these instructors tended to be especially suspicious, insular, and at times, cold. My first time really interacting with the Rollingwood DT instructors was in July 2018, when I observed DT Week, which was a week of training dedicated only to physical tactics, in which cadets learned how to strike, kick, use handcuffs, and take someone to the ground. Before then, I had spent most of my time at Rollingwood either watching scenario-based or classroom training. When I entered the DT gym that morning, the instructors had not yet arrived, and the gym was silent aside from a few whispers between cadets while they stretched and warmed up. There were blue mats laid out in the middle of the gym and seven or eight folding chairs set up on the far-right side from the main entrance. I took a seat and waited for the instructors to get there. A few minutes later, a group of men wearing the typical DT uniform—a red shirt and khaki tactical pants—walked through the doors and congregated in a circle by a table set up in the corner, far away from me. None of them greeted me, nor did they make any attempt to chat or fill me in on what was happening throughout the day.

I showed up again the next morning, despite my anxiety from the cold reception I had received the day prior. By the end of the second day, the dynamic had completely changed. David, one of the DT instructors, who had said all of three words to me on the first day, was now talking to me about his infertility issues with his wife and expressing frustration about how difficult and expensive it was to get through the adoption process. This shift came about for a few key reasons. First, the DT instructors learned that I had a friend who worked at Rollingwood. One of the instructors asked me, somewhat contemptuously, how I had gotten permission to be there. I explained that my friend Claire had recently graduated from the Rollingwood academy and put me in touch with Diego, the prior sergeant at the academy. "Why didn't you just say you were friends with Claire?" Rob asked, adding, "Claire really left you hanging. All she had to do was tell us you were coming." Later that day, Rob showed me a text conversation between him and Claire in which he asked her about me, and she replied that I was "super cool." "Now that we know you're cool," Rob said as he extended his arm toward me to shake hands, "my name is Rob."

For the entire second day, however, I was still being chaperoned, this time by Neil, one of the firearms instructors at the academy. Neil looked to be in his fifties, was white and tall, and had a round belly and brown hair. He was a bit of a jester, loudly poking fun at his coworkers and making conversation with everyone around him. Throughout the day, he and I talked about policing but also about many other topics, like philosophy podcasts, astrology charts, and comedians. Toward the end of the second day, Neil acknowledged that the DT instructors were not very welcoming the day before, adding, "I broke the silence. It was pretty apparent that no one was talking to you." He explained that he gave everyone the lowdown on me—that I was "cool"—so I could expect a much warmer reception from here on out. "Cool," in this case, I think meant that I was not being outwardly or explicitly hostile toward cops in our conversations about policing. Realizing then that as a firearms instructor he had no reason to be in the DT gym that day, I asked if he would have been there if I had not been observing. "You gotta understand," he replied, "you're an outsider," confirming that he was, in fact, instructed to spend the day with me to vet me for his coworkers.

On the third day of DT Week, the instructors were even more transparent about their initial wariness of my presence at the academy. Rob recounted seeing me on that first morning and immediately feeling "hostile" and, confirming my fears from that day, wondering, "Is she media? A journalist?" Chiming in, David added, "Yeah, do I need my lawyer present?" and the group all laughed. At this point, the instructors began initiating conversation with me, sharing information about the training, showing me pictures of their kids, inviting me to go shooting with them, and including me in their lunch plans.

The process of building rapport at Terryville, Hudson, and Clarkston went more smoothly, both because I was becoming more familiar with the organizational context and because at two of these departments—Terryville and Hudson—I was able to fully participate in the training. As I described earlier in this book, discipline and dedication are highly prized characteristics within policing and are mostly demonstrated through enduring physical discomfort and pain. That I was voluntarily running, lifting weights, doing push-ups and sit-ups, and learning defensive tactics alongside the cadets—often in extreme heat—elicited some degree of respect. Although they may not have all understood (or cared) what a dissertation was, they knew that I had a goal, and, like them, I was putting myself through hell to accomplish it.

The Political Meanings of Presence

Before I started this project, I had spent almost no time in highly regimented, masculine spaces. I did not come from a first responder or military family, I did not play sports in high school, and I grew up in a mostly politically liberal Jewish community. My social circles are composed primarily of dancers, artists, and academics, so I had very limited exposure to the world of policing before I began this fieldwork. I do, however, have family who identify with conservative politics, an aunt and uncle who worked as police officers for their entire careers, and friends who have worked in law enforcement. As part of a prior project, I had also spent time with gun owners, who generally identified strongly with conservative politics and supported the police. I am also white, which means I come from a racial background that has not historically been subjected to abuse by the police. These tensions in my own background and identity came up continually throughout my fieldwork as I tried to simultaneously occupy multiple worlds that were often in direct opposition to each other.

During my year at police academies, I found that I was often treated as a sort of foil: my presence in these spaces, and what that meant politically, was constantly being interpreted and negotiated. It was quite clear—both to my participants and to me—that I was an outsider to this institution. I was a woman, I was small, I was not particularly athletic, I had a nose ring, I was a PhD student, and I lived in a city that had a national reputation of being a liberal haven. This was a reality that I wrestled with in both small and big ways while in the field. As an example of something seemingly small, I could never quite figure out what to wear while I was conducting fieldwork. This concern was, of course, deeply shaped by my being a young woman entering a male-dominated and highly masculinized space. I wanted to strike a balance between looking professional and not too stuffy, while also drawing as little attention to my body as humanly possible. Initially, I decided to wear business professional clothing, like black jeans or slacks, a blouse, and loafers or flat shoes. After a day or two, a Rollingwood sergeant commented that my outfit made me look "high maintenance." I decided then to dress a bit more casually, shifting to jeans, a sweater, and basic sneakers. Noticing this switch, a Rollingwood sergeant joked that I looked like I was about to spend an afternoon sailing, once again making me self-conscious about my clothing choices. I knew, however, that it would not be read favorably if I dressed exactly like the instructors since I was, as they knew, not an officer. At that point, I ultimately decided that there would be no winning on this—no matter what I wore, the instructors or cadets would comment on it—so I just stuck with jeans and a sweater most of the time.

Other times, these negotiations around my identity and presence at these academies played out in larger, more significant ways. The academy structure, which included scenario-based training involving officer volunteers, meant that I was frequently meeting new officers who had no idea who I was or why I was there. Because of this, building rapport was not a process that ever really ended but, rather, one that continued for my entire year in the field.

For example, during one day of scenario-based training at Rollingwood, an officer I had never met before initiated a conversation with me by asking, "So you're a student or something?" When I met new officers at these academies, most of the time they had been given some pieces of information about me from a colleague, usually that I was a student or an intern doing a project. I responded to this new officer by confirming that I was indeed a student, adding that I was researching police training and had been hanging out with different departments around the state. Her face almost expressionless, she immediately followed up by asking, "So are you pro- or anti-police?" Having just met this officer moments prior, I was thrown off by both the timing and direct nature of her question, so I laughed. She shrugged her shoulders and said, "Sorry, I know I'm super blunt." "No, that's okay," I replied. "It's a legitimate question." A year prior, while conducting fieldwork at civilian firearms schools, I would often be asked the similarly phrased question of whether I was pro- or anti-gun. I had learned then that it was important to be honest, but strategic, in my response, as feigning neutrality understandably elicited suspicion. Although my opinion could legitimately be complex, it would have been absurd to pretend that I did not, in fact, have an opinion about policing. I explained to this officer that I thought her job was very hard, that I did not think I would be good at it, and that I believed there was some nuance to the job that critics of policing did not often consider. However, I went on, I also thought there were some major problems with the institution. She nodded her head, taking in my response, and asked, "Okay, so you're somewhere in the middle?" "Yeah, I guess so," I said. Importantly, in this case, and in others, my outsider status was primarily dependent on my gender and my being a student but never my race. There was never a situation in which a cadet or officer assumed that I would have been critical of the police because of my race. As a white person, I was not ever read—at least not explicitly—as being in opposition to the institution.

There were many times when this highlighting of my outsider status was done in a much more playful way. These mostly good-natured digs at me simultaneously demonstrated that I was not fully an insider but that I was "in" enough to participate in the affectionate teasing that happened almost constantly at these academies. Once, for example, I had to take a week or so off from fieldwork to attend events related to my graduate program back on my university's campus. When I returned to Rollingwood, Rob—one of the DT instructors—playfully asked, "How was your campus protest?" I laughed and replied, "Oh, great." "How many statues did you burn down?" he followed up. "Just two today," I responded. Another time, at Terryville, Kyle, the instructor who oversaw the pepper-spray training, made multiple comments throughout his lecture on crowd-control techniques about "hippies," making references to politically liberal cities. Knowing that I was from a liberal city, any time he made these kinds of references, he would briefly stop, look at me, and toss his chin back slightly, prompting the class to laugh. After a few times, I rolled my eyes and responded, "Yeah, all right, all right."

My presence sometimes revealed other boundaries or categories that were salient for police officers. For example, upon meeting me, a Rollingwood officer once asked me if I was from the local civilian oversight group for the department. Another time, a different Rollingwood officer asked if I was there spying on behalf of the "fourth floor," which was where the chief of police's office was located in the department's headquarters downtown. These questions about who I was and why I was there were important pieces of data, highlighting the many different adversaries that officers believed presented a potential threat to them and to the police more broadly.

The Physical Toll of Ethnography

Conducting an ethnography is necessarily a physical experience. My approach to this project drew heavily from feminist—and especially Black feminist—theories and methodologies that recognize the body as an important site of knowledge production.[1] This way of thinking about the body challenges conceptualizations of a mind-body split. Ethnographer Loïc Wacquant similarly considers the body as an essential element of knowledge production.[2] Wacquant's approach to a carnal sociology highlights the body's role in understanding social phenomena. The body, he explains, is not simply "socially constructed" but rather is a "socially constructing vector of knowledge, power, and practice."[3] Although I share other feminist scholars' critique of Wacquant for his neglect of existing feminist theories of embodied knowledge, the concept of carnal sociology does prove useful in its centering of the physical experience of ethnographic methods.[4]

In line with these traditions, my goal in conducting this ethnography was to understand not just what police training looked or sounded like but also how it felt. I strived to get myself as close as possible to an actual cadet's experience of academy training. This meant that, alongside the cadets, I woke up early, sat through hours of dense lectures, ran miles while in formation, learned basic drill commands, did push-ups on asphalt, lifted weights, and learned how to punch, kick, use pressure points, apply handcuffs, and take someone to the ground.

Over time, physically participating in police training started to shape my own embodiment. Other ethnographers have discussed this shaping process in their work. After years of fieldwork in Vietnam studying the relationship between global finance markets and intimacy industries, Kimberly Hoang described these embodied costs of fieldwork. While in the field, Hoang anxiously tried to adjust her body to local beauty standards, and she struggled with gendered expectations requiring her to enact subservience to men. Hoang recounts a time during fieldwork when she returned to her apartment, stood in front of her bathroom sink to wash off her makeup, and realized she could "no longer recognize [her] own face in the mirror."[5] These feelings and habits stayed with her even after she left the field, for example, in the way she shaped her eyebrows with makeup or served food first to others before taking a portion for herself.

Before I even began fieldwork for this project, my academic mentor brought up her concerns about the embodied process I was about to embark on at these police academies. If the police academy training was, as I suspected, an important site of socialization and transformation, she asked, what would make me immune from that process? Why did I think my experience at the academy would be different from anyone else's? What would stop me from becoming indoctrinated and becoming a police officer? Interestingly, I received a version of this question not just from my mentor but also from the officers I met in the field. At Hudson, while standing in the back of the classroom, one of the sergeants asked me, "You do know you'll have to go through all of this again when you decide you want to be a cop, right?" Another time, a different Hudson sergeant asked, "Want to be a cop yet?" I laughed and replied that no, I did not, but that he was not the first person to ask me that question. He explained that since I was going through the training, I might end up wanting to do it.

I never did end up wanting to pursue a career in law enforcement. I did, however, absorb the academy environment, soaking in the ethos of the space in ways that led to ideological, emotional, and physical changes. I started responding to questions with an added "sir" or "ma'am" and more often wore my hair up in a tight bun. I started to look forward to defensive tactics training, increasingly finding the physical exertion involved in fighting to be exciting. I became even more vigilant about my surroundings, often scanning parking lots at gas stations or grocery stores for anything that felt potentially dangerous. I also became much more comfortable with the constant yelling at the academy. Whereas initially, the shouting increased my heart rate and made me sweat, by the end of the year, I was completely unphased by it.

People around me noticed some of these changes. During a meeting with my mentor about my progress with fieldwork, she noted that I stood up straighter and took up more space in her office. Even the academy instructors made a few comments about this shift in my embodiment. About five months into my fieldwork at Terryville, I arrived at the firearms range and rang the doorbell by the front door of the mobile classroom that served as the primary office. I waited about a minute; no one answered, so I knocked on the door. Terry, the academy's captain, opened the door, and we walked together to the back of the classroom, where the other instructors were sitting together around a table. Kevin, whom I had come to know quite well by then, commented that I had "scared the shit out of them" with my knock on the door, which was apparently very loud and aggressive. Referencing the academy training, Kevin mused that I must be learning something. I laughed, explaining that I knocked hard because I was not sure they would hear me but that I must be getting used to being more authoritative. Yes, Kevin agreed, adding while laughing that it was a "solid" knock.

A perhaps less visible embodied cost of doing this work was the sexual harassment that I endured while in the field. I knew going into this project that I would probably be on the receiving end of some harassment, as I was likely to be one of very few women in a highly masculine, male-dominated space. However, despite this expectation, I was still caught off guard by the frequency and tenor of the harassment, which was much more direct and sometimes more alarming than I had originally anticipated. An added wrinkle to this dynamic was the fact that the people doing the harassing were themselves police officers, limiting and complicating the potential avenues of reporting the situation if it ever became dangerous for me. Some of this harassment included comments about my body or appearance. In one instance, when I was sitting in the defensive tactics gym with my legs crossed at my ankles and the heels of my feet visible out of my shoes, a sergeant tapped my shoulder and told me that my heels were nice and well-groomed. Another time, an instructor asked if I had any other piercings besides the one in my nose, immediately following up the question by inquiring about what kinds of men I typically dated. Another instructor once commented that the cadets might have trouble performing because there was a "hot girl" sitting there watching them.

These comments always unnerved me and made me feel uncomfortable. One situation in particular, though, left me feeling unsafe. At Rollingwood's academy, the firearms range was in a separate building from the primary classrooms, so I would sometimes go back and forth between the two buildings to watch the training and talk with each set of instructors. On one of these days, during a lull in the scenario-based training that was taking place in the main building, I headed over to the firearms range to see what was going on over there. When I arrived, Neil and his coworkers were sitting in their shared office talking about military contract work overseas. The group greeted me and asked if there were any "goodies" still over at the main building—during this week of training, an officer's mother brought in huge containers of baked goods for the instructors—and I replied that sadly, they were all gone. You had "one job," Andy joked, and Neil added, "Yeah, thanks a lot, Sam!"

Earlier in the day, Neil had suggested we shoot at the firearms range at some point. In the middle of the conversation about baked goods, Neil grabbed two full magazines and a pistol out of the bottom drawer of a filing cabinet. He turned his back to the other officers, so as not to point the gun at them, while he pulled the pistol's slide back to check if there was a round in the chamber, and then holstered the gun. He tilted his head up sharply and told me to follow him. I got up and walked with him out of the office toward the range. "We gotta make this quick," he added, explaining that they had a training session coming in soon.

I put on eye and ear protection and followed Neil into the range. There was an officer inside the range kneeling, maybe fifteen feet back from the targets, shooting from cover through different slots in a wooden structure. When he stopped shooting, Neil shouted out to him, telling him to hold fire for a second while he hung up a new target, which was a photo of a middle-aged white man aiming a pistol at us. The officer looked over and gave us a thumbs-up. Neil loaded the magazine into his pistol, an M&P 9, and asked, "You know what to do?" I replied, "I mean, yeah, I haven't shot in a couple years, but yeah, just," and I motioned racking a slide, "and then shoot." He nodded and handed me his gun. The pistol was heavy in my hands, and I felt nervous, my heart rate spiking and my hands shaking a bit since I had not shot in a while. I got my footing, bent my knees, gripped the gun, and lined up my sights. As I was adjusting my body into a shooting position, Neil commented on the jeans I was wearing, adding that I really "dressed down" today, with a suggestive twang in his tone. I tried to ignore his comment and instead focus on pulling the trigger.

After I finished shooting the first magazine, Neil asked, "What are you aiming for?" I lowered the gun, keeping it pointed downrange, and replied that at first, I was aiming for the man's head, but by the end of the magazine, I had switched to aim for the center of mass. I dropped the magazine, and Neil reloaded the next full magazine and handed me the pistol again, telling me to aim for the guy's forehead. "Okay," I responded, as I set myself up and started shooting. My aim got much better, and most of my shots ended up somewhere on the man's head. As I was shooting, Neil made another comment, this time telling me that my "ass" was "really bouncing" as I was shooting, again in a suggestive tone. I continued to shoot, but the nausea that comes with these kinds of experiences flooded through my body as I realized that the other officer had left the range, so I was now alone with Neil. "Nice job," he said, when I finished shooting. I dropped the magazine again and handed it to Neil. He took the pistol back, and I walked back over to the main building, feeling glad that I would not be back at Rollingwood for at least a week or two.

I do not know why Neil decided to make those comments at that particular moment, as we never discussed it afterward. Perhaps he wanted to remind me that even though I had a gun in my hands, he still had power over me as a man. Maybe he wanted me to feel alienated and unsafe, so that I was reminded that I was an outsider to the institution. Either way, these experiences of sexual harassment highlighted to me, in a very visceral way, what it meant to be a woman in these spaces. That Neil spoke to me in this way knowing full well that I was a researcher suggests that this kind of behavior is acceptable in this context and probably does not lead to negative consequences for officers. Neil was in a supervisory role at the academy and, as a result, had access to all incoming cadets and any current officers undergoing in-service training at the firing range, giving him ample opportunities to engineer these kinds of interactions for himself.

Although I can, and do, treat this information as data, the fact that this element of fieldwork is so rarely talked about reveals how ethnographic methods inherently expose different people to unique levels of risk. Feminist ethnographers Rebecca Hanson and Patricia Richards examine this kind of gendered and racialized harassment in the field, showing its prominence and arguing that its general absence from ethnographic narratives illuminates the concerning ways that the discipline requires ethnographers to write their bodies out of their research. By examining the experiences of women in the field, whose work has often been marginalized within ethnography, these scholars "disrupt dominant field narratives and raise questions about the taken for granted assumptions that undergird ethnography."[6] In addition to highlighting the unequal structures embedded within the research method itself, my experiences illuminated how some of the men at my field sites conceptualized women's role in these spaces, where the only legible way to interact with me was to sexually objectify me and my presence there.

There were instances throughout my time in the field when I did have to set boundaries to ensure my own health and well-being. Toward the end of my fieldwork, for example, I had to decide whether I was willing to, alongside the Terryville cadets, get sprayed in the face with pepper/OC spray and shot in the back with a TASER. Although I felt conflicted, I ultimately decided not to go through with either of these experiences. This conflict arose from, on the one hand, a sense that I needed to suffer to establish my legitimacy as an ethnographer, while on the other hand, knowing that I did want to do it and that I did not think I needed to put myself through that level of pain to do good research.

I realize now that the nagging feeling that I needed to go through pain and suffering to gain credibility within the world of ethnography is rooted in the same masculinist value system that characterizes police training. Not unlike the world of policing, the tradition of carnal ethnography often rewards scholars who endeavor to use their bodies to understand hypermasculine, violent worlds. Kimberly Hoang has highlighted this tendency, pointing out that what is even described as carnal ethnography hinges on this masculinized investment.[7] Hoang notes that men who pursue ethnographic projects about, for example, boxing, drug robberies, or firefighting are rewarded for their embodied dedication to their scholarship.[8] In contrast, Hoang, who studied gender and global capital flows through Vietnam's nightlife, or Ashley Mears, who conducted an ethnography of modeling markets, are often objectified and sexualized as a result of their exposure to these feminine-coded topics.[9]

My decision not to get sprayed in the face with OC spray or shot in the back with a TASER, just like all decisions in the field, came with a cost. I do not have the necessary information to write about what it physically felt like to be exposed to OC spray or to be shot with a TASER, which were both mandatory for academy cadets. These exercises, I was told, were required so that cadets would understand these weapons' level of force if they decided to use their OC spray or TASER while on duty. I also did lose some standing with the cadets for this decision, many of whom tried to get me to do it along with them and afterward expressed disappointment that I decided not to. At lunch on TASER Day, for example, Matt, one of the Terryville cadets, turned to me and said, "I really thought you'd take one for the team." Surprised, I asked him, "Did you actually think that I would do it?" He nodded and said he did, adding that he was disappointed. Later, as I walked to my car at the end of the day, Faith, one of the instructors, commented, "You really wussed out today. That was your one chance!"

Even with all these embodied costs and difficult decisions, I did still experience many moments of fun, joy, and positive, meaningful connection while in the field. These moments of joy and connection with participants came in many different forms, like joking around during lunch or cheering each other on during workouts or PT (physical training) tests. Many of these experiences of connection, though, were rooted in mutual or shared suffering. I especially felt a bond with the cadets on OC Spray Day at Terryville when each cadet was required to get sprayed in the face with OC.[10] Just as with TASER Day, I was told that the cadets were required to go through this exercise so that they would understand the effects of this weapon and what level of force it entailed. We spent the morning in the classroom with Dylan while he explained how OC spray works, described when it should be used, outlined the department's policy on its use, and showed videos of its deployment on people.

Dylan gave an overview of how the afternoon would run, explaining that one by one, each cadet would get sprayed in the face with OC spray, then go through a small DT-related obstacle course, and finish up by completing an arrest on a volunteer, which included putting the volunteer in handcuffs and then frisking them. Each cadet had a partner from the class whose job it was to ensure that they did not injure themselves while going through the exercise and recovering afterward. After they finished these tasks, Dylan instructed, they should immediately go to the water fountains set up for them to wash out their eyes, and then, unfortunately, they would just need to wait for the pain to pass. It would be very painful for about thirty-five to forty minutes, Dylan warned, and then it would start to ease up. The OC spray could reactivate for twenty-four to forty-eight hours, so any time the cadets' pores opened, for example, in the shower, the pain would come back. That did not mean that they should not shower for a week, Dylan smirked. They should also not do any "stupid shit," Dylan went on, like covering their face with sour cream or milk or washing it with baby shampoo. None of it will work, he said, so they should not bother. Just water, air, and time—that was it.

We took a forty-five-minute lunch break, and when we got back to the classroom, Dylan read out the first six names on his list. Those not in this first group, he explained, should help their partners through the course and then stay with them for the thirty-five to forty minutes afterward, monitoring them to make sure they did not injure themselves while pacing around the parking lot and to check that they were not having an allergic reaction. Dylan reminded the class again not to rub their eyes, not to keep their eyes wide open in front of the large fan outside, not to spend too much time under the water, and that again, the only thing that would help them would be time and cold air. If they just kept walking around and catching the breeze, he said, the pain should start to dissipate in about thirty-five to forty minutes. "Y'all are lucky," he added. "There's a cold front coming in, so the wind will feel great."

"All right," Dylan announced, "first six, you're up." We all rose to our feet and walked outside to the parking lot. The anxiety in the air was palpable and showed up on the cadets' bodies—some had nervous smiles stretched across their faces, while others were shaking their heads, uneasily moving their hands and arms, or jumping up and down to psych themselves up. Chase repeatedly furrowed his brow, grimaced, and told me that he was nervous. Dylan instructed the cadets to gather on the far side of the parking lot and get in order. Andrea realized that her usual partner, Garrett, was set to go through the exercise directly after her, so he would not be able to help her through it. Eyes wide with nerves, she turned to me and pleaded, "Sam, will you be my partner?!" "Of course," I said, and she replied, "Are you gonna walk with me?" "Yes," I said, reassuring her that I would make sure she was okay.

Once the instructors were set up at each station, we began. Aaron went first; he walked to the designated spot, about five feet away from Dylan, and closed his eyes. A moment later, Dylan yelled, "Pepper, pepper!" and a stream of OC spray hit Aaron on his brow line, right above his eyes. "All right, open your eyes," Dylan instructed. Aaron's eyelids apprehensively fluttered open, and a second later, his entire body jolted. His neck spasmed, his head swung sharpy to the right, and he jumped up and down. He groaned loudly, twisting and unable to keep his eyes open. "Arghhhh!" he yelled out.

Andrea and I stood together in line, watching each one of her classmates' dramatic physical reactions as the pain of the OC spray set in. When there was just one cadet left before us in line, Andrea glanced back at me and, in a panicked tone, asked, "You got me, right?" I smiled and assured her, "Yes, I got you, girl!" She nervously shook out her hands and swayed her head back and forth as we watched Gerardo, the cadet in front of us, go through the exercise. When Andrea was finally up, I started to feel nervous too. I did not want to mess up my job as her partner, and I did not want her to be in too much pain. Andrea walked to the designated spot, Dylan shouted, "Pepper, pepper!" and the stream of OC spray hit the top of her head, a little bit too far from her eyes to elicit an immediate reaction. Dylan tried again, this time spraying her across the cheeks and mouth. A moment later, she pressed her weight into her toes, lifting her heels off the ground, her shoulders raised into her neck, her head swung to the side, and she began walking toward me, where I was waiting to help direct her to the first station.

Andrea immediately reached up to rub her face, so following instructions, I pulled her arms down and reminded her not to touch her eyes. I placed one hand on her lower back and another on her forearm to guide her to Kevin, who was holding a punching bag at the first station. As directed, she delivered ten strikes to the bag with each hand. "Open your eyes, Andrea!" Kevin shouted. "I can't," she groaned. She raised her eyebrows as high as she could, trying to force her eyes open. I guided her to the next station, this time just holding the back of her belt. "I can't see," she said, panicked, as we walked together.

Once Andrea finished the rest of the stations, I grabbed her shoulder and directed her over to the water fountains, where she could wash out her eyes. Faith, one of the instructors, met us by the fountains to walk Andrea through it: she told Andrea to open her eye, let the water wash it out for a couple seconds, and then rinse off her face. Andrea forced each eye open with her thumb and pointer finger to rinse them out. Spit and mucus covered the front of Andrea's shirt from her attempts to wipe off her nose and mouth during each of the stations. She kept trying to wipe her eyes on her shirt, which now had OC spray on it, so I gently reminded her, "Don't wipe your eyes." "I'm not!" she snapped. "I'm just wiping my nose."

I spent the next forty-five minutes with Andrea, following her wherever she went to make sure she was okay and did not trip or fall. Andrea desperately attempted to sooth herself, trying anything to get some relief. She wanted to sit, so I helped her to the ground. A moment later, she wanted to get up, so I helped her back up. She wanted to pace around the parking lot, then she wanted to sit on a bench, then stand in front of the fans, then walk in the direction of the oncoming breeze, then stand over by the fence. While facing the fence, she grabbed the chain links and shook it back and forth while moaning in agony. She crouched down at the fence, holding it for support, head bowed down to the ground while repeatedly telling me that the burning would not stop. She wanted to go stand between the fence and the academy building, where someone told us there was a wind tunnel, so we went over there for a bit. She rinsed her face off again; but that did not help, so we tried the fan again. We just kept moving, trying anything that might calm the pain. Nothing did.

Eventually, the pain began to subside, and Andrea started to feel better. Afterward, she thanked me multiple times for helping her get through it. That experience has stayed with me as one of the more intense moments I had during fieldwork. Andrea and her classmates were in a position of complete physical and emotional vulnerability. They could not see, they were crying and wailing in pain, the skin on their faces was swollen and irritated, and they had spit and mucus hanging from their mouths and noses. To see someone at their worst, and to be charged with ensuring their safety and offering emotional support, was an intensely intimate experience. I felt responsible for Andrea's well-being that afternoon, and it was awful to watch her, and her classmates, endure such pain.

All these experiences, which were both intellectual and physical, of course shaped the research, but they all changed my own life. I have taken my time in the field with me in ways that I notice and probably in others that I do not. I am not, as my participants sometimes reminded me, a police officer, nor have I ever been. I have, however, watched and participated in the process of becoming a police officer, which has left an indelible mark on my worldview and physical embodiment.

Empathy and Power in the Field

Feeling emotions, whether that be frustration, fear, disappointment, nervousness, excitement, gratitude, or joy, is an important part of doing ethnographic fieldwork. Feminist scholars have long recognized the role of emotions in research. Rather than striving for a distanced, objective approach to scholarship, feminist and queer methodologies acknowledge the researcher's capacity to shape, and be shaped by, the research process.[11] Sociologist Reuben Jonathan Miller describes this proximity to the social worlds that we study as both a "goal and a gift." He suggests that empathy, in and of itself, is not enough and encourages scholars to "walk alongside the people you spend time with and to do your best to learn from and communicate something about their lives with all the tools that you have."[12]

This proximity is one of ethnography's greatest strengths and I think one of an ethnographer's biggest rewards and challenges. We enter other people's lives, ideally with open minds and hearts, to learn about who they are, what they think, and what they do. These people, whom we call our "participants," let us witness their lives, give us their time, and share with us their feelings and beliefs, usually for nothing in return. Scholars have noted the potentially exploitative nature of this relationship, as researchers often enter a field site, extract information, and then leave.[13] This dynamic is especially important to consider when researchers are studying people or communities that are socially marginalized and more vulnerable to harm.[14] Feminist methodologies have attempted to address some of the ethical issues that can arise from the potentially extractive nature of research, for example, by participating in shared authorship or coming back to the field site to present findings to the community.[15]

The ethical calculus of the researcher-participant relationship changes, however, when studying people, communities, and organizations with power.[16] What power does the researcher hold, and how should they think about this power, when they are studying powerful people? As feminist scholars have pointed out, the research practices that may be needed when studying marginalized populations simply are not appropriate when studying the elite and powerful.[17]

Studying the police—an organization that wields significant power—generated intense feelings of conflict for me. Many times, I was shocked by what I saw in the field. Once, I was so surprised by the things I was hearing and seeing that I started to feel like I was tricking my participants—"They do know I am a researcher, right?" I would ask myself. I consulted a mentor about this at the time, explaining that I felt guilty that many of these cadets and officers had started to trust me, which felt ethically murky. My mentor reminded me that everyone at my field sites knew who I was and why I was there, which was true, and that my job was to understand their world according to them.

However, I still often had trouble reconciling my approach to research as being rooted in an ethic of empathy with the violence, racism, and sexism I saw happening in real time. My fieldwork with the police was a crash course in the complexity of the human experience: I felt fond of people whose actions and beliefs I was disturbed by, and I did not know what to do with that feeling. I was not sure what role empathy should have in my approach to studying the police.

Even with all this conflict, I still think that furthering knowledge in any meaningful way necessarily requires empathy toward all human beings. Feeling empathy, however, does not negate the other feelings that may arise simultaneously, nor does it mean that we should not be cautious with what we then do with this empathy when it is directed toward people in institutionally powerful positions. The risk of this approach comes when this empathy supersedes accountability. We can, as researchers, strive to empathetically understand powerful respondents, but we must also always hold them accountable.

Notes

Preface

1 Harel Shapira and Samantha J. Simon, "Learning to Need a Gun," *Qualitative Sociology* 41, no. 1 (2018): 1–20.

2 Frances Robles, "Florida's 'Stand Your Ground' Law Applies to Police, Too, Court Rules," *New York Times*, December 14, 2018, sec. US, www.nytimes.com.

3 Greg Henderson and Scott Neuman, "Jury Acquits Zimmerman of All Charges," *NPR*, July 13, 2013, sec. America, www.npr.org.

4 Jelani Cobb, "The Matter of Black Lives," *New Yorker*, March 6, 2016, www.newyorker.com.

5 Monica Anderson, "The Hashtag #BlackLivesMatter Emerges: Social Activism on Twitter," *Internet, Science & Tech*, Pew Research Center (blog), August 15, 2016, www.pewresearch.org.

6 Anderson.

7 Obama White House, "President Obama Discusses Communities and Law Enforcement Working Together," YouTube, December 1, 2014, www.youtube.com/watch?v=5_OxlLEUSx4&t=525s.

8 Larry Buchanan, Quoctrung Bui, and Jugal K. Patel, "Black Lives Matter May Be the Largest Movement in U.S. History," *New York Times*, July 3, 2020, sec. US, www.nytimes.com.

9 J. David Goodman, "A Year after 'Defund,' Police Departments Get Their Money Back," *New York Times*, October 10, 2021, sec. US, www.nytimes.com; Grace Manthey, Frank Esposito, and Amanda Hernandez, "Despite 'Defunding' Claims, Police Funding Has Increased in Many US Cities," *ABC News*, October 16, 2022, https://abcnews.go.com.

Chapter 1. The Academy

1 Patricia Hill Collins, *Black Feminist Thought: Knowledge, Consciousness and the Politics of Empowerment* (New York: Routledge, 1990); Kimberlé Crenshaw, "Mapping the Margins: Intersectionality, Identity Politics, and Violence against Women of Color," *Stanford Law Review* 43, no. 6 (1991): 1241–99.

2 Loïc Wacquant, *Body and Soul: Notebooks of an Apprentice Boxer* (Oxford: Oxford University Press, 2006).

3 Buchanan, Bui, and Patel, "Black Lives Matter May Be the Largest"; Armed Conflict Location & Event Data Project, "US Crisis Monitor Releases Full Data for Summer 2020," August 31, 2020, https://acleddata.com; Kim Parker, Juliana Horowitz, and Monica Anderson, "Amid Protests, Majorities across Racial and Ethnic Groups Express Support for the Black Lives Matter Movement" (Pew Research Center, June 12, 2020).

4 Frank Donner, *Protectors of Privilege: Red Squads and Police Repression in Urban America* (Berkeley: University of California Press, 1992); Joey L. Mogul, Andrea J. Ritchie, and Kay Whitlock, *Queer (In)Justice* (Boston: Beacon, 2012); Alex S. Vitale, *The End of Policing* (London: Verso, 2017); Isabel Wilkerson, *Caste: The Origins of Our Discontents* (New York: Random House, 2020).

5 Rebecca Onion, "America's Lost History of Border Violence," *Slate*, May 5, 2016, https://slate.com; Vitale, *End of Policing*.

6 James W. Buehler, "Racial/Ethnic Disparities in the Use of Lethal Force by US Police, 2010–2014," *American Journal of Public Health* 107, no. 2 (December 20, 2016): 295–97, https://doi.org/10.2105/AJPH.2016.303575; Andres F. Rengifo and Morgan McCallin, "'You Don't Get Respect If You Give No Respect': How Black and Latino Youth Make Sense of Encounters with Police," *Sociological Focus* 50, no. 1 (January 2, 2017): 66–80, https://doi.org/10.1080/00380237.201 6.1218218; Victor M. Rios, *Punished: Policing the Lives of Black and Latino Boys* (New York: NYU Press, 2011); C. Solis, E. L. Portillos, and R. K. Brunson, "Latino Youths' Experiences with and Perceptions of Involuntary Police Encounters," *Annals of the American Academy of Political and Social Science* 623, no. 1 (May 1, 2009): 39–51, https://doi.org/10.1177/0002716208330487.

7 Mae M. Ngai, "The Architecture of Race in American Immigration Law: A Reexamination of the Immigration Act of 1924," *Journal of American History* 86, no. 1 (1999): 67–92; Vitale, *End of Policing*.

8 Matt Apuzzo and Joseph Goldstein, "New York Drops Unit That Spied on Muslims," *New York Times*, April 15, 2014, sec. New York, www.nytimes.com.

9 Sally E. Hadden, *Slave Patrols: Law and Violence in Virginia and the Carolinas* (Cambridge, MA: Harvard University Press, 2003); Samuel Walker, *The Police in America: An Introduction* (Boston: Macmillan/McGraw-Hill School, 1980).

10 Hadden, *Slave Patrols*, 9.

11 Gary Potter, "The History of Policing in the United States" (Eastern Kentucky University Police Studies Online, 2013); Philip L. Reichel, "The Misplaced

Emphasis on Urbanization in Police Development," *Policing and Society* 3, no. 1 (October 1, 1992): 1–12, https://doi.org/10.1080/10439463.1992.9964653; Walker, *Police in America.*

12 Hadden, *Slave Patrols*; Philip L. Reichel, "Southern Slave Patrols as a Transitional Police Type," *American Journal of Police* 7 (1988): 51; Reichel, "Misplaced Emphasis."

13 Reichel, "Southern Slave Patrols," 68.

14 Hadden, *Slave Patrols*, 217.

15 Michelle Alexander and Cornel West, *The New Jim Crow: Mass Incarceration in the Age of Colorblindness* (New York: New Press, 2012); Khalil Gibran Muhammad, *The Condemnation of Blackness: Race, Crime, and the Making of Modern Urban America* (Cambridge, MA: Harvard University Press, 2011); Wilkerson, *Caste.*

16 Muhammad, *Condemnation of Blackness.*

17 Douglas S. Massey and Nancy A. Denton, *American Apartheid: Segregation and the Making of the Underclass* (Cambridge, MA: Harvard University Press, 1993).

18 Richard Williams, Reynold Nesiba, and Eileen Diaz McConnell, "The Changing Face of Inequality in Home Mortgage Lending Residential Segregation in the Post Civil Rights Era," *Social Problems* 52, no. 2 (2005): 181–208.

19 Devah Pager and Lincoln Quillian, "Walking the Talk? What Employers Say versus What They Do," *American Sociological Review* 70, no. 3 (June 2005): 355–80, https://doi.org/10.1177/000312240507000301; Devah Pager and Hana Shepherd, "The Sociology of Discrimination: Racial Discrimination in Employment, Housing, Credit, and Consumer Markets," *Annual Review of Sociology* 34, no. 1 (July 7, 2008): 181–209, https://doi.org/10.1146/annurev. soc.33.040406.131740; Jennifer Cheeseman Day and Eric C. Newburger, "The Big Payoff: Educational Attainment and Synthetic Estimates of Work-Life Earnings" (US Census Bureau, July 2002).

20 EdBuild, "Nonwhite School Districts Get $23 Billion Less than White Districts Despite Serving the Same Number of Students" (February 2019); Century Foundation, "Closing America's Education Funding Gaps" (July 22, 2020).

21 Carol Anderson and Dick Durbin, *One Person, No Vote: How Voter Suppression Is Destroying Our Democracy* (New York: Bloomsbury, 2018); Frances Fox Piven, Lorraine Carol Minnite, and Margaret Groarke, *Keeping Down the Black Vote: Race and the Demobilization of American Voters* (New York: New Press, 2009); Christopher Uggen and Jeff Manza, "Democratic Contraction? Political Consequences of Felon Disenfranchisement in the United States," *American Sociological Review* 67, no. 6 (December 2002): 777–803, https://doi. org/10.2307/3088970.

22 Kylea L. Liese, Mulubrhan Mogos, Sarah Abboud, Karen Decocker, Abigail R. Koch, and Stacie E. Geller, "Racial and Ethnic Disparities in Severe Maternal Morbidity in the United States," *Journal of Racial and Ethnic Health Disparities*

6, no. 4 (August 1, 2019): 790–98, https://doi.org/10.1007/s40615-019-00577-w; Emily E. Petersen, "Racial/Ethnic Disparities in Pregnancy-Related Deaths—United States, 2007–2016," *Morbidity and Mortality Weekly Report* 68 (2019), https://doi.org/10.15585/mmwr.mm6835a3.

23 Elizabeth Arias and Jiaquan Xu, "United States Life Tables, 2018," National Vital Statistics Reports (US Department of Health and Human Services, Centers for Disease Control and Prevention, November 17, 2020); David R. Williams and Michelle Sternthal, "Understanding Racial-Ethnic Disparities in Health: Sociological Contributions," *Journal of Health and Social Behavior* 51, no. S (2010): S15–27.

24 Katheryn Russell-Brown, *The Color of Crime*, 3rd ed. (New York: NYU Press, 2021).

25 Jeannine Bell, "Dead Canaries in the Coal Mines: The Symbolic Assailant Revisited," *Georgia State University Law Review* 34, no. 3 (2018): 534.

26 Alexander and West, *New Jim Crow*; David E. Barlow and Melissa Hickman Barlow, "Racial Profiling: A Survey of African American Police Officers," *Police Quarterly* 5, no. 3 (2002): 334–58; Rod K. Brunson, "'Police Don't Like Black People': African-American Young Men's Accumulated Police Experiences," *Criminology & Public Policy* 6, no. 1 (2007): 71–101; Rod K. Brunson and Jody Miller, "Gender, Race, and Urban Policing: The Experience of African American Youths," *Gender & Society* 20, no. 4 (August 1, 2006): 531–52, https://doi.org/10.1177/0891243206287727; J. Buehler, "Racial/Ethnic Disparities"; Charles R. Epp, Steven Maynard-Moody, and Donald Haider-Markel, *Pulled Over: How Police Stops Define Race and Citizenship*, Chicago Series in Law and Society (Chicago: University of Chicago Press, 2014); Ann Arnett Ferguson, *Bad Boys: Public Schools in the Making of Black Masculinity* (Ann Arbor: University of Michigan Press, 2001); Phillip Atiba Goff, Tracey Lloyd, Amanda Geller, Steven Raphael, and Jack Glaser, "The Science of Justice: Race, Arrests, and Police Use of Force" (Center for Policing Equity, July 2016); Delores Jones-Brown, "Forever the Symbolic Assailant: The More Things Change, the More They Remain the Same Special Issue: Race and Policing: Reaction Essay," *Criminology and Public Policy* 6, no. 1 (2007): 103–22; Rios, *Punished*; Douglas A. Smith and Christy A. Visher, "Two Papers on Crime: Street-Level Justice: Situational Determinants of Police Arrest Decisions," *Social Problems* 29, no. 2 (1982 1981): 167–77.

27 Brunson, "Police Don't Like Black People"; Brunson and Miller, "Gender, Race, and Urban Policing"; Forrest Stuart and Ava Benezra, "Criminalized Masculinities: How Policing Shapes the Construction of Gender and Sexuality in Poor Black Communities," *Social Problems* 65, no. 2 (May 1, 2018): 174–90, https://doi.org/10.1093/socpro/spx017.

28 Brunson and Miller, "Gender, Race, and Urban Policing"; Shannon Malone Gonzalez, "Making It Home: An Intersectional Analysis of the Police Talk,"

Gender & Society 33, no. 3 (June 1, 2019): 363–86, https://doi. org/10.1177/0891243219828340.

29 Susan E. Martin, *Breaking and Entering: Policewomen on Patrol* (Berkeley: University of California Press, 1982).

30 Martin.

31 Janis Appier, *Policing Women: The Sexual Politics of Law Enforcement and the LAPD* (Philadelphia: Temple University Press, 1998).

32 Martin, *Breaking and Entering.*

33 Mary E. Hamilton, *Policewoman: Her Service and Ideals* (New York: Arno, 1924).

34 Appier, *Policing Women.*

35 Appier; Marilyn Corsianos, *Policing and Gendered Justice: Examining the Possibilities* (Toronto: University of Toronto Press, 2009).

36 Walker, *Police in America.*

37 Susan E. Martin, "Women on the Move?," *Women & Criminal Justice* 1, no. 1 (October 13, 1989): 21–40, https://doi.org/10.1300/J012v01n01_03.

38 David B. Muhlhausen, "Women in Policing: Breaking Barriers and Blazing a Path" (National Institute of Justice, July 2019).

39 Steven Leinen, *Black Police, White Society* (New York: NYU Press, 1984).

40 National Advisory Commission on Civil Disorders, "Report of the National Advisory Commission on Civil Disorders" (1967).

41 National Advisory Commission on Civil Disorders; Walker, *Police in America.*

42 David Alan Sklansky, "Not Your Father's Police Department: Making Sense of the New Demographics of Law Enforcement," *Journal of Criminal Law & Criminology* 96, no. 3 (Spring 2006): 1209–43.

43 Martin, *Breaking and Entering,* 79.

44 Martin.

45 Susan E. Martin, "'Outsider within' the Station House: The Impact of Race and Gender on Black Women Police," *Social Problems* 41, no. 3 (1994): 383–400, https://doi.org/10.2307/3096969.

46 Eugene Beard, Lee P. Brown, and Lawrence E. Gary, *Attitudes and Perceptions of Black Police Officers of the District of Columbia Metropolitan Police Department* (Washington, DC: Institute for Urban Affairs and Research, 1976); Kenneth Bolton and Joe Feagin, *Black in Blue: African-American Police Officers and Racism* (New York: Routledge, 2004).

47 Martin, "'Outsider within' the Station House."

48 Joan Acker, "Hierarchies, Jobs, Bodies: A Theory of Gendered Organizations," *Gender & Society* 4, no. 2 (1990): 139–58, https://doi. org/10.1177/089124390004002002; Rosabeth Moss Kanter, *Men and Women of the Corporation,* 2nd ed. (New York: Basic Books, 1977); Victor Ray, "A Theory of Racialized Organizations," *American Sociological Review* 84, no. 1 (2019): 26–53.

49 Acker, "Hierarchies, Jobs, Bodies"; Joan Acker, "Inequality Regimes: Gender, Class, and Race in Organizations," *Gender & Society* 20, no. 4 (2006): 441–64, https://doi.org/10.1177/0891243206289499.

50 R. W. Connell and James W. Messerschmidt, "Hegemonic Masculinity: Rethinking the Concept," *Gender & Society* 19, no. 6 (December 1, 2005): 829–59, https://doi.org/10.1177/0891243205278639; Candace West and Don H. Zimmerman, "Doing Gender," *Gender & Society* 1, no. 2 (June 1, 1987): 125–51, https://doi.org/10.1177/0891243287001002002.

51 Jennifer Brown, "From Cult of Masculinity to Smart Macho: Gender Perspectives on Police Occupational Culture," in *Police Occupational Culture: New Debates and Direction*, Sociology of Crime, Law and Deviance 8 (Bingley, UK: Emerald Group, 2007), 206–26; Martin, *Breaking and Entering*; Anastasia Prokos and Irene Padavic, "'There Oughtta Be a Law against Bitches': Masculinity Lessons in Police Academy Training," *Gender, Work & Organization* 9, no. 4 (August 1, 2002): 439–59, https://doi.org/10.1111/1468-0432.00168; Frank J. Barrett, "The Organizational Construction of Hegemonic Masculinity: The Case of the US Navy," *Gender, Work & Organization* 3, no. 3 (1996): 129–42, https://doi.org/10.1111/j.1468-0432.1996.tb00054.x; Dana M. Britton and Christine L. Williams, "'Don't Ask, Don't Tell, Don't Pursue': Military Policy and the Construction of Heterosexual Masculinity," *Journal of Homosexuality* 30, no. 1 (1995): 1–21; Jana L. Pershing, "Men and Women's Experiences with Hazing in a Male-Dominated Elite Military Institution," *Men and Masculinities* 8, no. 4 (April 1, 2006): 470–92, https://doi.org/10.1177/1097184X05277411; Randol Contreras, *The Stickup Kids: Race, Drugs, Violence, and the American Dream* (Berkeley: University of California Press, 2012); Valerie Jenness and Sarah Fenstermaker, "Forty Years after Brownmiller: Prisons for Men, Transgender Inmates, and the Rape of the Feminine," *Gender & Society* 30, no. 1 (February 1, 2016): 14–29, https://doi.org/10.1177/0891243215611856; Hank Nuwer, *Wrongs of Passage: Fraternities, Sororities, Hazing, and Binge Drinking* (Bloomington: Indiana University Press, 2002); Peggy Reeves Sanday, *Fraternity Gang Rape: Sex, Brotherhood, and Privilege on Campus*, 2nd ed. (New York: NYU Press, 2007); C. J. Pascoe, *Dude, You're a Fag: Masculinity and Sexuality in High School*, 2nd ed. (Berkeley: University of California Press, 2011); Jennifer Carlson, *Citizen-Protectors: The Everyday Politics of Guns in an Age of Decline* (Oxford: Oxford University Press, 2015); Harel Shapira and Samantha J. Simon, "Learning to Need a Gun," *Qualitative Sociology* 41, no. 1 (March 1, 2018): 1–20, https://doi.org/10.1007/s11133-018-9374-2; Angela Stroud, *Good Guys with Guns: The Appeal and Consequences of Concealed Carry* (Chapel Hill: University of North Carolina Press, 2015).

52 Pascoe, *Dude, You're a Fag*.

53 Steve Herbert, "'Hard Charger' or 'Station Queen'? Policing and the Masculinist State," *Gender, Place and Culture: A Journal of Feminist Geography* 8, no. 1 (2001): 55–71; Jack R. Greene and Stephen D. Mastrofski, eds., *Community Policing: Rhetoric or Reality* (New York: Praeger, 1988); Robert Trojanowicz and Bonnie Bucqueroux, *Community Policing: A Contemporary Perspective* (New York: Routledge, 1999).

54 Herbert, "'Hard Charger' or 'Station Queen'?," 56.

55 Radley Balko, *Rise of the Warrior Cop: The Militarization of America's Police Forces* (New York: PublicAffairs, 2014); Egon Bittner, *The Functions of the Police in Modern Society* (Rockville, MD: National Institute of Mental Health, Center for Studies of Crime and Delinquency, 1973); Martin, *Breaking and Entering.*

56 UK Parliament, "Metropolitan Police," accessed April 25, 2023, www.parliament.uk.

57 G. L. Kelling and M. H. Moore, "The Evolving Strategy of Policing" (US Department of Justice, 1988); Stewart Mott, James K. Stewart, and Mark H. Moore, "Debating the Evolution of American Policing" (US Department of Justice, 1988); Samuel Walker, "The Engineer as Progressive: The Wickersham Commission in the Arc of Herbert Hoover's Life and Work," *Marquette Law Review* 96, no. 4 (Summer 2013): 1165–97.

58 Allen Z. Gammage, *Police Training in the United States* (Springfield, IL: Charles C. Thomas, 1963).

59 Gammage; August Vollmer and Albert Schneider, "School for Police as Planned by Berkeley," *Journal of Criminal Law and Criminology* 7, no. 6 (1917): 877–98.

60 Gammage, *Police Training in the United States.*

61 President's Commission on Law Enforcement and Administration of Justice, *The Challenge of Crime in a Free Society* (Washington, DC: President's Commission on Law Enforcement and Administration of Justice, 1967).

62 Michael S. McCampbell, "Field Training for Police Officers: The State of the Art" (National Institute of Justice, US Department of Justice, 1987).

63 James V. Cotter, "Law Enforcement Accreditation: A Big Step toward Professionalism," *FBI Law Enforcement Bulletin* 52 (1983): 19.

64 "Police Officer Standards and Training Commissions (POST Commissions)," in *Encyclopedia of Law Enforcement*, ed. Larry E. Sullivan, Marie Simonetti Rosen, and Dorothy M. Schulz, and Maria Haberfeld, vol. 1 (Thousand Oaks, CA: Sage, 2004), 349–51.

65 Emily D. Buehler, "State and Local Law Enforcement Training Academies, 2018—Statistical Tables" (Bureau of Justice Statistics, US Department of Justice, July 2021); Brian A. Reaves, "State and Local Law Enforcement Training Academies, 2013" (Bureau of Justice Statistics, US Department of Justice, July 2016).

66 E. Buehler, "State and Local Law Enforcement Training Academies."

67 John Van Maanen, "Observations on the Making of Policemen," *Human Organization* 32, no. 4 (1973): 407–18; Michael Sierra-Arévalo, "The Commemoration of Death, Organizational Memory, and Police Culture," *Criminology* 57, no. 4 (2019): 632–58, https://doi.org/10.1111/1745-9125.12224.

68 Van Maanen, "Observations on the Making of Policemen," 411.

Chapter 2. A Few Good Officers

1 After each interview, I asked the interviewee to fill out a demographic form, which included blank spaces for them to write in their gender, age, race, marital status, number of children, and years of law enforcement experience. In my descriptions of interviewees in this book, I use the gender and racial identities that they wrote on their demographic form.

2 Terryville provided me with the spreadsheet the hiring officers used to track attrition through the hiring process for its incoming academy class. The percentages of applicants who were eliminated at each stage of Terryville's hiring process that I report in this chapter are based on the numbers provided to me in the spreadsheet that Terryville hiring officers used.

3 Mark Harris, "The Lie Generator: Inside the Black Mirror World of Polygraph Job Screenings," *Wired*, October 1, 2018, www.wired.com.

4 The hiring officers explained to me that they often recorded their phone conversations with applicants so that they had an official record of what was said.

5 The department's parameters regarding drug use were based on the number of times a drug was used, what kind of drug, and the time passed since last use.

6 Suzanne M. Bianchi, Liana C. Sayer, Melissa A. Milkie, and John P. Robinson, "Housework: Who Did, Does or Will Do It, and How Much Does It Matter?," *Social Forces* 91, no. 1 (September 1, 2012): 55–63, https://doi.org/10.1093/sf/sos120; Megan Brenan, "Women Still Handle Main Household Tasks in U.S." (Gallup, January 29, 2020); Kim Parker and Wendy Wang, "How Mothers and Fathers Spend Their Time," chap. 4 in *Modern Parenthood: Roles of Moms and Dads Converge as They Balance Work and Family* (Washington, DC: Pew Research Center, March 14, 2013); Parker and Wang, "Time in Work and Leisure, Patterns by Gender and Family Structure," chap. 6 in *Modern Parenthood*; Cynthia Hess, M. Phil Tanima Ahmed, and Jeff Hayes, "Providing Unpaid Household and Care Work in the United States: Uncovering Inequality" (Institute for Women's Policy Research, January 2020).

7 Zachary Oberfield, "Motivation, Change, and Stability: Findings from an Urban Police Department," *American Review of Public Administration* 44, no. 2 (March 1, 2014): 210–32, https://doi.org/10.1177/0275074012461297; James L. Perry and Lois Recascino Wise, "The Motivational Bases of Public Service," *Public Administration Review* 50, no. 3 (1990): 367–73, https://doi.org/10.2307/976618.

8 Aliya Hamid Rao and Megan Tobias Neely, "What's Love Got to Do with It? Passion and Inequality in White-Collar Work," *Sociology Compass* 13, no. 12 (2019): e12744, https://doi.org/10.1111/soc4.12744.

9 Ilana Gershon, *Down and Out in the New Economy* (Chicago: University of Chicago Press, 2017).

10 During a speech at a fundraiser for the 2016 presidential campaign, Hillary Clinton said, "You could put half of Trump's supporters into what I call the 'basket of deplorables.'" In response, people in support of Donald Trump reappropriated the phrase, adopting the moniker to describe themselves.

11 Mark Baker, *Cops: Their Lives in Their Own Words* (New York: Simon and Schuster, 1985); Bethan Loftus, "Police Occupational Culture: Classic Themes, Altered Times," *Policing and Society* 20, no. 1 (March 1, 2010): 1–20, https://doi.org/10.1080/10439460903281547; Robert Reiner, *The Politics of the Police* (London: Harvester Wheatsheaf, 1992).

12 Lisa Donovan, "Chicago Police Union Endorses President Trump's Reelection Bid," *Chicago Tribune*, September 9, 2020, www.chicagotribune.com; Abigail Hauslohner, Mark Berman, and Aaron C. Davis, "As Police Unions Endorse Trump, Some Worry Officers Displaying Bias Could Be Intimidating at the Polls, Affect Voting," *Washington Post*, October 31, 2020, www.washingtonpost.com; Tom Jackman, "Fraternal Order of Police Union Endorses Trump," *Washington Post*, September 16, 2016, www.washingtonpost.com.

13 Simone Weichselbaum and Tom Meagher, "When Warriors Put on the Badge" (Marshall Project, March 30, 2017), www.themarshallproject.org.

14 Pierre Bourdieu, *The Logic of Practice*, trans. Richard Nice (Stanford, CA: Stanford University Press, 1992).

15 Jennifer M. Reingle Gonzalez, Stephen A. Bishopp, Katelyn K. Jetelina, Ellen Paddock, Kelley Pettee Gabriel, and M. Brad Cannell, "Does Military Veteran Status and Deployment History Impact Officer Involved Shootings? A Case-Control Study," *Journal of Public Health* 41, no. 3 (September 2019): e245–e252, https://doi.org/10.1093/pubmed/fdy151; Simone Weichselbaum, "Police with Military Experience More Likely to Shoot" (Marshall Project, October 15, 2018), www.themarshallproject.org.

16 Hadden, *Slave Patrols*; Muhammad, *Condemnation of Blackness*.

17 Richard R. Bennett and Theodore Greenstein, "The Police Personality: A Test of the Predispositional Model," *Journal of Police Science & Administration* 3, no. 4 (1975): 439–45; Zachary W. Oberfield, "Socialization and Self-Selection: How Police Officers Develop Their Views about Using Force," *Administration & Society* 44, no. 6 (September 1, 2012): 702–30, https://doi.org/10.1177/0095399711420545; Alexander B. Smith, Bernard Locke, and Abe Fenster, "Authoritarianism in Policemen Who Are College Graduates and Non-College Police," *Journal of Criminal Law, Criminology, and Police Science* 61, no. 2 (1970): 313–15, https://doi.org/10.2307/1142226.

18 Andrew Ford, "NJ Police Tests Fail Women Recruits. Here's How It Hurts Your Safety and Your Wallet," *Asbury Park Press*, July 29, 2019; Muhlhausen, "Women in Policing"; Civil Rights Division, US Department of Justice, "The Civil Rights Division's Pattern and Practice Police Reform Work: 1994–Present" (January 2017).

Chapter 3. Us vs. Them

1 William Westley, *Violence and the Police: A Sociological Study of Law, Custom, and Morality* (Cambridge, MA: MIT Press, 1970), 780.

2 Loftus, "Police Occupational Culture," 1–2.

3 Dan Lamothe, "Vietnam Veteran Andrew Brannan Executed for Murder after PTSD Defense Fails," *Washington Post*, January 13, 2015, www.washingtonpost.com.

4 Thomas Lake, "The Endless Death of Kyle Dinkheller," *CNN Politics*, August 2017, www.cnn.com.

5 Edward R. Maguire, Justin Nix, and Bradley A. Campbell, "A War on Cops? The Effects of Ferguson on the Number of U.S. Police Officers Murdered in the Line of Duty," *Justice Quarterly* 34, no. 5 (July 29, 2017): 739–58, https://doi.org/10.1080/07418825.2016.1236205.

6 "2 Persons of Interest Sought in Shooting of Camden Detectives," *ABC 6 Action News*, August 9, 2018; Sarah Mervosh, "2 Undercover Officers in Camden Are Ambushed and Shot at Red Light, Police Say," *New York Times*, August 8, 2018, sec. US, www.nytimes.com.

7 Tom Steele and Naheed Rajwani, "Man Who Fatally Shot Houston-Area Deputy Killed Himself a Day Later, Police Say," *Dallas Morning News*, April 10, 2017, sec. Crime, www.dallasnews.com.

8 Maguire, Nix, and Campbell, "War on Cops?"; John A. Shjarback and Edward R. Maguire, "Extending Research on the 'War on Cops': The Effects of Ferguson on Nonfatal Assaults against U.S. Police Officers," *Crime & Delinquency* 67, no. 1 (2019): 3–26, https://doi.org/10.1177/0011128719890266.

9 Travis L. Dixon, Cristina L. Azocar, and Michael Casas, "The Portrayal of Race and Crime on Television Network News," *Journal of Broadcasting & Electronic Media* 47, no. 4 (December 1, 2003): 498–523, https://doi.org/10.1207/s15506878jobem4704_2; Travis L. Dixon and Daniel Linz, "Overrepresentation and Underrepresentation of African Americans and Latinos as Lawbreakers on Television News," *Journal of Communication* 50, no. 2 (June 1, 2000): 131–54, https://doi.org/10.1111/j.1460-2466.2000.tb02845.x; Robert M. Entman, "Modern Racism and the Images of Blacks in Local Television News," *Critical Studies in Mass Communication* 7, no. 4 (December 1, 1990): 332–45, https://doi.org/10.1080/15295039009360183; Robert M. Entman, "Representation and Reality in the Portrayal of Blacks on Network Television News," *Journalism Quarterly* 71, no. 3 (September 1, 1994): 509–20, https://doi.

org/10.1177/107769909407100303; Franklin D. Gilliam Jr., Shanto Iyengar, Adam Simon, and Oliver Wright, "Crime in Black and White: The Violent, Scary World of Local News," *Harvard International Journal of Press/Politics* 1, no. 3 (June 1, 1996): 6–23, https://doi.org/10.1177/1081180X96001003003; CalvinJohn Smiley and David Fakunle, "From 'Brute' to 'Thug:' The Demonization and Criminalization of Unarmed Black Male Victims in America," *Journal of Human Behavior in the Social Environment* 26, nos. 3–4 (May 18, 2016): 350–66, https://doi.org/10.1080/10911359.2015.1129256.

10 Erin Ash, Yiwei Xu, Alexandria Jenkins, and Chenjerai Kumanyika, "Framing Use of Force: An Analysis of News Organizations' Social Media Posts about Police Shootings," *Electronic News* 13, no. 2 (June 1, 2019): 93–107, https://doi.org/10.1177/1931243119850239.

11 Paul J. Hirschfield and Daniella Simon, "Legitimating Police Violence: Newspaper Narratives of Deadly Force," *Theoretical Criminology* 14, no. 2 (May 1, 2010): 155–82, https://doi.org/10.1177/1362480609351545.

12 Charles F. Klahm IV, Jordan Papp, and Laura Rubino, "Police Shootings in Black and White: Exploring Newspaper Coverage of Officer-Involved Shootings," in *The Politics of Policing: Between Force and Legitimacy*, ed. Mathieu Deflem, Sociology of Crime, Law and Deviance 21 (Bingley, UK: Emerald Group, 2016), 197–218.

13 Natasha Shrikant and Rahul Sambaraju, "'A Police Officer Shot a Black Man': Racial Categorization, Racism, and Mundane Culpability in News Reports of Police Shootings of Black People in the United States of America," *British Journal of Social Psychology* 60, no. 4 (2021): 1196–1217, https://doi.org/10.1111/bjso.12490.

14 Travis L. Dixon, "Black Criminals and White Officers: The Effects of Racially Misrepresenting Law Breakers and Law Defenders on Television News," *Media Psychology* 10, no. 2 (June 29, 2007): 270–91, https://doi.org/10.1080/15213260701375660; Dixon and Linz, "Overrepresentation and Underrepresentation"; Dixon, Azocar, and Casas, "Portrayal of Race and Crime"; Entman, "Modern Racism"; Entman, "Representation and Reality"; Gilliam et al., "Crime in Black and White"; Smiley and Fakunle, "From 'Brute' to 'Thug.'"

15 Alexander and West, *New Jim Crow*; Barlow and Barlow, "Racial Profiling"; Brunson, "Police Don't Like Black People"; Brunson and Miller, "Gender, Race, and Urban Policing"; J. Buehler, "Racial/Ethnic Disparities"; Epp, Maynard-Moody, and Haider-Markel, *Pulled Over*; Ferguson, *Bad Boys*; Goff et al., "Science of Justice"; Jones-Brown, "Forever the Symbolic Assailant"; Shannon Malone Gonzalez, "Black Girls and the Talk? Policing, Parenting, and the Politics of Protection," *Social Problems* 69, no. 1 (February 2022): 22–38, https://doi.org/10.1093/socpro/spaa032; Rios, *Punished*; Smith and Visher, "Two Papers on Crime."

16 Alexander and West, *New Jim Crow*; Barlow and Barlow, "Racial Profiling"; Brunson, "Police Don't Like Black People"; Brunson and Miller, "Gender, Race, and Urban Policing"; J. Buehler, "Racial/Ethnic Disparities"; Epp, Maynard-Moody, and Haider-Markel, *Pulled Over*, 2014; Ferguson, *Bad Boys*; Goff et al., "Science of Justice"; Jones-Brown, "Forever the Symbolic Assailant"; Malone Gonzalez, "Black Girls and the Talk?"; Rios, *Punished*; Smith and Visher, "Two Papers on Crime."

17 Matthew J. Hickman, "Citizen Complaints about Police Use of Force," NCJ 210296 (Bureau of Justice Statistics, US Department of Justice, June 2006); William Terrill and Jason R. Ingram, "Citizen Complaints against the Police: An Eight City Examination," *Police Quarterly* 19, no. 2 (June 1, 2016): 150–79, https://doi.org/10.1177/1098611115613320.

18 Terrill and Ingram, "Citizen Complaints against the Police."

19 Bocar Abdoulaye Ba and Roman Rivera, "Police Think They Can Get Away with Anything. That's Because They Usually Do," *Washington Post*, June 8, 2020, www.washingtonpost.com.

20 Hickman, "Citizen Complaints about Police Use of Force."

21 Ba and Rivera, "Police Think They Can Get Away with Anything"; Terrill and Ingram, "Citizen Complaints against the Police."

22 Peter B. Kraska and Victor E. Kappeler, "To Serve and Pursue: Exploring Police Sexual Violence against Women," *Justice Quarterly* 12, no. 1 (1995): 86–111; Timothy M. Maher, "Police Sexual Misconduct: Officers' Perceptions of Its Extent and Causality," *Criminal Justice Review* 28, no. 2 (September 1, 2003): 355–81, https://doi.org/10.1177/073401680302800209; Cara E. Rabe-Hemp and Jeremy Braithwaite, "An Exploration of Recidivism and the Officer Shuffle in Police Sexual Violence," *Police Quarterly* 16, no. 2 (June 1, 2013): 127–47, https://doi.org/10.1177/1098611112464964; Philip Matthew Stinson Sr., John Liederbach, Steven L. Brewer Jr., and Brooke E. Mathna, "Police Sexual Misconduct: A National Scale Study of Arrested Officers," *Criminal Justice Policy Review* 26, no. 7 (October 1, 2015): 665–90, https://doi.org/10.1177/0887403414526231.

23 Stinson et al., "Police Sexual Misconduct."

24 Maher, "Police Sexual Misconduct"; International Association of Chiefs of Police, "Addressing Sexual Offenses and Misconduct by Law Enforcement: Executive Guide" (June 23, 2011).

25 Loftus, "Police Occupational Culture"; Peter K. Manning, *Police Work: The Social Organization of Policing* (Cambridge, MA: MIT Press, 1977); Robert Reiner, *The Politics of the Police* (Oxford: Oxford University Press, 2000); Jonathan Rubinstein, *City Police* (New York: Farrar, Straus and Giroux, 1980); John Van Maanen, "Police Socialization: A Longitudinal Examination of Job Attitudes in an Urban Police Department," *Administrative Science Quarterly* 20,

no. 2 (1975): 207–28, https://doi.org/10.2307/2391695; Westley, *Violence and the Police*.

26 Maguire, Nix, and Campbell, "War on Cops?"

Chapter 4. Police Work as Warfare, Officers as Warriors

1 Elizabeth Hinton, "'A War within Our Own Boundaries': Lyndon Johnson's Great Society and the Rise of the Carceral State," *Journal of American History* 102, no. 1 (June 1, 2015): 100–112, https://doi.org/10.1093/jahist/jav328; James Forman Jr., *Locking Up Our Own: Crime and Punishment in Black America* (New York: Farrar, Straus and Giroux, 2018).

2 Herbert, "'Hard Charger' or 'Station Queen'?"; Martin, *Breaking and Entering*.

3 Seth Stoughton, "Law Enforcement's Warrior Problem," *Harvard Law Review Forum* 128 (2014): 217, 228.

4 Radley Balko, "A Day with 'Killology' Police Trainer Dave Grossman," *Washington Post*, February 14, 2017, www.washingtonpost.com; Bryan Schatz, "'Are You Prepared to Kill Somebody?': A Day with One of America's Most Popular Police Trainers," *Mother Jones*, March 2017, www.motherjones.com.

5 Otwin Marenin, "Cheapening Death: Danger, Police Street Culture, and the Use of Deadly Force," *Police Quarterly* 19, no. 4 (December 1, 2016): 461–87, https://doi.org/10.1177/1098611116652983; Michael Sierra-Arévalo, "American Policing and the Danger Imperative," *Law & Society Review* 55, no. 1 (2021): 70–103.

6 Jennifer Carlson, "Police Warriors and Police Guardians: Race, Masculinity, and the Construction of Gun Violence," *Social Problems* 67, no. 3 (2019): 6, https://doi.org/10.1093/socpro/spz020.

7 Herbert, "'Hard Charger' or 'Station Queen'?"; Greene and Mastrofski, *Community Policing*; Trojanowicz and Bucqueroux, *Community Policing*.

8 Kelling and Moore, "Evolving Strategy of Policing"; Herbert, "'Hard Charger' or 'Station Queen'?"

9 Iris Marion Young, "The Logic of Masculinist Protection: Reflections on the Current Security State," *Signs: Journal of Women in Culture and Society* 29, no. 1 (September 1, 2003): 4, https://doi.org/10.1086/375708.

10 Carlson, *Citizen-Protectors*; Carlson, "Police Warriors and Police Guardians"; Shapira and Simon, "Learning to Need a Gun"; Stroud, *Good Guys with Guns*.

11 James William Gibson, *Warrior Dreams: Violence and Manhood in Post-Vietnam America* (New York: Hill and Wang, 1994); Susan Jeffords, *Hard Bodies: Hollywood Masculinity in the Reagan Era* (New Brunswick, NJ: Rutgers University Press, 1993).

12 Britton and Williams, "Don't Ask, Don't Tell, Don't Pursue."

13 Eduardo Bonilla-Silva, *Racism without Racists: Color-Blind Racism and the Persistence of Racial Inequality in America*, 3rd ed. (Lanham, MD: Rowman and Littlefield, 2009).

14 Eduardo Bonilla-Silva, "The Structure of Racism in Color-Blind, 'Post-Racial' America," *American Behavioral Scientist* 59, no. 11 (2015): 7, https://doi.org/10.1177/0002764215586826.

15 Charles W. Mills, *The Racial Contract* (Ithaca, NY: Cornell University Press, 1997); Charles W. Mills, "White Ignorance," in *Race and Epistemologies of Ignorance*, ed. Shannon Sullivan and Nancy Tuana (Albany: State University of New York, 2007), 13–38.

16 Mills, *Racial Contract*, 11.

17 Mills, 18.

18 Jennifer C. Mueller, "Producing Colorblindness: Everyday Mechanisms of White Ignorance," *Social Problems* 64, no. 2 (May 1, 2017): 147, https://doi.org/10.1093/socpro/spw061.

19 Bell, "Dead Canaries in the Coal Mines"; Melissa Hickman Barlow, "Race and the Problem of Crime in 'Time' and 'Newsweek' Cover Stories, 1946 to 1995," *Social Justice* 25, no. 2 (72) (1998): 149–83; Barlow and Barlow, "Racial Profiling"; Lincoln Quillian and Devah Pager, "Black Neighbors, Higher Crime? The Role of Racial Stereotypes in Evaluations of Neighborhood Crime," *American Journal of Sociology* 107, no. 3 (November 1, 2001): 717–67, https://doi.org/10.1086/338938; Hadden, *Slave Patrols*; Muhammad, *Condemnation of Blackness*; Russell-Brown, *Color of Crime*.

20 Patricia Hill Collins, *Black Sexual Politics: African Americans, Gender, and the New Racism* (New York: Routledge, 2005); Jones-Brown, "Forever the Symbolic Assailant"; Mogul, Ritchie, and Whitlock, *Queer (In)Justice*; Muhammad, *Condemnation of Blackness*; Russell-Brown, *Color of Crime*; Jerome H. Skolnick, *Justice without Trial: Law Enforcement in Democratic Society*, 4th ed. (New Orleans: Quid Pro Books, 1966).

21 Barlow, "Race and the Problem of Crime," 151.

22 Kate Antonovics and Brian G Knight, "A New Look at Racial Profiling: Evidence from the Boston Police Department," *Review of Economics and Statistics* 91, no. 1 (February 1, 2009): 163–77, https://doi.org/10.1162/rest.91.1.163; Barlow and Barlow, "Racial Profiling"; Epp, Maynard-Moody, and Haider-Markel, *Pulled Over*; US General Accounting Office, "Racial Profiling: Limited Data Available on Motorist Stops" (March 2000); Sunghoon Roh and Matthew Robinson, "A Geographic Approach to Racial Profiling: The Microanalysis and Macroanalysis of Racial Disparity in Traffic Stops," *Police Quarterly* 12, no. 2 (June 1, 2009): 137–69, https://doi.org/10.1177/1098611109332422; Michael R. Smith and Matthew Petrocelli, "Racial Profiling? A Multivariate Analysis of Police Traffic Stop Data," *Police Quarterly* 4, no. 1 (March 1, 2001): 4–27, https://doi.org/10.1177/1098611101004001001.

23 Epp, Maynard-Moody, and Haider-Markel, *Pulled Over*, 12.

24 W. E. B. Du Bois, *The Souls of Black Folk* (Cambridge, MA: G&D Media, 1903); Patricia Hill Collins, "Learning from the Outsider Within: The Sociological

Significance of Black Feminist Thought," *Social Problems* 33, no. 6 (December 1, 1986): s14–32, https://doi.org/10.2307/800672.

25 W. E. B. Du Bois, "Strivings of the Negro People," *The Atlantic*, August 1, 1897, www.theatlantic.com.

26 Patricia Hill Collins, "Reflections on the Outsider Within," *Journal of Career Development* 26, no. 1 (Fall 1999): 86.

27 Barlow and Barlow, "Racial Profiling"; Michelle Conlin, "Off Duty, Black Cops in New York Feel Threat from Fellow Police," *Reuters*, December 23, 2014, www.reuters.com; John Paul and Michael Birzer, "The Experiences of Black Police Officers Who Have Been Racially Profiled: An Exploratory Research Note," *Journal of African American Studies* 21 (August 1, 2017): 1–18, https://doi.org/10.1007/s12111-017-9382-4.

28 New York State Task Force on Police-on-Police Shootings, "Reducing Inherent Danger: Report of the Task Force on Police-on-Police Shootings" (2010).

29 Josiah McC. Heyman, "U.S. Immigration Officers of Mexican Ancestry as Mexican Americans, Citizens, and Immigration Police," *Current Anthropology* 43, no. 3 (June 2002): 479–507, https://doi.org/10.1086/339527; Cesar Cuauhtemoc Garcia Hernandez, "La Migra in the Mirror: Immigration Enforcement and Racial Profiling on the Texas Border," *Notre Dame Journal of Law, Ethics & Public Policy* 23 (2009): 167; Jennifer G. Correa and James M. Thomas, "The Rebirth of the U.S.-Mexico Border: Latina/o Enforcement Agents and the Changing Politics of Racial Power," *Sociology of Race and Ethnicity* 1, no. 2 (April 1, 2015): 239–54, https://doi.org/10.1177/2332649214568464.

30 Correa and Thomas, "Rebirth of the U.S.-Mexico Border"; Irene I. Vega, "Empathy, Morality, and Criminality: The Legitimation Narratives of U.S. Border Patrol Agents," *Journal of Ethnic and Migration Studies* 44, no. 15 (November 18, 2018): 2544–61, https://doi.org/10.1080/1369183X.2017.1396888.

31 Kanter, *Men and Women of the Corporation.*

32 Kanter; Mary Dodge and Mark Pogrebin, "African-American Policewomen: An Exploration of Professional Relationships," *Policing: An International Journal of Police Strategies & Management* 24, no. 4 (January 1, 2001): 550–62, https://doi.org/10.1108/13639510110409601; Martin, *Breaking and Entering*; Martin, "'Outsider within' the Station House"; Mark Pogrebin, Mary Dodge, and Harold Chatman, "Reflections of African-American Women on Their Careers in Urban Policing. Their Experiences of Racial and Sexual Discrimination," *International Journal of the Sociology of Law* 28, no. 4 (December 1, 2000): 311–26, https://doi.org/10.1006/ijsl.2000.0131.

33 Martin, "'Outsider within' the Station House."

34 Pogrebin, Dodge, and Chatman, "Reflections of African-American Women."

35 Martin, *Breaking and Entering.*

36 Roddrick Colvin, "Shared Perceptions among Lesbian and Gay Police Officers: Barriers and Opportunities in the Law Enforcement Work Environment," *Police Quarterly* 12, no. 1 (March 1, 2009): 86–101, https://doi. org/10.1177/1098611108327308; Christine M. Galvin-White and Eryn Nicole O'Neal, "Lesbian Police Officers' Interpersonal Working Relationships and Sexuality Disclosure: A Qualitative Study," *Feminist Criminology* 11, no. 3 (July 1, 2016): 253–84, https://doi.org/10.1177/1557085115588359; Susan L. Miller, Kay B. Forest, and Nancy C. Jurik, "Diversity in Blue: Lesbian and Gay Police Officers in a Masculine Occupation," *Men and Masculinities* 5, no. 4 (April 1, 2003): 355–85, https://doi.org/10.1177/0095399702250841.

Chapter 5. Training for War

1 According to a 2021 study by the Department of Justice, in 2018, the highest number of instructional hours at police academies was dedicated to firearms (seventy-three hours), then defensive tactics (sixty-one hours), and patrol procedures (fifty-two). Thus, the emphasis on tactical training at the academies I studied was consistent with national trends in police academy training.

2 "Clearing a weapon" refers to a set of actions that ensure that a firearm does not have any ammunition in it. When clearing a pistol, this usually means putting the safety on (if the pistol has one), dropping the magazine (the piece of equipment that holds the bullets) out of the pistol, and pulling and locking the slide back to ensure that there are no rounds of ammunition in the chamber.

3 The details of the video showing this incident were described in chapter 3. The video shows dash-camera footage from a 1998 incident in which Deputy Dinkheller, a young white man, pulls over Andrew Brannan, a middle-aged white man, for speeding. Brannan gets out of the car, starts dancing, and then repeatedly verbally threatens the deputy. The deputy shouts commands at Brannan to "get back" several times. Brannan returns to his truck and retrieves a rifle, all while the officer continues to shout commands. Brannan then fatally shoots Deputy Dinkheller.

4 For cadets with prior military or police experience, some of these embodiments were already learned.

5 Nigel Fielding, "Cop Canteen Culture," in *Just Boys Doing Business? Men, Masculinities and Crime*, ed. Tim Newburn and Elizabeth A. Stanko (London: Routledge, 1994); Prokos and Padavic, "There Oughtta Be a Law against Bitches."

6 Pascoe, *Dude, You're a Fag.*

7 After cadets graduate from the academy, they typically complete several months of field training on patrol. New officers are assigned one or more field training officers, who are tasked with new officers' on-the-job training.

8 The FBI tracks the number of law enforcement officers who are feloniously killed each year. Between 1996 and 2019, on average, fifty-four officers were

feloniously killed annually. The lowest number of felonious deaths within this time range occurred in 2013, when twenty-seven officers were killed; the highest number of felonious deaths within this time range occurred in 1996, when seventy-four officers were killed.

Chapter 6. Pushed Out of Policing

1 E. Buehler, "State and Local Law Enforcement Training Academies."

2 At the academies I studied, this number was usually three.

3 Anima Adjepong, "'They Are like Badges of Honour': Embodied Respectability and Women Rugby Players' Experiences of Their Bruises," *Sport in Society* 19, no. 10 (November 25, 2016): 1489–1502, https://doi.org/10.1080/17430437.2015. 1133602; Wacquant, *Body and Soul*; Dale C. Spencer, "Narratives of Despair and Loss: Pain, Injury and Masculinity in the Sport of Mixed Martial Arts," *Qualitative Research in Sport, Exercise and Health* 4, no. 1 (March 1, 2012): 117–37, https://doi.org/10.1080/2159676X.2011.653499; Kevin Young, Philip White, and William McTeer, "Body Talk: Male Athletes Reflect on Sport, Injury, and Pain," *Sociology of Sport Journal* 11, no. 2 (June 1, 1994): 175–94, https://doi.org/10.1123/ssj.11.2.175.

4 Nicholas Bogel-Burroughs, "A Drunken Hazing, a Fatal Fall and a Cornell Fraternity's Silence," *New York Times*, March 13, 2021, sec. New York, www. nytimes.com; Gentry R. McCreary and Joshua W. Schutts, "Why Hazing? Measuring the Motivational Mechanisms of Newcomer Induction in College Fraternities," *Journal of Cognition and Culture* 19, nos. 3–4 (August 7, 2019): 343–65, https://doi.org/10.1163/15685373-12340063; Nuwer, *Wrongs of Passage*; Stephen Sweet, "Understanding Fraternity Hazing: Insights from Symbolic Interactionist Theory," *Journal of College Student Development* 40, no. 4 (1999): 355–63; C. Huysamer and E. M. Lemmer, "Hazing in Orientation Programmes in Boys-Only Secondary Schools," *South African Journal of Education* 33, no. 3 (August 1, 2013): 1–22, https://doi. org/10.15700/201503070756; Brett G. Stoudt, "'You're Either In or You're Out': School Violence, Peer Discipline, and the (Re)Production of Hegemonic Masculinity," *Men and Masculinities* 8, no. 3 (January 1, 2006): 273–87, https://doi.org/10.1177/1097184X05282070; Sandra L. Kirby and Glen Wintrup, "Running the Gauntlet: An Examination of Initiation/Hazing and Sexual Abuse in Sport," *Journal of Sexual Aggression* 8, no. 2 (July 1, 2002): 49–68, https://doi.org/10.1080/13552600208413339; Michael A. Robidoux, *Men at Play: A Working Understanding of Professional Hockey* (Montreal: McGill-Queen's University Press, 2001); Barrett, "Organizational Construction of Hegemonic Masculinity"; Pershing, "Men and Women's Experiences with Hazing"; Dave Philipps, "Ex-Marine Describes Violent Hazing and the Lies That Covered It Up," *New York Times*, September 30, 2016, sec. US, www.nytimes.com.

5 Ben Kesslen, "Ohio College Student in Critical Condition, Organs to Be Donated after Alleged Hazing Incident," *NBC News*, March 7, 2021.

6 Catherine Porter, "St. Michael's, a Toronto All-Boys School, Is Rocked by Accusations of Sexual Assaults," *New York Times*, November 23, 2018, sec. World, www.nytimes.com.

7 Patrick Fazio, "5 Football Players Charged with 2016 Wheaton College Hazing Incident," *NBC5 Chicago*, September 18, 2017.

8 Dan Lamothe, "Military Hazing Is Often Horrifying—and the Pentagon Has No Idea How Often It Happens," *Washington Post*, February 12, 2016, www.washingtonpost.com.

9 Aldo Cimino, "The Evolution of Hazing: Motivational Mechanisms and the Abuse of Newcomers," *Journal of Cognition and Culture* 11, nos. 3–4 (January 1, 2011): 241–67, https://doi.org/10.1163/156853711X591242; McCreary and Schutts, "Why Hazing?"

10 Kate Wilcox and Bianca Buono, "Handcuffs and Hoods: Goodyear Police Officers Detail 'Hell Day' Hazing," *12News*, April 15, 2021, www.12news.com; Matthew Prendergast and Phil Prazan, "Five Austin Cadets Sent to Hospital after Physical Fitness Training," *KXAN*, October 3, 2019, www.kxan.com; Alana Semuels, "Society Is Paying the Price for America's Outdated Police Training Methods," *Time*, November 20, 2020; Laura Hutchinson, "Police Academy & Instructors Sued for Harassment, Hazing," *22News WWLP*, March 5, 2015; WAFB Staff, "LSP Responds to Allegations of Hazing, Cheating Scandal at Training Academy," *WAFB9*, October 15, 2019.

11 Wilcox and Buono, "Handcuffs and Hoods."

12 Michael Barajas, "The 'Culture of Violence' inside Austin's Police Academy," *Texas Observer*, February 15, 2021, www.texasobserver.org.

Chapter 7. The Future of Policing

1 30×30, "About 30×30," accessed November 30, 2022, https://30x30initiative.org.

2 Cheryl Corley, "Increasing Women Police Recruits to 30% Could Help Change Departments' Culture," *NPR*, July 31, 2022, www.npr.org; Robert Klemko, "This Police Chief Is Hiring More Female Officers to Fix 'Toxic' Policing," *Washington Post*, March 26, 2022, www.washingtonpost.com; Ashley Fantz and Casey Tolan, "Want to Reform the Police? Hire More Women," *CNN*, June 23, 2020, www.cnn.com.

3 Shannon Malone Gonzalez, Samantha J. Simon, and Katie Kaufman Rogers, "The Diversity Officer: Police Officers' and Black Women Civilians' Epistemologies of Race and Racism in Policing," *Law & Society Review* 56, no. 3 (2022): 477–99, https://doi.org/10.1111/lasr.12623.

4 Karen E. Fields and Barbara J. Fields, *Racecraft: The Soul of Inequality in American Life* (New York: Verso, 2014).

5 Maguire, Nix, and Campbell, "War on Cops?"; Shjarback and Maguire, "Extending Research on the 'War on Cops'"; Michael Sierra-Arévalo and Justin Nix, "Gun Victimization in the Line of Duty: Fatal and Nonfatal Firearm Assaults on Police Officers in the United States, 2014–2019," *Criminology & Public Policy* 19 (2020): 1041–66; Michael D. White, Lisa M. Dario, and John A. Shjarback, "Assessing Dangerousness in Policing," *Criminology & Public Policy* 18, no. 1 (2019): 11–35, https://doi.org/10.1111/1745-9133.12408; Michael D. White, "Ambush Killings of the Police, 1970–2018: A Longitudinal Examination of the 'War on Cops' Debate," *Police Quarterly* 23, no. 4 (2020): 451–71, https://doi.org/10.1177/1098611120919441.

6 National Commission on Law Observance and Enforcement, *Report on Lawlessness in Law Enforcement* (Washington, DC: National Commission on Law Observance and Enforcement, 1931), 66–67.

7 President's Commission on Law Enforcement and Administration of Justice, *Challenge of Crime in a Free Society*.

8 President's Task Force on 21st Century Policing, *Final Report of the President's Task Force on 21st Century Policing* (Washington, DC: Office of Community Oriented Policing Services, 2015), https://cops.usdoj.gov.

9 Vitale, *End of Policing*, 27.

10 Vitale, 27.

11 Derecka Purnell, "How I Became a Police Abolitionist," *The Atlantic*, July 6, 2020, www.theatlantic.com.

12 Angela Davis, *Abolition Democracy* (New York: Seven Stories, 2005), 73.

13 Charmaine Chua, "Abolition Is a Constant Struggle: Five Lessons from Minneapolis," *Theory & Event* 23, no. 5 (2020): 141.

14 Chua, 131.

15 Mona Chalabi, "Gun Homicides and Gun Ownership Listed by Country," *The Guardian*, July 22, 2012, sec. News, www.theguardian.com; Nurith Aizenman and Marc Silver, "How the U.S. Compares with Other Countries in Deaths from Gun Violence," *NPR*, August 5, 2019, sec. Health, www.npr.org.

16 David Hemenway, Deborah Azrael, Andrew Conner, and Matthew Miller, "Variation in Rates of Fatal Police Shootings across US States: The Role of Firearm Availability," *Journal of Urban Health* 96, no. 1 (2018): 63–73, https://doi.org/10.1007/s11524-018-0313-z.

17 Aaron J. Kivisto, Bradley Ray, and Peter L. Phalen, "Firearm Legislation and Fatal Police Shootings in the United States," *American Journal of Public Health* 107, no. 7 (July 2017): 1068–75, https://doi.org/10.2105/AJPH.2017.303770.

Methodological Appendix

1 Collins, *Black Feminist Thought*; Crenshaw, "Mapping the Margins"; Donna Haraway, "Situated Knowledges: The Science Question in Feminism and the Privilege of Partial Perspective," *Feminist Studies* 14, no. 3 (1988): 575–99;

Dorothy E. Smith, *The Everyday World as Problematic: A Feminist Sociology* (Toronto: University of Toronto Press, 1987).

2 Wacquant, *Body and Soul.*

3 Loïc Wacquant, "Putting Habitus in Its Place: Rejoinder to the Symposium," *Body & Society* 20, no. 2 (2014): 118.

4 Kimberly Kay Hoang, "Gendering Carnal Ethnography: A Queer Reception," in *Other, Please Specify: Queer Methods in Sociology*, ed. D'Lane Compton, Tey Meadow, and Kristen Schilt (Oakland: University of California Press, 2018), 230–45; Victoria Pitts-Taylor, "A Feminist Carnal Sociology? Embodiment in Sociology, Feminism, and Naturalized Philosophy," *Qualitative Sociology* 38, no. 1 (March 1, 2015): 19–25, https://doi.org/10.1007/s11133-014-9298-4.

5 Kimberly Kay Hoang, *Dealing in Desire: Asian Ascendancy, Western Decline, and the Hidden Currencies of Global Sex Work* (Oakland: University of California Press, 2015), 193.

6 Rebecca Hanson and Patricia Richards, *Harassed: Gender, Bodies, and Ethnographic Research* (Oakland: University of California Press, 2019), 5.

7 Hoang, "Gendering Carnal Ethnography."

8 Wacquant, *Body and Soul*; Randol Contreras, *The Stickup Kids: Race, Drugs, Violence, and the American Dream* (Berkeley: University of California Press, 2012); Matthew Desmond, *On the Fireline: Living and Dying with Wildland Firefighters* (Chicago: University of Chicago Press, 2007).

9 Hoang, *Dealing in Desire*; Ashley Mears, *Pricing Beauty: The Making of a Fashion Model* (Berkeley: University of California Press, 2011).

10 Cadets were required to complete this exercise in order to be issued OC spray to carry on their duty belt. Although technically it was an option for cadets not to complete this exercise, and thus not to carry OC spray on duty, I never heard of a case in which a cadet voluntarily opted out.

11 Collins, *Black Feminist Thought*; Compton, Meadow, and Schilt, *Other, Please Specify*; Georgiann Davis and Torisha Khonach, "The Paradox of Positionality: Avoiding, Embracing, or Resisting Feminist Accountability," *Fat Studies* 9, no. 2 (May 3, 2020): 101–13, https://doi.org/10.1080/21604851.2019.1628604; Kim V. L. England, "Getting Personal: Reflexivity, Positionality, and Feminist Research," *Professional Geographer* 46, no. 1 (February 1, 1994): 80–89, https://doi.org/10.1111/j.0033-0124.1994.00080.x; Alison Rooke, "Queer in the Field: On Emotions, Temporality, and Performativity in Ethnography," *Journal of Lesbian Studies* 13, no. 2 (April 13, 2009): 149–60, https://doi.org/10.1080/10894160802695338.

12 Reuben Jonathan Miller, *Halfway Home: Race, Punishment, and the Afterlife of Mass Incarceration* (New York: Little, Brown, 2021), 288, 289.

13 Dawn Goodwin, Catherine Pope, Maggie Mort, and Andrew Smith, "Ethics and Ethnography: An Experiential Account," *Qualitative Health Research* 13, no. 4 (April 1, 2003): 567–77, https://doi.org/10.1177/1049732302250723; Kimberly

Huisman, "'Does This Mean You're Not Going to Come Visit Me Anymore?':
An Inquiry into an Ethics of Reciprocity and Positionality in Feminist
Ethnographic Research," *Sociological Inquiry* 78, no. 3 (2008): 372–96, https://
doi.org/10.1111/j.1475-682X.2008.00244.x; Judith Stacey, "Can There Be a
Feminist Ethnography?," *Women's Studies International Forum* 11, no. 1 (January
1, 1988): 21–27, https://doi.org/10.1016/0277-5395(88)90004-0.

14 Raul Pacheco-Vega and Kate Parizeau, "Doubly Engaged Ethnography:
Opportunities and Challenges When Working with Vulnerable Communities,"
International Journal of Qualitative Methods 17, no. 1 (December 1, 2018),
https://doi.org/10.1177/1609406918790653; L. Mun Wong, "The Ethics of
Rapport: Institutional Safeguards, Resistance, and Betrayal," *Qualitative Inquiry*
4, no. 2 (June 1, 1998): 178–99, https://doi.org/10.1177/107780049800400203.

15 Sarah Becker and Brittnie Aiello, "The Continuum of Complicity: 'Studying
Up'/Studying Power as a Feminist, Anti-racist, or Social Justice Venture,"
Women's Studies International Forum 38 (May 1, 2013): 63–74, https://doi.
org/10.1016/j.wsif.2013.02.004; Gloria González-López, "Mindful Ethics:
Comments on Informant-Centered Practices in Sociological Research,"
Qualitative Sociology 34, no. 3 (July 22, 2011): 447, https://doi.org/10.1007/
s11133-011-9199-8.

16 Luis L. M. Aguiar and Christopher J. Schneider, *Researching amongst Elites:
Challenges and Opportunities in Studying Up* (New York: Routledge, 2016).

17 Becker and Aiello, "Continuum of Complicity."

Index

Page numbers in italics indicate Figures and Tables.

abolition movement, 77, 213–16
academies. *See* police academies
Acker, Joan, 15
activists, x, xi, 7, 14, 74, 214; BLM movement, 85, 88; police vs., 64, 83–90, 99; scenario-based training and, 85–86; videos, 84, 89–90
adrenaline, 43, 44
Air Force, US, 49
Alabama, firearm prevalence, 217
alcohol, 27, 35, 193
All in the Family (TV show), 106–7
"All Lives Matter," 120–21
ambushing, of police, 69–74, *73*, 78, 100, 107
American police flag, 46–47, *47*
anti-Asian sentiment, 8
anti-Blackness, 124
antisemitism, 107
applicants, for recruitment: acceptance rates, 30; attrition rates, 27, 28, 30, 256n2; background investigations, 24, 26–29, 31–34, 41, 45, 48–50, 52–53, 55–56; board interviews, 26–27, 32–34, 36, 38, 40–41, 44–45, 50, 54–57; conservatives, 59–60; hiring, 23–30; history statement, 27, 28–29, 45; making the cut, 30–60; personality types, 31–40, 59; politics and, 47–52; polygraph exam and, 29–30, 32; reasons for applying, 40–47; violence and, 52–60; wrong reasons for applying, 43–44, 45
Army, US, 49, 53, 115; racial profiling of Black men in, 121–22; veterans, vii–viii, ix, 21–23, 80, 162, 168–69
arrests, 12, 97, 154, 185; of Black people, 9–10; mechanics, 3, 145–46; searches and, 149–50
arson, 30
Asians, 8, 93; cadets, 37, 40, 96–97, 186–87, 191–92; women instructors, 129–30
"ask, tell, make," 147

Atlanta, Georgia, 193
attrition rates: firings, 43, 167, 183–84, 185, 195, 196, 198; police academies and, 19, 182, 183; recruitment applicants, 27, 28, 30, 256n2; resignations, 43, 183–84, 188–90, 192, 193, 196, 199, 200, 201, 202
Austin, Texas, 49, 193, 194
Australia, gun ownership in, 216

background investigators, with hiring, 24, 26–29, 31–34, 41, 45, 48–50, 52–53, 55–56
bad guys, 42, 64, 98, 103, 127; cadets and, 65–69, 99, 102, 210–11, 216; guns and disarming, 165–66; police as, 77; profiling, 106–24; warrior-guardian framework and, 105, 137–38
Baltimore, Maryland, 193
Barlow, Melissa H., 114
Baton Rouge, Louisiana, 119, 193
baton strikes, 140, 153, 154, 155
The Battousai (YouTube channel), 84
Bell, Jeannine, 11
benefits, pay and, 43
"be on the lookout" sheet (BOLO), 146
Berkeley Police Department, 17
Biden, Joe, xi
biracial officers, 116–17
Black children, police and, 11, 121, 122–23
Black City Mother's Bureau, 13
Black Codes, 9
Black communities, police violence in, 209–10
Black feminist thought, 6, 235
Black Lives Matter (BLM) movement, 77, 115, 119, 120; activists, 85, 88; growth of, x, 7, 224
Black men: Army veterans, 21–23; background investigators, 41, 52–53, 55; Black women officers and, 15; cadets, 149–50; criminalization of, 10–11,

109–10, 116, 137; on hiring boards, 41; instructors, 80, 88–89, 115–16, 119, 121–22, 172–74, 190–92, 198–99; police shootings of, x, 7, 11, 80, 81, 82, 83, 87–88, 116, 119, 120–21, 224; in policing, 13–14; recruiting officers, 21–23, 30, 34–35, 36, 55, 57; sergeants, 80, 88–89, 115–16, 119, 121–22, 172–74, 190–92, 198–99; stereotypes of, 11; as threat, 106, 137; in US Army with racial profiling, 121–22; veterans as firearms instructors, 80
Blackness, 9–10, 11, 114, 116, 124
Black officers: double consciousness and, 123; men, 21–23, 30, 34–35, 36, 55, 57; police shootings of, 123; populations, 14; racial profiling of, 123, 137; racism and, 15; as warrior officers, 115–24, 137; women, 12–13, 15, 117–18, 122–23
Black people: arrests of, 9–10; criminalization of, 10–11, 82–83, 113–14; double consciousness and, 123; life expectancy, 10; police shootings of, 118, 119; racial stereotypes of, 11, 15, 93, 131; racism and, 106–7; surveillance of, 103, 212
Black Visions Collective, 214
Black women: Black City Mother's Bureau and, 13; instructors, 66–67; as liabilities on patrol, 131; maternal morbidity and, 10; as outsider, 123; police sexual misconduct and, 11; police shootings of, xi, 7, 78; racialized sexual exploitation of, 13; racialized stereotypes of, 15, 131; with racism and sexism, 137
Black women officers: with harassment and racism, 15; hiring, 12–13; with outsider concept, 123; on racial profiling, 117–18, 122–23
Black Youth Project, 214

BLM movement. *See* Black Lives Matter movement
Blue Lives Matter, 224
board interviews, 36, 50; dishonesty in, 32–34; questions, 26–27, 38, 40–41, 44–45, 54–57
body: brachial plexus origin, 152–53; cameras, 78, 96–97; center of mass, 159, 162, 239; choke holds, 134, 157; embodied costs of fieldwork, 236–37, 240–42, 246; hand placement, 108–9, 136, 165; hurting, 38–39, 71, 141, 150–58, 181, 184–85, 190–91, 193–94, 200, 231, 243–46; knowledge production and, 6, 235; language, 90, 107, 109, 112, 143; movements, 108, 136, 165; physical control, 148–50, 179; pre-attack indicators, 108, 109; pressure points, 150–53, 236; redman exercise and, 139–42; trusting gut hunches, 109. *See also* training
BOLO ("be on the lookout" sheet), 146
Bonilla-Silva, Eduardo, 112
Border Patrol, US, 8, 115, 123–24
Boston, Massachusetts, 17
Bowling Green State University, 193
brachial plexus origin, 152–53
Brannan, Andrew, 67–68, 264n3
"Breakout Workout," 168–69
bribes, 36
brotherhood, 44, 103, 120, 127, 159
Brown, Michael, x, 7, 11, 83, 87–88, 224
brutality, 17, 86, 212

cadets: Asian, 37, 40, 96–97, 186–87, 191–92; attrition rates, 19, 43, 167, 182–85, 188–90, 192–93, 195–96, 198–202; bad guys and, 65–69, 99, 102, 210–11, 216; Black men, 149–50; career trajectory, 264n7; on DT training experience, 197; gradua-

tion, 5, 6, 18, 81, 172, 180–82, 183, 185, 187, 189, 192, 199; hazing of, 193–94; Latinas, 137, 146, 148, 186; Latinos, 163–64, 168–69; on news media, 81; "recycled," 185; transformation of, 4–5, 6, 98, 143; US veterans as, 72, 75, 131, 168–69, 186–87, 191–92, 197, 199, 204, 264n4; white men, 155–56; women, 2–5, 7, 11, 68, 72, 129–35, 137, 146–48, 151–53, 156, 157, 163, 165–67, 168–70, 178–79, 181, 186, 189, 200–204, 208–9, 244–46. *See also* defensive tactics (DT) training; physical training; scenario-based training; warfare training
CALEA (Commission on Accreditation for Law Enforcement Agencies), 18
California, 12–13, 18, 49
calling, policing as, 41–42, 43, 45, 59, 102
Camden County Police Department, 70–71
cameras: body, 78, 96–97; footage from dash, 67, 147, 264n3
Canada, gun ownership in, 216
captains, 162, 181, 237
career fairs, recruitment, 6, 21–23, 34, 53, 226
Caribbean, slavery in, 8
Carlson, Jennifer, 104
carnal ethnography, 6, 241
carnal sociology, 235
Carolinas, colonists in, 8
carrying. *See* license to carry
Carson, Roger, 66
case law, 4, 101, 126
Castile, Philando, x
castle doctrine, viii
center of mass, aiming for, 159, 162, 239
The Challenge of Crime in a Free Society report (1967), 212
Chicago, with crime, 125, 126
Chicago Police Department, 52, 95

chiefs of police, ix, 71, 235; at graduation, 181–82; with leadership, 13,
17, 51, 206–7, 209; on police sexual
misconduct, 97
children, x, 3, 13, 35, 79, 103, 110, 117–18;
family and officers, 36–37, 70, 127,
181, 231, 256n1; as innocents to be
protected, ix, 105, 129, 137; police and
Black, 11, 121, 122–23; Police Explorer
Program and, 145–46
CHL (concealed handgun license), vii
choke holds, 134, 157
Chua, Charmaine, 215
Civil Rights Act (1964), 10, 13
Clark, Stephon, x
class A offense, 24–25
class B offense, 24–25
"clearing a weapon," 264n2
Clinton, Hillary, 85, 257n10
CNN, 209
cognitive tests, 26
Collins, Patricia Hill, 123
colonization, slavery and, 8
color-blind ideology, 112–13, 120–21
commanders, 24, 44, 66, 93, 207, 227
commands: giving, 68, 143–47, 149, 154,
156, 157, 178; verbal, 67, 147–48, 177,
264n3
Commission on Accreditation for Law
Enforcement Agencies (CALEA),
18
Commission on Law Enforcement and
Administration of Justice, 18, 212
communities: with day and night
watches, 9; foot patrols, 14, 16, 104,
173; police violence in Black and
Latino, 209–10; residential segregation, 10
community policing, 16, 104, 136, 207
complaints, 54, 94–99, 100
compliance, 54, 142, 144, 147, 150, 174,
178, 205

concealed handgun license (CHL), vii
Connecticut, firearm prevalence, 217
conservatives, 34, 59–60, 213–14; gun
ownership, 49, 232; news media, 48,
77; officers as, 50, 51–52; Republicans, 48–51
"cop culture," 168, 209
cop eyes, 73
corruption, 17, 35, 36, 212
COVID-19, xi
credit history, 25, 35–36
crime, 81–83, 87–88, 114, 125, 126, 212
Crime Control Act (1973), 13
crime-fighter image, 16, 103, 104, 136
criminality, 46–47, 109–14, 116–18, 124,
136
criminalization, race and, 9–11, 82–83,
109–10, 113–14, 116, 137
criminal law, 9, 187
Critical Resistance, 214
critical thinking skills, 27
culture, cop, 168, 209

damage, doing, 150
dash-camera footage, 67, 147, 264n3
data collection, statistical, 10
Davis, Angela, 214
day watches, night and, 9
deadly force, killing and, x, 72, 91, 102,
103, 120, 158–59, 207
death: and children, ix–x, 79; of civilians
by officers, xi, 7, 78, 79, 83, 86–87, 92,
99, 178, 179, 213; from college fraternity hazing, 193; dying and killing,
126–28, 136, 142, 158, 178; funerals,
127, 177; killing, x, 72, 91, 102–3, 120,
126–28, 136, 142, 158–62, 175–76, 178,
207; by lethal injection, 68; mytholo-
gizing, 104; of officers, 19, 66–69,
72–73, 73, 74, 103, 147, 177, 210, 216,
264n3, 264n8; suicide, 73, 174–75;
survivability, 158

de-escalation: as nothing new, 172–79; training, 67–68, 77–78, 90–91, 94, 108–9, 147, 173–75, 177–79, 215, 224; verbal skills, 173, 211

defensive solidarity, 64

defensive tactics (DT) training: arrest mechanics, 145–46; arrests and searches, 149–50; bad guy and, 65; "Breakout Workout," 168–69; cadets on, 197; disarming bad guy with gun, 165–66; discipline and correction, 165–66, 168, 216; ethnography and, 237; failures and termination, 167, 182; fighting, 162–68, 178; final exam, 52, 146–47, 149–50, 153–55, 166–68; giving commands, 143–47, 149, 154, 156, 157, 178; gun retained in fight, 167–68; guns, 145, 146, 147, 154, 165–68, 195–96, 201, 216–17; gym, 3, 61–62, 142–43, 230–31, 238; handcuffing, 142–43, 156–57; hurting, 150–58; injuries, 141, 156, 157, 181; instructional hours dedicated to, 264n1; instructors, 42–44, 47–48, 52–53, 62–63, 69, 142–47, 149–68, 171–77, 184, 186–87, 190–91, 194–99, 229–31, 234; killing, 158–62; OC Spray, 74–76, 77, 89–90, 234, 241–45, 268n10; oxygen deprivation and, 153–54; physical control, 148–50, 179; redman exercise and, 139–42, 154; sexism and, 168–70; strikes and, 47, 75, 144, 164, 186, 194, 230, 245; "taking it easy" on women during, 130, 131–32; TASER Day, 76, 170–72, 241–42; week, 47–48, 61–63, 186–87, 194–95, 229–31; women and, 3, 130–32. See also scenario-based training

"defunding the police," xi, 213–15

Democrats, 51

demographic form, 256n1

Demographic Unit, NYPD, 8

Department of Justice, US, 7, 95, 182, 264n1

Diallo, Amadou, 82

Dinkheller, Kyle, 67–68, 147, 177, 264n3

discipline: DT training with correction and, 165–66, 168, 216; femininity and gendered, 170–72; in personalities, 37–39; with sexism, 168–70

discrimination, 10, 13, 84, 92, 106, 107

dishonesty, 30–34, 35, 99, 109, 185

dishonorable discharge, US military, 25

dispatch, 96, 145

dispatchers, 911, viii, 214

distrust, x, xi, 45, 210

diversity: cultural, 84; hiring initiatives, 11, 53, 208–10, 212, 215, 224; policing and demographic, 117

"doing damage," 150

domestic disturbances, 4

domestic violence, 53

dominance, masculinity and, 15–16

domination, violence and, 17, 178

double consciousness, 123

drivers, racial profiling, 114

driving violations, 25

drugs, 27, 34, 108, 193; illegal, 25, 93, 94, 122, 146; use and hiring, 29–30, 33, 35, 41, 256n5

DT. See defensive tactics (DT) training

Du Bois, W. E. B., 123

dying. See death

eligibility requirements, recruitment, 25

emotional strength, 185, 190, 246

emotions, 16, 34, 170

empathy and power, with ethnography, 246–48

Epp, Charles, 114

ethics, professionalism and, 43–44, 77, 93

ethnography, 23, 223; carnal, 6, 241;
with empathy and power, 246–48;
physical toll of, 235–46; women and,
236–37, 240–42
exams. *See* tests
exploitation, with sex and race, 13

Facebook, x
"Fairview" Sheriff's Office, 6, 119, 159
family, 136, 183, 185; brotherhood, 44,
103, 120, 127, 159; fellow officers as,
64, 98; officers and, 36–37, 70, 127,
181, 231, 256n1. *See also* children
FBI (Federal Bureau of Investigation),
18, 74, 264n8
femininity, 16, 187; with gendered
disciplining, 170–72; sexism and,
168–70
feminist methodologies, 247
feminist theories, 235
Ferguson, Missouri, x, 74, 79, 83, 87–88,
224
Ferguson Police Department, 7, 87–88
field sites: description of, *228*; in mid-to
large-size cities in southern states,
5–6, 228; selecting, 227–28
field training officer (FTO), 109, 111,
129–30, 175
fieldwork: embodied costs of, 236–37,
240–42, 246; empathy and power
with, 246–48
"Fight (Will to Win) Day," 162–65
fighting: back, 56, 166; bad at, 195–96,
197, 198, 199, 200–203; crime-fighter
image, 16, 103, 104, 136; DT training,
162–68, 178; grappling, 61–62, 132,
154–57, 166–67; gunfights, viii, 72,
158, 159; with gun retained, 167–68;
hiring and experience with, 52–58;
takedowns, 47, 156–57, 186–87, 194–
95; women with, 56–58, 203. *See also*
warfare training

Filipinas, 129–30
finances, 25, 35–36
firearms: "clearing a weapon," 264n2;
guns, vii–viii, ix, 37, 49, 65, 76, 105,
108–9, 141, 144–47, 154, 160–72,
195–96, 201, 207, 216–18, 223, 232,
241–42; instructional hours dedicated to, 264n1; instructors, 46, 63,
65, 71–73, 76, 80, 119, 158–63, 170,
172, 187, 195, 223–24, 230–31, 238–40,
242–43; license-to-carry, vii–ix, xii,
49, 223; marksmanship and, 65, 71,
158; "post-engagement checklist,"
159–60; range, 159, 160–61, 237–40;
range master and, 65, 71; scenario-
based training, 160–62, 216–17. *See
also* shootings
firearms-training classes, for civilians, ix,
xi, 16, 223–24, 227
firing, of cadets and attrition rates, 43,
167, 183–84, 185, 195, 196, 198
flags, 181, 188; American police, 46–47,
47; US military, 48, 128
flashlights, 160
Florida, "Stand Your Ground" law, ix–x
Floyd, George, xi, 7, 83, 213
Foltz, Stone, 193
foot patrols, 14, 16, 104, 173
force: deadly, x, 72, 91, 102, 103, 120,
158–59, 207; excessive, 94, 118–19,
198; improper, 95; options, 51, 94,
101, 102–3, 126–28; physical, 57–58,
143, 147, 173, 175–78; use of, viii, 52–
58, 68, 77, 82, 88, 91, 100–101, 118, 119,
141, 147, 161–66, 184, 201–2, 207, 229
Fort Sill, Oklahoma, 21–23
Fox News, 48, 77
Fraternal Order of Police, 52
frisks, 85–86, 95–97, 110, 112, 148–49,
216, 242
FTO (field training officer), 109, 111,
129–30, 175

Fundamentals of Marksmanship class, 65, 71, 158
funerals, 127, 177

gangs, 32, 109–10
Garner, Eric, 86–87, 92, 99
Garza, Alicia, x
gender, 93, 256n1; discipline and femininity, 170–72; fighting and, 56–58; frisks and searches, 95–97; PT tests and, 25–26, 38; race and, ix, 11–17, 42, 106, 109–10, 130–31, 188, 209, 213, 226; with women as warrior officers, 129–35, 137
geography, criminality and, 111
Georgia, 193, 217
Gershon, Ilana, 46
Gilmore, Ruth, 214
The Good, the Bad, and the Ugly (film), 176
Goodyear, Pennsylvania, 193, 194
graduations, police academies, 5, 6, 18, 81, 172, 180–82, 183, 185, 187, 189, 192, 199
Graham v. Connor, 118
grappling, 61–62, 132, 154–57, 166–67
Gray, Freddie, x
Greenwood, Clinton, 73
Grossman, David, 104
group solidarity, 63–64, 98, 193
guardians: framework, 206–7, 212; warriors and, 102–6, 124–26, 128–30, 132, 135–38, 206–7
gunfights, viii, 72, 158, 159
gun nut, 49
guns, 65, 144, 207; body placement with, 108–9; CHL, vii; DT training, 145, 146, 147, 154, 165–68, 195–96, 201, 216–17; fighting and retaining, 167–68; ownership, vii–viii, ix, 49, 105, 216–18, 223, 232; redman exercise and, 141; scenario-based training and,

160–62, 216–17; TASER, 37, 76, 170–72, 201, 241–42; warfare training, 162–72. *See also* firearms; shootings, civilians; shootings, police
gut hunches, trusting, 109

Hadden, Sally, 8
Haider-Markel, Donald, 114
Hamilton, Mary E., 12
handcuffing, 3, 109, 142–43, 156–57, 194
hand placement, 108–9, 136, 165
Hanson, Rebecca, 239
Harris County Sheriff's Office, 72–73, 73
hazing, 193–94
"Hell Day," 194
Heraclitus, 102
Herbert, Steve, 16
heterosexuality, 12, 104–5, 137
hiring: background investigators with, 24, 26–29, 31–34, 36, 41, 45, 48–50, 52–53, 55–56; Black women as officers, 12–13; conservative ethos with training and, 34, 48–49, 51; decisions, 23; disqualifications, 25, 27, 32–34, 45, 53; diversity initiatives in, 11, 53, 208–10, 212, 215, 224; drug use and, 29–30, 33, 35, 41, 256n5; fighting experience and, 52–58; initiatives and women, 208–9; institutional fit and, 186–205; occupational fit and evaluations, 182–83; officers and board interviews, 26–27, 32–34, 36, 38, 40–41, 44–45, 50, 54–57; politics and, 48–49; practices and institutionalized policing, 59–60; practices and racism, 59; qualifications for, 183–86; units, 21–34, 36–41, 44–45, 48–50, 52–53, 55–57, 184, 226; warfare training and future of policing, 208–11; white men and exclusionary practices, 12

hiring officers, 24, 226; attrition rates and, 256n2; making the cut and, 30–31, 36, 38–39, 41, 50, 52–57; personalities, 62; with polygraph exams, 30; recruitment interviews and, 198, 256n4. *See also* recruitment

Hispanic men, on hiring units, 24–27, 28–30, 31

history statement, applicants, 27, 28–29, 45

Hoang, Kimberly, 236, 241

homophobia, 135, 170, 193, 208

Hoover, Herbert, 212

Human Factor Science, 151

humiliation, 8, 165, 168, 172, 186–87, 192–93, 196, 206

hunches, trusting gut, 109

hurting: injuries, 141, 156, 157, 181, 184, 185, 193, 194; pain, 38, 39, 71, 150, 190, 191, 200, 231, 243–46; warfare training and, 150–58

ICE (Immigration and Customs Enforcement), US, 51, 111

Idaho, firearm prevalence, 217

identity, 92, 93, 135, 256n1. *See also* warriors, officers as

Immigration and Customs Enforcement (ICE), US, 51, 111

INCITE, 214

"Increasing Women Police Recruits to 30% Could Help Change Departments' Culture" (NPR), 209

initiation rituals, 193–94

injuries: DT training, 141, 156, 157, 181; hazing, 193, 194; PT, 184, 185, 194

institutional fit: being bad at violence, 194–99; doing whatever it takes, 188–94, 204; "good," 187–92, 203; policing and, 186–205; unwillingness to use violence, 195, 199–205

instructors: on ambushes, 70–71; Black men, 80, 88–89, 115–16, 119, 121–22, 172–74, 190–92, 198–99; Black women, 66–67; with cadets and graduation, 180–82; with de-escalation training, 67–68, 77–78, 90–91, 94; DT, 42–44, 47–48, 52–53, 62–63, 69, 142–47, 149–68, 171–77, 184, 186–87, 190–91, 194–99, 229–31, 234; firearms, 46, 63, 65, 71–73, 76, 80, 119, 158–63, 170, 172, 187, 195, 223–24, 230–31, 238–40, 242–43; force options, 101–3, 126–28; on gender, frisks and searches, 95–96; with hazing, 193–94; on institutional fit, 189–90; on killing and dying, 126–28, 136, 178; Latinos, 42–43, 47–48, 52–53, 63, 151–53, 155–56, 163, 171, 183; license-to-carry, vii–ix, xii; multiculturalism classes, 84, 106–8, 109, 111, 112; on news media, 64, 77–81; OC spray and, 75–77, 242–45; police academies, 1–3; with politics, 47–48, 50–51; PT, 38–39, 129–30, 189; on PT, 185; on race and racism, 115–16; on racial profiling, 107–14, 121–22; on rigors of police academy, 192, 204–5; on using violence, 199–200; white men, vii–ix, xii, 1, 3, 43–44, 46, 48, 51, 63, 65, 71–73, 76–78, 84–85, 89, 94, 101, 106–7, 109, 111–12, 130, 135, 142–45, 151–53, 157–60, 163, 171–72, 174–77, 187, 195–96, 198, 207, 230–31, 234, 238–40, 242–44; women, 38–39, 66–67, 76, 109, 111, 129–30, 149–50

International Association of Chiefs of Police, 97

interviews, 55, 198, 225, 256n4. *See also* board interviews

Jackson, Jesse, 79

Jean, Botham, x

Johnson, Lyndon B., 14, 18, 212
justice, 7, 18, 95, 182, 212, 264n1

Kaba, Mariame, 214
Kenny, William Francis, 73
Kerner Commission (National Advisory Commission on Civil Disorders), 14
killing: deadly force, x, 72, 91, 102, 103, 120, 158–59, 207; dying and, 126–28, 136, 142, 158, 178; murder and, 126–27; warfare training and, 158–62, 175–76. *See also* death
"killology," 104
knowledge: production, 6, 45–46, 235; white ignorance, 112–13
Ku Klux Klan, 9, 59, 115

labor strikes, 7–8
labor unions, 52, 166, 214
LAPD (Los Angeles Police Department), 12–13
LAPD City Mother's Bureau, 13
Latin America, slavery in, 8
Latinas: background investigators, 50, 55, 56; cadets, 137, 146, 148, 186; instructors, 149–50; with racism and sexism, 137
Latinos: cadets, 163–64, 168–69; criminality of, 124; instructors, 42–43, 47–48, 52–53, 63, 151–53, 155–56, 163, 171, 183; sergeants, 42, 224–25, 230; teenagers with Police Explorer Program, 145–46
Latinos/as: Border Patrol officers, 123–24; communities and police violence, 209–10; criminalization of, 109–10; with discrimination, 10; surveillance of, 212
Laurens County Sheriff's Department, 67

laws: Black Codes, 9; case, 4, 101, 126; CHL, vii; Civil Rights Act, 10, 13; Crime Control Act, 13; criminal, 9, 187; Metropolitan Police Bill and UK, 17; National Origins Act, 8; "Stand Your Ground," ix–x
lawsuits, 64, 94, 193–94
lethal injection, 68
LGBTQ, 8, 51
liberals, 46, 51, 85, 215, 232; cities, 49, 50, 89, 235; news media, 77, 100; as threat to white men, 105
license to carry: classes, vii–viii, 223; instructors, vii–ix, xii; laws, 49
lieutenants, white men, 35–36, 38, 42, 51, 84–85, 106–7, 109, 111–12, 173–74, 184, 226, 229
life expectancy, Black people, 10
Loftus, Bethan, 64
Los Angeles Police Department (LAPD), 12–13
Louisville Metro Police Department, 17
low light situations, guns in, 65, 160

Marines, US, 42, 48, 49, 75, 86, 164, 166–68, 175–76, 193
marketing videos, 206–7
marksmanship, 65, 71, 158
Martin, Susan, 14–15, 130, 134–35
Martin, Trayvon, ix–x
masculinity, 15, 105, 191, 193; crimefighter image and, 16, 103, 104; gendered discipline and, 170–72; ideals, 195–96; sexism and, 168–70; whiteness and, xi, 12, 187
Massachusetts, 17, 193, 217
maternal morbidity, 10
Mattis, James (General), 175–76
Maynard-Moody, Steven, 114
Mears, Ashley, 241
media, entertainment, 106–7, 176, 215

media, news: ambushing of police in, 70–71, 78; cadets on, 81; conservative, 48, 77; with criminalization of Black people, 10–11, 82; instructors on, 77–81; liberal, 77, 100; with police accounts of violence privileged, 82, 100; with police interactions on video, 77–79, 84; police shootings of Black men in, 80, 81, 83, 87, 116; on police violence, 79–81, 82–83, 87, 90; police vs., 64, 74–83, 87–90, 99, 100, 229; the public inflamed by, 80–81, 88–89, 99; with race and crime-related stories, 81–83, 87–88; study of police shootings in, 82–83; on women and hiring initiatives, 209

men: Asian, 37, 40, 96–97, 186–87; of color as military veterans, 53; ethnography and, 241; officers on women coworkers, 132–34; South Asian, 37, 96–97. *See also* Black men; Latinos; white men

mental health, 19, 22, 78, 202

mental strength, 185, 190

Metropolitan Police Bill, UK, 17

Mexicans, 8, 85–86

Mexico border, with US, 111

military, US: Air Force, 49; Army, vii–viii, ix, 21–23, 49, 53, 80, 115, 121–22, 162, 168–69; dishonorable discharge, 25; flags, 48, 128; heterosexuality and, 105; Marines, 42, 48, 49, 75, 86, 164, 166–68, 175–76, 193; men and women of color overrepresented in, 53; Navy, 37, 41, 49, 61–62, 197. *See also* veterans

Miller, Reuben Jonathan, 246

Mills, Charles W., 112–13

mind-set: mental health and, 19, 22, 78, 202; mental strength, 185, 190; warrior, 102, 125, 126, 137, 196, 205; weak,

43, 189, 201–3. *See also* whatever it takes

minorities: police shootings of, 44; as threat, 105

Mueller, Jennifer, 113

Muhammad, Khalil Gibran, 9

multiculturalism, 51, 83–84, 106–8, 109, 111, 112, 163

Muslims, 8

National Academy of the Federal Bureau of Investigation (FBI), 18

National Advisory Commission on Civil Disorders (Kerner Commission), 14

National Commission on Law Observance and Enforcement (Wickersham Commission), 212

nationality, with race and criminality, 111

National Origins Act (1924), 8

National Public Radio (NPR), 209

National Rifle Association (NRA), 49

Native Americans, 8

Navy, US, 37, 41, 49, 61–62, 197

neoliberal economies, 46

New York, firearm prevalence, 217

New York Police Department (NYPD), 8, 12, 17, 52, 86–87

New York Times (newspaper), xi

night watches, day and, 9

911, viii, 131, 214

Nixon, Richard, 103

nonwhites, 8, 19, 106, 112–13

NPR (National Public Radio), 209

NRA (National Rifle Association), 49

NYPD (New York Police Department), 8, 12, 17, 52, 86–87

Obama, Barack, x, 7, 212

Occupy protests, 89–90

OC (oleoresin capsicum, pepper) spray, 74–76, 77, 89–90, 234, 241–45, 268n10

"officer friendly" programs, 103
officers: biracial, 116–17; Black, 12–15,
    21–23, 30, 34–36, 55, 57, 115–24,
    137; Border Patrol, 123–24; civilians
    shooting, 67–68, 70–71, 72–73, 73,
    78, 119, 147, 177, 264n3; death of, 19,
    66–69, 72–73, 73, 74, 103, 147, 177,
    210, 216, 264n3, 264n8; death of civil-
    ians by, xi, 7, 78, 79, 83, 86–87, 92, 99,
    178, 179, 213; with family, 36–37, 70,
    127, 181, 231, 256n1; family and fellow,
    64; rapport-building with, 228–32;
    recruiting, 21–23; safety of, 91, 100,
    108–9, 147, 166, 173–74, 176–77;
    white men, 130–31; white women,
    12. See also hiring officers; warriors,
    officers as
oleoresin capsicum (OC, pepper) spray,
    74–76, 77, 89–90, 234, 241–45,
    268n10
outsider, Black women as, 123
ownership, guns: civilian, vii–viii,
    217, 218, 223; conservative, 49, 232;
    lowering, 217–18; in other countries,
    216; police shootings and, 217; police
    violence and civilian, 217, 218; white
    men, ix, 105
oxygen deprivation, 153–54, 184

pain: compliance, 150; firearms training
    and, 71; inflicting, 200; OC spray
    and, 243–46; physical, 38, 39, 200,
    231; tolerance, 190, 191
Pantaleo, Daniel, 86–87
Parliament, UK, 17
part-time gigs (side jobs), ix, 24, 27
Pascoe, C. J., 16, 170
passion, for policing, 43, 45–46, 183, 189
patrol procedures, 185, 264n1
pay (salaries), 43, 58
Peace Officer and Training Standards
    (POST) organizations, 18

Peel, Robert (Sir), 17
pepper spray. See OC spray
personalities: desirable traits, 31, 35,
    36–37, 59; with discipline, 37–39;
    dishonesty, 31–34, 35; DT instruc-
    tors, 62; hiring officers, 62; recruit-
    ment applicants with right, 31–40,
    59; teamwork and reliability, 39–40,
    56; tests, 26
Pew Research Center, x
Philadelphia, with crime, 125, 126
physical control, warfare training and,
    148–50, 179
physical exam, 30, 32
physical fitness, 4, 38–39, 129, 156, 181
physical force, 57–58, 143, 147, 173,
    175–78
physical training (PT), 6, 228; class,
    188–89; injuries, 184, 185, 194;
    instructors, 38–39, 129–30, 189; tests,
    25–26, 38–39, 57, 184, 185, 186, 187,
    199, 242; training, 84, 184–85, 192,
    204
Pi Kappa Alpha, Bowling Green State
    University, 193
plainclothes detectives, 8, 70–71, 93
police: American police flag, 46–47,
    47; as bad guys, 77; defunding, xi,
    213–15; Fraternal Order of Police, 52;
    interacting with, viii; reform, 77, 178,
    208–9, 211–15, 224; role of, 124–26;
    stereotypes, 93; unions, 52, 166. See
    also specific topics
police academies: attrition rates, 19,
    182, 183; graduations, 5, 6, 18, 81,
    172, 180–82, 183, 185, 187, 189, 192,
    199; highest number of instructional
    hours at, 264n1; with lawsuits for
    hazing, 193–94; origins and history,
    17–20; requirements, 19; rigors, 192–
    93, 204–5; wall of honor, 66. See also
    cadets

police departments, formation of US, 9. *See also specific departments*

Police Explorer Program, 145–46

Police Memorial Week, 66

PoliceOne.com, 70

police violence: in Black and Latino communities, 209–10; civilian gun ownership and, 217, 218; fighting experience and, 54–55; news media on, 79–81, 82–83, 87, 90; with privileged accounts in news media, 82, 100; racist, xi, 8, 52, 54, 59–60, 83, 208–9; as state violence, 207–8

policing: Black men in, 13–14; as calling, 41–42, 43, 45, 59, 102; career trajectory for cadets, 264n7; children with career in, 70; community, 16, 104, 136, 207; demographic diversity and, 117; evolution of, 119–20, 159, 172–73; hiring practices and institutionalized, 59–60; institutional fit, 186–205; masculinity and, 16; passion for, 43, 45–46, 183, 189; political era of, 17; power with race and, 92, 93; promotions in, 12, 14, 15; qualifications for, 183–86; race and gender in, 11–17; as safer over time, 74; Task Force on 21st Century Policing, x, 7, 212; white women in, 12–15, 130; Wickersham Commission on, 212; women in, 4–5, 12–13, 14–15, 19

policing, future of: with hiring and warfare training, 208–11; pathways forward, 211–19; reform, 77, 178, 208–9, 211–15, 224; violence and, 207–8

political era of policing, 17

political meanings of presence, 232–35

politics: background investigators and, 48–49; with "defunding the police" ads, 213–14; Democrats, 51; recruitment applicants with right, 47–52;

Republicans, 48–51. *See also* conservatives; liberals

polygraph exam, 29–30, 32

"post-engagement checklist," firearms, 159–60

POST (Peace Officer and Training Standards) organizations, 18

post-traumatic stress disorder (PTSD), 68, 199

power: fieldwork with empathy and, 246–48; with race and policing, 92, 93; racial profiling and abuse of, 122; violence and, 43, 44

PPCT (pressure point control tactics), 151

pre-attack indicators, 108, 109

prejudice, discrimination and, 84, 92, 106, 107

presence, political meanings of, 232–35

pressure point control tactics (PPCT), 151

pressure points, body, 150–53, 236

professionalism and ethics class, 43–44, 77, 93

profiling: bad guys, 106–24; criminality, 109–14, 116–18, 136; race-neutral concepts with, 116, 117; racial, 107–14, 116–18, 121–23, 136, 137

promotions, in policing, 12, 14, 15

protests, x, xi, 7, 14, 74, 89–90

psychiatric evaluation, 30

PT. *See* physical training

PTSD (post-traumatic stress disorder), 68, 199

public-servant image, 102–3, 136, 182

the public: ambushing of police by, 69–74, 73, 78, 100, 107; with complaints, 94–99, 100; firearms-training classes for civilians, ix, xi, 16, 223–24, 227; frisks and searches of, 95–97; news media inflaming, 80–81, 88–89, 99; police relations with, 79–80, 82, 85–

87, 88–89, 92–93, 100, 104, 105–6, 137, 145–46, 207, 209–12; police vs., 64, 79–81, 85–100
Puerto Ricans, 161, 162
The Purge (film), 215
Purnell, Derecka, 214

quantitative skills, 26
queer bars, raids on, 8
quitting. *See* attrition rates; resigning

race, 77, 89; civilian complaints and, 95; color-blind ideology and, 112–13, 120–21; crime and, 114; criminality, nationality and, 111; criminalization and, 9–11, 82–83, 109–10, 113–14, 116, 137; gender and, ix, 11–17, 42, 106, 109–10, 130–31, 188, 209, 213, 226; identity and, 92, 93, 256n1; injustice, x, xi, 85, 86; Kerner Commission on inequality, 14; news media on crime and, 81–83, 87–88; as organizational trait, 15; power with policing and, 92, 93; profiling, 107–14, 116–18, 121–23, 136, 137; racism and, 111–13, 115–16, 121; sex with exploitation and, 13. *See also* stereotypes, racialized; *specific races*
race-neutral concepts, with profiling, 116, 117
racism: anti-Blackness and, 124; anti-semitism, 107; Black people and, 106–7; Black women officers with harassment and, 15; children with, 117–18; entertainment media with, 106–7; hiring practices and, 59; with police violence, xi, 8, 52, 54, 59–60, 83, 208–9; race and, 111–13, 115–16, 121; scenario-based training and, 85–86; sexism and, 137, 247–48; systemic, 9–10, 11; violence and, 7, 44, 54, 218; white officers and, 15; white

women officers with, 15; women with sexism and, 137
raids, on queer bars, 8
range master, 65, 71
rape, 97, 193
reading comprehension, 26
reasonableness, 78, 88, 118–19, 121, 162
recruitment: applying and, 23–30; career fairs, 6, 21–23, 34, 53, 226; eligibility requirements, 25; hiring officers and, 24, 30–31, 36, 38–39, 41, 50, 52–57, 62, 198, 226, 256n2, 256n4; interviews, 55, 198, 256n4; of military veterans, 21–23, 53–55; networks, 28–29; officers, 21–23, 30, 34–35, 36, 55, 57; women and hiring initiatives, 208–9. *See also* applicants, for recruitment
"recycled," cadets, 185
redman exercise, 139–42, 154
reform, police, 77, 178, 208–9, 211–15, 224
Reichel, Philip, 9
reliability, teamwork and, 39–40, 56
Republicans, 48–51
residential segregation, 10
resigning, cadets quitting, 43, 183–84, 188–90, 192, 193, 196, 199, 200, 201, 202
Richards, Patricia, 239
rituals, 75, 139, 162–64, 193–94, 197
Robinson, Georgia Ann, 13
Rockwell, Norman, 104
romantic relationships, 130
Runaway (painting), 104
Russell-Brown, Katheryn, 10–11

safety, of officers, 91, 100, 108–9, 147, 166, 173–74, 176–77
St. Michael's College School, Toronto, 193
salaries (pay), 43, 58

San Jose Police Department, 18
scenario-based training, 5, 6, 56, 69, 173, 226, 228, 233, 238; activists, racism and, 85–86; authority and giving commands, 143–47; discipline and correction, 165–66, 216; domestic disturbance, 4; failing, 196–97; firearms, 160–62, 216–17; force options, 101; role of, 145; use-of-force, 161–66, 201–2, 207, 229; violence and, 128, 165–66, 206–7
Scott, Walter, x
searches: arrests and, 149–50; frisks and, 95–97, 110, 216
Sebastian, Charles, 13
segregation, residential, 10
self-defense, viii, ix–x
"sensory overstimulation," 155
sergeants, 30, 53, 188, 227, 233, 236, 238; Black men, 80, 88–89, 115–16, 119, 121–22, 172–74, 190–92, 198–99; Latinos, 42, 224–25, 230; white men, 39–40, 49–50, 61–62, 69–71, 78–81, 94, 124–26, 169–70, 185, 189–90, 192, 199–200, 206–7, 226, 228–29; white women, 32–33, 36, 41, 55–56
sex, 10, 130, 145; assault, 13, 95, 97, 193; heterosexuality, 12, 104–5, 137
sexism, 137, 168–70, 194, 247–48
sexual harassment, 237–38, 239, 240, 241
sexual misconduct, police, 11, 64, 95, 96–97, 99, 100
Shapira, Harel, 223
Sharpton, Al, 79
shock knife, 155
shootings, civilians, viii, ix–x; of officers, 67–68, 70–71, 72–73, 73, 78, 119, 147, 177, 264n3; suicides, 173, 174–75
shootings, police: of Black men, x, 7, 11, 80, 81, 82, 83, 87–88, 116, 119, 120–21, 224; of Black officers, 123; of Black people, 118, 119; of Black women, xi,

7, 78; of children, 79; gun ownership rates and, 217; of minorities, 44; "post-engagement checklist," 159–60; study on media coverage of, 82–83; videos, 78, 79, 178
side jobs (part-time gigs), ix, 24, 27
slave patrols, 8–9, 59
slavery, 8, 9, 10
Snively, Clarence, 13
social isolation, 64, 98
socialization: process, 7, 19–20, 194; into state violence, 5, 20, 100, 64, 106, 124, 183, 208; transformation and, 236
sociologists, 6, 19–20, 45–46, 173, 212–13, 246
sociology, carnal, 235
solidarity, group, 63–64, 98, 193
South Asians, 37, 96–97
South Carolina, slave patrols, 9
Springfield, Massachusetts, 193
"Stand Your Ground" law, Florida, ix–x
staph infections, 148
state-mandated curriculum, vii, 6, 66, 106, 228
stereotypes, of police, 93
stereotypes, racialized: Asians, 93, 187; of Black people, 11, 15, 93, 131; of women, 12, 15, 93, 131
Sterling, Alton, x, 119
Stoughton, Seth, 103
strikes: baton, 140, 153, 154, 155; brachial, 152–53; DT and, 47, 75, 144, 164, 186, 194, 230, 245; labor, 7–8
suicides, civilians, 73, 174–75
Supreme Court, US, 118
surveillance, 103, 116, 212, 214
survivability, 158
SWAT units, 115, 194

Tactical Communications (Verbal Judo) course, 77
tactical strategies, gunfights, viii

takedowns, 47, 156–57, 186–87, 194–95

TASERs, 37, 76, 170–72, 201, 241–42

Task Force on 21st Century Policing, x, 7, 212

Taylor, Breonna, xi, 7

Team Building class, 66

teamwork, reliability and, 39–40, 56

tests: cognitive, 26; DT final exam, 52, 146–47, 149–50, 153–55, 166–68; failures, 26, 27, 32, 38, 45, 85, 158, 166, 167, 182, 184, 185, 196–97; personality, 26; physical exam, 30, 32; polygraph exam, 29–30, 32; psychiatric evaluation, 30; PT, 25–26, 38–39, 57, 184, 185, 186, 187, 199, 242; written exams, 26, 32, 177, 184

Texas, vii–viii, x, 8, 49, 119, 193

Texas Rangers, 8

thin blue line, 46–47, 127

30×30 Initiative, women and, 209

"This Police Chief Is Hiring Female Officers to Fix 'Toxic' Policing" (*Washington Post*), 209

"threshold evaluation," 140, 154

tokens, workplace and women as, 129, 137

training, civilians: firearms, ix, xi, 16, 223, 227; violence and, ix

training, officers: civilian training versus, ix; conservative ethos with hiring and, 34, 48–49, 51; in de-escalation, 67–68, 77–78, 90–91, 94, 108–9, 147, 173–75, 177–79, 215, 224; origins and history, 17–18; privately run workshops, 103–4; socialization process, 19–20. *See also* cadets; defensive tactics (DT) training; physical training(PT); scenario-based training; warfare training

transformation: of cadets, 4–5, 6, 98, 143; socialization and, 236

Trump, Donald, xi, 48–49, 50, 52, 213–14, 257n10

2 vs. 1 takedown, 186–87, 194–95

UK (United Kingdom), 17, 216

Uniform Crime Report, 10

unions, 214

unions, police, 52, 166

United Kingdom (UK), 17, 216

United States (US): American police flag, 46–47, 47; Border Patrol, 8, 115, 123–24; border with Mexico, 111; Department of Justice, 7, 95, 182, 264n1; gun ownership in, 216; ICE, 51, 111; police department formation in, 9; Supreme Court, 118. *See also* military, US

University of Texas at Austin, 49

US. *See* United States

use of force, viii, 52–53, 55–58, 68, 77, 82, 88, 91, 101, 147; complaints, 54, 100; policies, 118–19, 184; reports, 141; scenarios, 161–66, 201–2, 207, 229

US-Mexico border, 111

Van Maanen, John, 19

verbal arguments, 85

verbal commands, 67, 147–48, 177, 264n3

Verbal Judo (Tactical Communications) course, 77

verbal reasoning, 26

verbal skills, de-escalation, 173, 211

veterans, US military, vii–viii, ix, 61; Black recruiting officers, 21–23, 30, 34, 36, 55, 57; with board interviews, 55; as cadets, 72, 75, 131, 168–69, 186–87, 191–92, 197, 199, 204, 264n4; as de-escalation training instructors, 67–68, 90–91; as DT instructors, 62; with fighting experience, 52, 54–55; firearms instructors, 80, 161, 162; with PTSD, 68, 199; recruiters and trainers, 53; recruitment of, 21–23, 53–54; with violence, 54

video games, violence and, 105

videos, 208, 225, 242; activists, 84, 89–90; camera footage, 67, 78, 96–97, 147, 264n3; civilians shooting officers, 67–68, 177, 264n3; civilian suicides, 174–75; college fraternity hazing, 193; de-escalation before physical force, 175, 178; marketing, 206–7; news media and police interaction, 77–79, 84; OC Spray, 75, 76, 89–90; officers killed or beaten, 19, 67–68, 74, 103, 177, 216, 264n3; officers shooting civilians, 78, 79, 178; TASER, 172

vigilante groups, 9

violence: activist movements and, 74; being bad at, 194–99; brutality and, 17, 86, 212; domestic, 53; domination and, 17, 178; with emancipation, 9; hiring and warfare training, 208–11; power and, 43, 44; racism and, 7, 44, 54, 218; recruitment applicants with right kind of, 52–60; scenario-based training and, 128, 165–66, 206–7; state, 5, 20, 64, 100, 106, 124, 183, 207–8, 213; training civilians and, ix; unnecessary, 44; unwillingness to use, 195, 199–205; US veterans with, 54; video games and, 105; with warrior-officers doing whatever it takes, 124–38; willingness to use, 192; women officers and, 134–35. See also police violence; warfare training

Virginia, colonists in, 8

Vitale, Alex, 212–13

Vollmer, August, 17

voter suppression, 10

Wacquant, Loïc, 235

wall of honor, police academies, 66

"Want to Reform the Police? Hire More Women" (CNN), 209

warfare, with officers as warriors, 103

warfare training: de-escalation as nothing new, 172–79; fighting, vii, 16, 47, 52–58, 61–62, 72, 103–4, 132, 136, 154–59, 162–68, 178, 186–87, 194–203; giving commands, 143–47, 149, 154, 156, 157; guns, 162–72; handcuffing, 142–43, 156–57; with hiring and future of policing, 208–11; hurting, 150–58; killing, 158–62, 175–76; physical control, 148–50, 179; redman exercise, 139–42. See also warriors, officers as

"war on cops," 69–70, 74, 224

War on Poverty, 103

warriors, officers as: biracial, 116–17; Black officers, 115–24, 137; with de-escalation, 175; fighting, 165; "killology" and, 104; mind-set, 102, 125, 126, 137, 196, 205; nonwhite, 106; profiling bad guys and, 106–24; with redman exercise, 139–42; violence and doing whatever it takes, 124–38; warfare with, 103; warrior-guardian framework, 102–6, 124–26, 128–30, 132, 135–38, 206–7; with women and gender, 129–35, 137

war room, 206–7

Washington Post (newspaper), 209

weapon check, 160

Wells, Alice S., 12

Westley, William, 63

whatever it takes: institutional fit and doing, 188–94, 204; warrior officers with violence doing, 124–38

Wheaton College football, 193

white ignorance, 112–13

white men, 16, 17, 34, 60; applicants, 55; cadets, 155–56; exclusionary hiring practices for, 12; gun owners, ix, 105; institution, 116, 137, 195; instructors, vii–ix, xii, 1, 3, 43–44, 46, 48, 51, 63, 65, 71–73, 76–78, 84–85, 89, 94, 101,

106–7, 109, 111–12, 130, 135, 142–45, 151–53, 157–60, 163, 171–72, 174–77, 187, 195–96, 198, 207, 230–31, 234, 238–40, 242–44; liberal threat to, 105; in license-to-carry classes, viii; lieutenants, 35–36, 38, 42, 51, 84–85, 106–7, 109, 111–12, 173–74, 184, 226, 229; military veterans, 169; murder of officers, 67, 264n3; officers, 104, 105, 130–31; officer shootings of, 80; officers with racialized stereotypes, 15, 130–31; as protectors, ix, 105, 130, 132, 137; sergeants, 39–40, 49–50, 61–62, 69–71, 78–81, 94, 124–26, 169–70, 185, 189–90, 192, 199–200, 206–7, 226, 228–29
whiteness, masculinity and, xi, 12, 187
white supremacy, 104; Ku Klux Klan, 9, 59, 115; white ignorance and, 112–13
white women: background investigators, 32–34, 36, 41, 45, 55–56; cadets, 146–48, 151–52, 156, 157, 163; conservatives, 213–14; LAPD City Mother's Bureau and, 13; as liabilities on patrol, 131; in license-to-carry classes, viii; officers with racism, 15; in policing, 12–15, 130; protection of, ix, 105, 129, 130, 132, 137; racialized stereotypes of, 12, 15, 131; with racism and sexism, 137; sergeants, 32–33, 36, 41, 55–56
Wickersham Commission (National Commission on Law Observance and Enforcement), 212

"Will to Win (Fight) Day," 162–65
Wilson, Darren, x
women: Asian instructors, 129–30; board interviews and, 36, 44–45, 57; cadets, 2–5, 7, 11, 68, 72, 129–35, 137, 146–48, 151–53, 156, 157, 163, 165–67, 168–70, 178–79, 181, 186, 189, 200–204, 208–9, 244–46; of color as military veterans, 53; discrimination against, 13; DT training and, 3, 130–32; ethnography and, 236–37, 240–42; with fighting experience, 56–58, 203; as foils, 49, 168–70, 232; gun clubs, 223; hiring initiatives, 208–9; instructors, 38–39, 66–67, 76, 109, 111, 129–30, 149–50; as liabilities on patrol, 131; officers and family, 36–37; officers and violence, 134–35; in policing, 4–5, 12–13, 14–15, 19; profiling, 110; racial stereotypes of, 12, 15, 93, 131; with racism and sexism, 137; as threat, 105; as tokens in workplace, 129, 137; as warrior officers, 129–35, 137. *See also* Black women; Latinas; white women
workplace, women as tokens in, 129, 137
workshops, privately run training, 103–4
written exams, 26, 32, 177, 184

YouTube, 84, 89, 225

Zimmerman, George, ix–x

About the Author

Samantha J. Simon is Assistant Professor in the School of Government & Public Policy and the School of Sociology at The University of Arizona.